T0049730

family handyman.

WHOLE HOUSE
QUICK & EASY
PROJECTS

family handyman

Text, photography and illustrations for *Whole House Quick & Easy Projects* are based on articles previously published in *Family Handyman* magazine (2915 Commers Dr., Suite 700, Eagan, MN 55121, familyhandyman.com). For information on advertising in *Family Handyman* magazine, call (646) 518-4215.

Whole House Quick & Easy Projects is published by Home Service Publications, Inc., a subsidiary of Trusted Media Brands, Inc. ©2021. All rights reserved. This volume may not be reproduced in whole or in part without written permission from the publisher. *Family Handyman* is a registered trademark of Trusted Media Brands, Inc.

Image Credits
24 EricVega/Getty Images; **177** *tl* Kemiko Concrete Stains; **177** *tr* Quikrete Companies; **38, 94, 134, 172, 192, 220, 262** illustrated by Steve Björkman
All other photographs by Tom Fenenga, Jeff Gorton, Mike Krivit, Bill Zuehlke
All other illustrations by Ron Chamberlain, Marion Ferro, John Hartman, Susan Jessen, Bruce Kieffer, Frank Rohrbach III

Text Credits
Family Handyman wishes to thank *Australian Handyman* for the use of projects "Magazine stand" and "Rolling storage box" and all technical art and images contained therein.

Hardcover ISBN: 978-1-62145-584-4
Paperback ISBN: 978-1-62145-585-1
ePub ISBN: 978-1-62145-586-8
Component number: 116400104H
LOCC: 2021938424

PRINTED IN THE UNITED STATES OF AMERICA
10 9 8 7 6 5 4 3 2 1

A NOTE TO OUR READERS: All do-it-yourself activities involve a degree of risk. Skills, materials, tools and site conditions vary widely. Although the editors have made every effort to ensure accuracy, the reader remains responsible for the selection and use of tools, materials and methods. Always obey local codes and laws, follow manufacturer instructions and observe safety precautions.

SAFETY FIRST–ALWAYS!

Tackling home improvement projects and repairs can be endlessly rewarding. But as most of us know, with the rewards come risks. DIYers use chain saws, climb ladders and tear into walls that can contain big, hazardous surprises.

The good news is that armed with the right knowledge, tools and procedures, homeowners can minimize risk. As you go about your projects and repairs, stay alert for these hazards:

Aluminum wiring

Aluminum wiring, installed in about 7 million homes between 1965 and 1973, requires special techniques and materials to make safe connections. This wiring is dull gray, not the dull orange characteristic of copper. Hire a licensed electrician certified to work with it. For more information, go to cpsc.gov and search for "aluminum wiring."

Spontaneous combustion

Rags saturated with oil finishes, like Danish oil and linseed oil, and oil-based paints and stains can spontaneously combust if left bunched up. Always dry them outdoors, spread out loosely. When the oil has thoroughly dried, you can safely throw the rags in the trash.

Vision and hearing protection

Safety glasses or goggles should be worn whenever you're working on DIY projects that involve chemicals, dust or anything that could shatter or chip off and hit your eye. Sounds louder than 80 decibels (dB) are considered potentially dangerous. Sound levels from a lawn mower can be 90 dB and from shop tools and chain saws can be 90 to 100 dB.

Lead paint

If your home was built before 1979, it may contain lead paint, which is a serious health hazard, especially for children six and under. Take precautions when you scrape or remove it. Contact your public health department for detailed safety information or call (800) 424-LEAD (5323) to receive an information pamphlet. Or visit epa.gov/lead.

Buried utilities

A few days before you dig in your yard, have your underground water, gas and electrical lines marked. Just call 811 or go to call811.com.

Smoke and carbon monoxide (CO) alarms

The risk of dying in reported home structure fires is cut in half in homes with working smoke alarms. Test your smoke alarms every month, replace batteries as necessary and replace units that are more than 10 years old. As you make your home more energy efficient and airtight, existing ducts and chimneys can't always successfully vent combustion gases, including potentially deadly carbon monoxide (CO). Install a UL-listed CO detector, and test your CO and smoke alarms at the same time.

Five-gallon buckets and window-covering cords

Anywhere from 10 to 40 children a year drown in five-gallon buckets, according to the U.S. Consumer Products Safety Commission. Always store empty buckets upside down and ones containing liquid with the covers securely snapped.

According to Parents for Window Blind Safety, hundreds of children in the United States are injured every year after becoming entangled in looped window-treatment cords. For more information, visit pfwbs.org.

Working up high

If you have to get up on your roof to do a repair or installation, always install roof brackets and wear a roof harness.

Asbestos

Texture sprayed on ceilings before 1978, adhesives and tiles for vinyl and asphalt floors before 1980, and vermiculite insulation (with gray granules) all may contain asbestos. Other building materials made between 1940 and 1980 could also contain asbestos. If you suspect that materials you're removing or working around contain asbestos, contact your health department or visit epa.gov/asbestos for information.

Learn More

For additional information about home safety, visit **homesafetycouncil.org**. This site offers helpful information about dozens of home safety issues.

CONTENTS

Chapter one
WINDOWS & DOORS

Chapter two
BACKYARD

Chapter three
KITCHEN & BATHROOM

Chapter four
GARAGE & WORKSHOP

Chapter five
FLOORS

Chapter **six**
WALLS & CEILINGS

Chapter **seven**
FURNITURE & SHELVING

Special **section**
THREE-DAY PROJECTS

WINDOWS & DOORS

Window planter

You can build and finish several of these simple window planters in a day.

Cut the 1x10 and 1x3 to length (see photos for dimensions). Pot diameters vary, so size the holes by scribing and cutting out a 6-in. circle from cardboard to ensure that the pot will rest on its rim **(Photo 1)**. Keep testing until you find the size. Then lay out and cut the openings.

Use a 5-gallon pail lid to scribe bracket curves **(Photo 2)**. Make sure the grain runs parallel to the shelf for strength. Smooth off the rough edges and paint the parts before you assemble—especially if you want the two-tone look. Then screw the parts together with 2-in. exterior screws.

Mount the shelf to the wall by screwing through the hanging strip into the wall framing.

WHAT IT TAKES		
TIME 2 hours	**COST** Less than $50	**SKILL LEVEL** Beginner
TOOLS Compass, drill, Speed square, jig saw, 5-gallon pail lid		

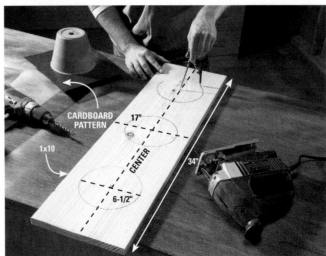

1 Mark the 6-in.-diameter holes with a compass. Then drill 1/2-in. starter holes and cut out the openings with a jigsaw.

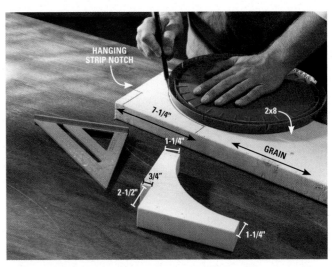

2 Mark the notch for the hanging strip and both 1-1/4-in. ends on the brackets. Draw the curve and cut the openings with a jigsaw.

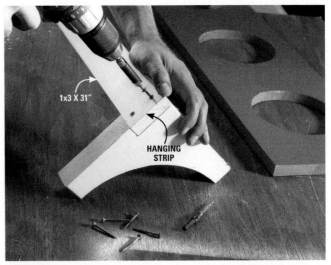

3 Predrill and screw the hanging strip to the brackets. Then center and screw the shelf to the brackets and to the hanging strip.

FIN COMB

1 Comb out the mats. Match the correct end of the fin comb to the fin spacing on your coils. Insert the comb and pull up to straighten the fins. Wear leather gloves to prevent nasty cuts.

2 Clean out the crud. Suck up all the spider webs, leaves, dust and dirt before you spray the coils.

3 Apply a foam cleaner. Shoot the spray over the entire surface of both coils and let the foam do the work for you. If the buildup is heavy, brush in the direction of the fins with a nylon-bristle brush.

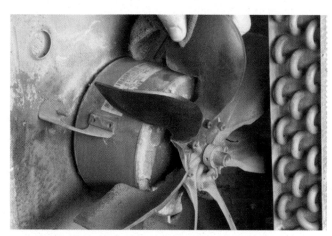

4 Service the fan motor. Pop off the plastic or rubber caps on the motor's oiling ports. Then squeeze a few drops into each port and recap.

Window AC care

Most people assume warm air from their AC unit means it's low on refrigerant. That is not always the cause.

Many times, window and through-the-wall AC units can't blow cold air because the evaporator and condenser coils or cooling fins are clogged. You can clean a window unit yourself in about an hour. Here's how to clean your window AC unit.

First remove the plastic filter holder/trim panel. It usually snaps off. Then remove the AC from the window or slide it out of the wall (get help—it's heavy). If you're working on a window unit, remove the mounting frame and case. The case screws are usually located along the bottom edge. Note the location of any odd-length screws since they have to go back in the same spots upon reassembly.

Then straighten the bent cooling fins with a fin comb **(Photo 1)**. Buy two cans of AC coil cleaner. Vacuum all visible buildup from both coils **(Photo 2)**. Then spray both coils with the cleaner **(Photo 3)**.

While the foam works, clean fan blades with household cleaner and a rag. If the fan motor has plastic- or rubber-capped oiling ports, pop them and squeeze in a few drops of electric motor oil (pros use the Zoom-Spout oiler).

Wash (or replace) the air filter and reinstall the unit. You will be pleased to note that your hard work has left it much cleaner and more efficient than before.

WHAT IT TAKES		
TIME 1 hour	**COST** Less than $50	**SKILL LEVEL** Beginner
TOOLS Fin comb, screwdriver		

Apply heat-reducing window film

Heat-control window film will help keep a room cooler, and you can install it yourself.

These films reflect the sun's heat and ultraviolet rays, and they reduce glare without obscuring the view. The more direct sunlight coming through the window, the more the film will help (and it may lower your air-conditioning bills!).

Applying the film takes approximately 30 minutes per window. The film should last about 10 years. Prices vary with film size and type of film. A film sized to cover two to three windows costs anywhere from $8 to $50 and up, depending on type. The film is sold at home centers and hardware stores. Different types of film are available, so get the one designed for heat control. The film can be applied to any window, including double-pane low-e windows, although they already reduce radiant heat loss and gain.

One drawback is that the film may void the manufacturer's warranty for the seal on double-pane windows, although the film shouldn't affect the seal. If the window warranty has already expired or reducing excessive heat is more important to you than possibly jeopardizing a warranty, then apply the film. Otherwise, consider other options, such as installing shades, awnings or shutters over the windows or planting a tree on the west side to block the sun.

ABOVE: Heat-control film is composed of treated micro-thin layers of film that block ultraviolet rays and reduce the summer heat that comes through the window. **BELOW:** Window film can be installed in about 30 minutes. The hazy appearance will disappear after 10 days.

WHAT IT TAKES		
TIME 30 minutes	**COST** $50-$100	**SKILL LEVEL** Beginner
TOOLS Scissors, blow dryer		

1 Close the door and tap the hinge pins loose with a hammer and nail.

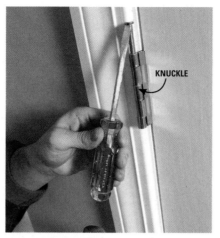

2 Tap the pin up until it's loose enough to pull out.

3 Open the door partway and pull it to the side so it drops off the hinges.

Remove a heavy door

Follow these instructions to keep your fingers from getting pinched.

To make this job go smoothly, first close and latch the door. Then remove the hinge pins by tapping on the bottom of each hinge pin with a nail (**Photo 1**). Don't try to drive the pins all the way out with the nail—you might damage the trim with the hammer. After the pins pop up an inch or so, try pulling them free with your fingers. If they're stubborn, just drive up on the underside near the knuckle with a flat-head screwdriver (**Photo 2**). Slide a piece of cardboard under the door to protect the floor, then ease the door off the hinges by lifting slightly at the knob with one hand and under one of the hinges with the other hand (**Photo 3**). If the weight of the door makes it difficult to separate the hinges, wedge a pry bar under the door to take weight off the hinges.

To put the door back on the hinges, grab the door at the center and tip it slightly toward the top, engaging the knuckles of the top hinge. With the weight of the door hanging on the top hinge, work the others together. Push a hinge pin into whichever lines up first, then tap in the remaining pins. If one of the hinges seems slightly low and the others won't fit together, place a pry bar under the center of the door and—with the lowest set of hinge leaves engaged—lever the door up until the other hinge leaves fit together (**Photo 4**).

Close the door most of the way and hold it firmly for this step—the pry bar may try to push the door in or out as well as up.

4 Replace the door on the hinges, using a pry bar if necessary to get the hinge leaves to fit together.

WHAT IT TAKES		
TIME 5 minutes	**COST** $0	**SKILL LEVEL** Beginner

TOOLS & MATERIALS
Hammer, pry bar, flat-head screwdriver

DOOR STOP

A.

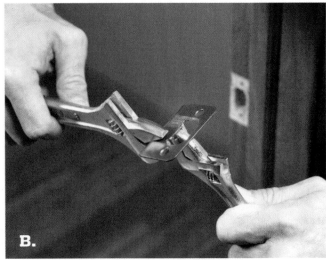

B.

CORK DOT

DOOR STOP

C.

Rattling doors

A door will rattle when there's too much space between the door and the door stop. The solution is to reduce or remove the gap.

FIX A: MOVE THE STOP

Knock the door stop flush with a hammer and a scrap piece of wood. If the stop is more than 1/16 in. out of whack, you may end up with an unfinished spot where the door stop used to be, especially on painted doors. Add a couple of brads or finish nails to the stop if it's a door that gets slammed.

FIX B: BEND THE STRIKE PLATE TAB

Many strike plates have an adjustable tab. Some of these tangs can be adjusted in place with a regular flat-head screwdriver. Others need to be removed and adjusted with pliers or an adjustable wrench. The more you bend the tab toward the

door, the farther the door has to travel before it is able to latch shut.

FIX C: FILL THE GAP WITH A BUMPER

Another simple fix is to install a cabinet door pad/bumper on the part of the door stop that contacts the door. Felt, cork or rubber will all work fine.

Cabinet bumpers vary in thickness, so check out the size of the gap between the slab and the stop before you head to the home center. You'll find the bumpers you need near the cabinet hardware section (although you can also find them online from several retailers).

Interior door repairs

Even if your door has been binding for years, we'll show you how to repair it quickly and inexpensively.

PROBLEM A: DOOR BINDS ALONG BOTTOM EDGE

If the door rubs on the latch-side bottom edge, look for fastener failure. In most cases, the lower jamb has shifted or pulled loose from its nails, resulting in an out-of-plumb opening. To reset the jamb, pry away the bottom section of casing and renail the jamb **(Photo A)**. If there are no shims, install them if necessary to allow for a 1/8-in. gap between the closed door and the jamb. Then nail with 10d casing nails and tack the casing back into place.

PROBLEM B: DOOR BINDS ALONG ENTIRE EDGE

If the door is binding along the length of the latch-side edge and other fixes haven't helped, the door has probably swollen from high humidity. First check to make sure all the edges are either painted or varnished. When a door isn't sealed on all four edges, moisture can enter and swell it as much as 1/4 in. If your door isn't well sealed, wait for the dry season to see if it will shrink back to a good fit. Then seal it with a primer/paint or stain/varnish combo.

If you want immediate results, you'll have to remove the door from its hinges and plane or sand down the latch side, removing just enough material so it can shut smoothly once again **(Photo B)**. Remove as little as possible to ensure a tight fit, then seal unfinished edges with paint or varnish.

To support the work, we used a clamping-style workbench to hold the door on end and adhered masking tape to the rubbing edge as a guide for the belt sander. Once you rehang the door and are happy with the fit, make sure you reseal the sanded edge to keep out moisture.

CAUTIONARY INSTRUCTIONS
If your home was built before 1978, the paint may contain lead, a hazardous material. Either have it tested (contact your local health department for testing labs) or follow safe scraping and sanding techniques. Dispose of the waste according to local regulations.

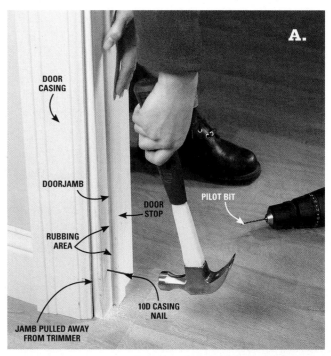

DOOR CASING

DOORJAMB

DOOR STOP

RUBBING AREA

PILOT BIT

10D CASING NAIL

JAMB PULLED AWAY FROM TRIMMER

A.

Pry out the inside casing with a stiff putty knife, then drive a 10d casing nail through the jamb and existing shim into the trimmer stud. Punch the nail slightly below the wood surface with a nail set, then putty the hole, sand the surface smooth and refinish with varnish or paint.

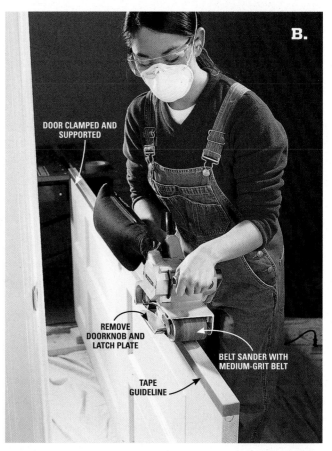

DOOR CLAMPED AND SUPPORTED

REMOVE DOORKNOB AND LATCH PLATE

BELT SANDER WITH MEDIUM-GRIT BELT

TAPE GUIDELINE

B.

With the door installed, mark the trim line with tape, using the jamb as a guide. Then remove the door, support it and sand it down to the tape with a belt sander.

WHAT IT TAKES

TIME	COST	SKILL LEVEL
1 day	More than $500	Intermediate

TOOLS
Hammer, pry bar, tape measure, level, caulking gun, utility knife, drill, nail set, saw, miter saw (optional)

Install a new front door

Here you'll learn how to order a door that'll fit like a glove. Then you'll learn, step by step, how to get your old door out and the new one in.

It's not often you can complete a project in a weekend that will save you money and dramatically improve the looks of your house. But that's what will happen when you replace a worn, drafty front door with a stylish, energy-efficient new one. And since each new door comes prehung in a weather-stripped frame, you don't have to be a master carpenter to do a first-class job.

If you can handle basic carpentry tasks, you'll have no trouble installing a new prehung door in a day. Figure on another day to finish the details and to start painting the door. You can complete most of the job with basic hand tools. You'll need a hammer, pry bar, tape measure, level, utility knife, nail set and saw. If you decide to install new interior trim, you'll also need a miter saw.

LEFT: A bright, shiny new door is just a couple of days away. ABOVE: Most new doors come prehung, which means the jamb, door and trim are already assembled. This makes replacing your old door much faster.

For this installation, a top-quality prehung wood door (Simpson Bungalow No. 7228) was ordered from a local lumberyard. Including the special 2-1/2-in.-wide exterior trim (casing), the total cost was $1,100. You could purchase a steel or fiberglass door for much less, but the style and crisp detailing of the wood door matched the house perfectly. The door arrived about two weeks after it was ordered.

MEASURE YOUR OLD DOOR

In most cases, simply order a new door the same size as the old one. If you alter the size or add sidelights, you'll have to reframe the opening and alter many details. This usually doubles or triples the size of the job. Here are the four sets of measurements you'll need to order a door.

For door size, measure the width and height of your old door. Round these up to full inches to find the size of the replacement door you'll need. If, for example, your door measures 35-3/4 in. wide and 79-1/2 in. tall, you'll order a 36 in. by 80 in. door.

For jamb width, measure from the back side of the interior trim to the back side of the exterior trim **(Figure A)**. Specify this jamb width when you order your new prehung door. This guarantees that the interior trim will fit flush to the wall without adding "jamb extensions."

Remove the interior trim to get accurate measurements of the rough opening. Measure the opening width between framing members and from the bottom of the sill to the top of the opening. Compare these measurements to the rough opening requirements of your new door to make sure it fits.

For the exterior opening (or "masonry opening" if you have a brick or stone door surround), measure to the outsides of the exterior casing and then from the bottom of the sill to the top of the trim. Compare these measurements with those of a prehung door that has standard 2-in.-wide "brick molding" trim. If the framed door with standard trim is too small to completely fill the space or if you want a different trim style, you have three options. The best solution is to order a door with wider, flat casing to fit the opening. You can always add a piece of decorative molding overtop to approximate the style of your existing exterior trim. (Here 2-1/2-in. flat casing was ordered and the existing decorative molding was reinstalled.) Second, you can order your door with standard molding and

1 Tap the hinge pins loose with a hammer and nail set, and then swing the door open and lift it off. Protect the floor with a drop cloth, since the old door will be heavy.

2 Pry the interior trim loose from the door frame. Protect the wall with a wide putty knife. If you plan to reuse the trim, first score the intersection between the molding and jamb with a utility knife.

FIGURE A. MEASURING

fill the gap with additional strips of wood. The last option is to order the door without exterior molding and make your own to fit.

START BY TEARING OUT YOUR OLD DOOR AND PREPARING THE OPENING

Photos 1 – 4 show how to take out the old door and frame. If you plan to reuse the interior moldings, pull the nails through the back side with pliers or a nipper to avoid damaging the face. Cutting through one side jamb makes it easy to tear out the entire frame **(Photo 4)**.

After the door frame is out, check the condition of the framing and the subflooring in the sill area. Cut out and replace any rotted wood. If the sill on your new door is thinner than the one you removed, you may have to build up the sill area as shown in **Photo 5**. Set the sill height so the door just clears your carpeting or rugs when it swings inward.

Photo 6 shows how to protect the sill from water intrusion. Buy the flashing tape from a lumberyard or home center. If you're installing a door in a newly constructed wall, you can buy a special plastic sill flashing kit instead. One brand is Jamsill (jamsill.com; call 800-526-7455 for ordering information). Details will vary depending on the doorway situation. The idea is to channel water away from the wood. If your home is built on a concrete slab, the door frame will probably rest directly on the slab.

If your door is exposed to the weather, direct water away from the door with a metal drip cap overtop **(Figure C)**. Brick openings like this one and doors protected by porches with roofs don't require a drip cap. You'll find drip caps at home centers and lumberyards. If the drip cap is damaged or missing, install a new one before you set the door frame in the opening. Cut the metal drip cap to

3 Slice the caulk joint between the siding (brick) and exterior trim, and pry the trim from the doorjamb with a pry bar.

4 Cut completely through the side jamb with a handsaw. Pry the jambs loose and pull them out of the opening.

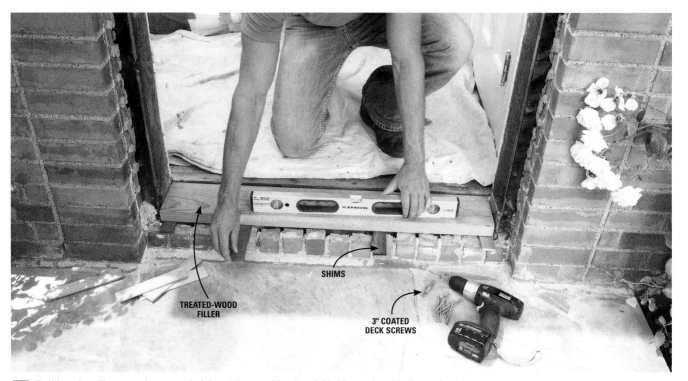

5 Build up the sill area to the proper height with treated lumber. Add shims to level it. Fasten it with coated deck screws.

SELF-STICKING FLASHING TAPE

6 Cover the rough sill area with self-sticking flashing tape. Wrap tape up the sides of the opening and over the front edge. Set the door in the opening, plumb it and check the fit.

CAULK

7 Apply a bead of caulk along the sides and top of the door opening and at the sill according to the instructions from the door manufacturer. Then set the door in the opening.

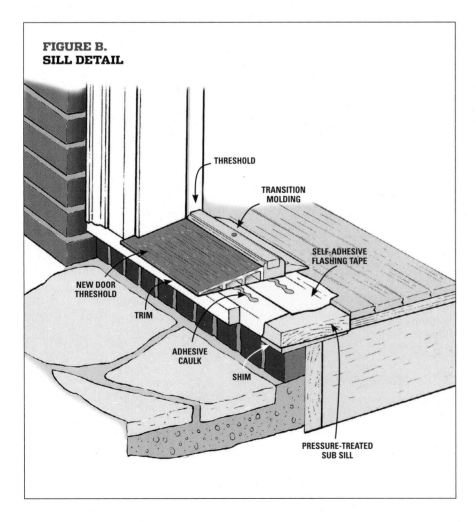

**FIGURE B.
SILL DETAIL**

THRESHOLD

TRANSITION MOLDING

SELF-ADHESIVE FLASHING TAPE

NEW DOOR THRESHOLD

TRIM

ADHESIVE CAULK

SHIM

PRESSURE-TREATED SUB SILL

fit, and slide it under the siding and building paper **(Figure C)**. If nails are in the way, slip a hacksaw blade under the siding and cut them.

SOLID SHIMMING IS THE KEY TO LONG-LASTING, TROUBLE-FREE DOOR OPERATION

Here the brick opening was level and plumb, but this isn't always the case. Start by checking the sill area with a 2-ft. level. If you're building it up as shown in **Photo 5**, it's easy to level it with shims at the same time. Otherwise, level the sill area with pairs of shims spaced about 4 in. apart.

Set the door in the opening for a test fit. Hold a level against the hinge jamb, and adjust the door and frame until the jamb is plumb. Check to see how the casing fits against the siding. If the siding is so far out of plumb that the door frame and casing don't fit in, either cut back the siding or trim the casing. Mark the casing in areas that need trimming. Then take the door out and trim the casing with a belt sander or circular saw.

Make sure the building paper is intact around the frame edges. If not, slide strips of 15 lb felt behind the siding and tack it to the framing with staples. When you're sure the door will fit, caulk along the sill and behind the casing, and tip the door into the opening. **Photos 8 – 10** show how to shim and nail the door. The goal is to center the door in the opening and shim the sides until they're plumb and straight.

Adjust the pairs of shims until the gap between the door and the jamb is consistent on the sides and on the top of the door. When you're happy with the fit, nail through the jamb into the framing at each shim location. Then go ahead and in each hinge replace one screw closest to the inside with one long enough to reach the framing **(Photo 11)**.

8 Make sure the doorsill is level. Then center the top of the door in the opening and tack it into place with galvanized casing nails. Plumb the hinge-side jamb and tack the bottom corners.

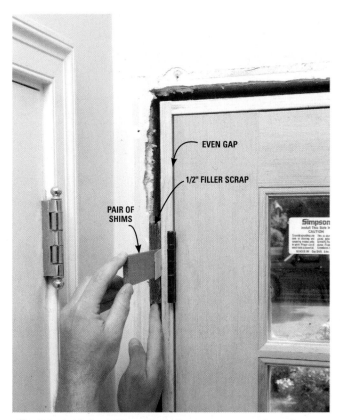

9 Shim behind each hinge. For large spaces, start with small squares of plywood. Then finish with pairs of shims. Make sure the hinge-side jamb remains plumb.

10 Shim at the top, middle and bottom of the latch-side jamb and at the top until the gap between the door and the doorjamb is consistent. Score the shims with a utility knife and break them off.

11 Replace a screw in each hinge with a 3-in. screw driven into the framing. Drive additional casing nails every 16 in. along the sides and top of the exterior trim.

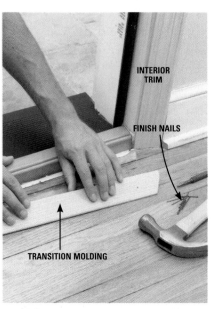

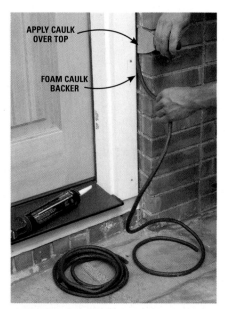

12 Fill the space between the doorjamb and framing with minimal expanding foam insulation. After the foam has expanded and skinned over, loosely stuff extra space with strips of fiberglass insulation.

13 Cut and install new interior trim, or reinstall the old trim. If there's a gap between the new sill and the existing flooring, cover it with a beveled transition.

14 Press foam caulk backer into the siding/trim gap. Apply a neat bead of caulk between the siding and the door trim. Cut a trim board to fit under the sill and screw it to the framing.

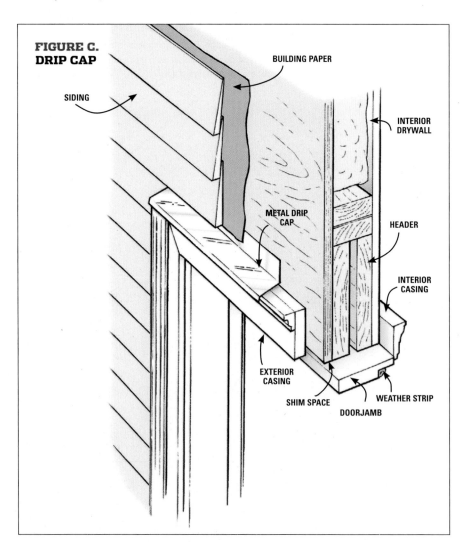

FIGURE C. DRIP CAP

- SIDING
- BUILDING PAPER
- INTERIOR DRYWALL
- METAL DRIP CAP
- HEADER
- INTERIOR CASING
- EXTERIOR CASING
- SHIM SPACE
- WEATHER STRIP
- DOORJAMB

Materials List

ITEM	QTY.
Treated lumber to build up the sill (optional)	
Roll of flexible self-sticking flashing tape	
Polyurethane caulk	2 tubes
Shims	3 packages
Minimal expanding foam	2 cans
Roll of foam caulk backing (optional)	
Transition molding (optional; photo 13)	
12d and 16d galvanized casing nails	1 lb. ea.
3 in. coated deck screws	1 lb.
4d, 6d and 10d finish nails	

After insulating the space around the door (**Photo 12**), install the interior trim. **Photo 13** shows how to cover a gap between the doorsill and flooring. Complete the job by caulking the exterior (**Photo 14**).

For gaps wider than 3/16 in., insert a foam backer and apply caulk over it. Most doors require an additional trim board under the sill to support its outer edge. Finally, remove the door and paint or stain and varnish your new door, jamb and trim.

As a last step, sit back and admire your brand-new door. No matter what color or which door you chose, you have a beautiful new entryway to your home.

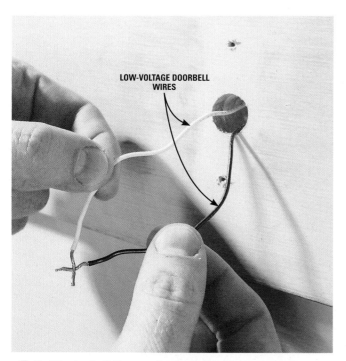

LOW-VOLTAGE DOORBELL WIRES

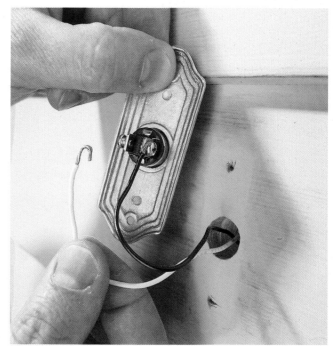

1 Test the doorbell. Unscrew the doorbell button to remove it from the wall. Loosen the screws on the back of the button and disconnect the wires. Then touch the two wires together. If the chime rings, the button is bad. If not, the chime, transformer or wiring is bad.

2 Replace the button. Connect the wires to the new button (it doesn't matter which screw the wires are attached to). Screw the button to the wall, and you're done.

How to fix a dead doorbell

Before you go out and buy a new doorbell, test your old one—the most likely culprit is a button not working properly.

A wireless doorbell is an easy solution: Just mount the button by the front door and place the chime anywhere indoors. But before you spend money on a new one, you should check your current doorbell's button. The button is connected to low-voltage wiring, so you don't have to worry about getting shocked. **Photos 1 and 2** show you how.

WHAT IT TAKES		
TIME 15 minutes	**COST** Less than $50	**SKILL LEVEL** Beginner
TOOLS Screwdriver		

Clean the chime armature, too

Sometimes a doorbell will stop ringing simply because the armature that actually rings the bell is clogged with dust and grime. Take the chime cover off, brush away all the dust and clean the armature with rubbing alcohol until it moves freely. If the bell still won't ring, there's either a break in the wire somewhere or you need a new transformer.

CHIME ARMATURE

Need new windows?

Here's how to tell if your dreams should be reality.

A.

On a windy or cold day, move a smoking incense stick along the perimeter of your "drafty" windows to detect either incoming or outgoing airflows. Make sure to note whether leakage occurs around the window sash itself or around the trim.

B.

Probe exposed wood corners annually with a screwdriver or other sharp tool, looking for soft spots that indicate rot. Check the lower edges of wood trim as well.

New windows can be the most exciting and dramatic improvement you can make to your home—changing how it looks and feels, and even raising its market value. Unfortunately, new windows are expensive, even if you do all the installation yourself. Here are the top five problems with old windows and how you can solve them.

A. YOUR HOUSE FEELS DRAFTY

If your house feels cool and drafty in the winter, chances are you have leaky windows. Turning up the thermostat and putting on a sweater won't always bring comfort, especially on a windy or downright frigid day.

New windows will solve this problem instantly. When properly installed, they are virtually airtight and your house will be free of most drafts. Depending on the leakage of your old windows, you could also see a 10 to 30 percent reduction in your bills—old windows can account for up to one-third of a home's energy loss.

BE SURE NEW WINDOWS ARE THE ANSWER

Drafts may seem like they're coming from windows even when they're not.

For example, air leaks can occur around the trim rather than around the sash. You can usually fix this yourself by removing trim and insulating. (Go to thefamilyhandyman.com and search for "stop window drafts.") If the leaks occur around only a few, frequently opened windows, you may be able to fix them with new weather stripping, latches or closers. Or call a window repair specialist for an estimate. The cost of professional window repair might seem high, but it may be less than new windows.

B. WINDOWS DON'T OPEN AND SHUT EASILY, ARE ROTTING OR HAVE BROKEN HARDWARE

It's frustrating when you have to struggle to open or close a window because the sash sticks or won't stay up, the crank won't turn, the sash won't latch or the hinges are broken. Installers tell us that they see these problems in homes only 10 years old. The original windows in many homes are not top quality.

On the other hand, new windows, especially those of a major brand, will operate smoothly and easily, and should give you years of trouble-free service.

FIX OR REPLACE?

To answer this question, first inspect your windows for signs of wear. Common problems include binding sashes, hardware that's not working, cracks in vinyl and wood rot. Installers tell us that most of the mechanical parts on lower-quality windows tend to fail at about the same time.

If only a few have problems, have a window repair specialist give you a bid. Then compare it with the cost of complete replacement. You can replace most types of hardware yourself. This is a good strategy if only a few windows have hardware problems. The trick is to find identical replacement parts. Finding replacement parts for major brand windows is fairly easy.

First look for a manufacturer label on the top, the bottom or the edge of the sash, or at the corner of the glass. Then call the manufacturer and ask about parts sources. If you're having a hard time finding the manufacturer's name, you can check local hardware stores and home centers for replacement hardware. Or you can conduct a search online for "window repair parts" or for "window weather stripping replacement." Up to a point, you can also fix wood rot. First, eliminate the source of moisture if you

Low-maintenance exteriors on new windows eliminate the painting chore and allow cleaning from the inside. Nice!

can—for example, a leaking gutter or ineffective flashing. Replace rotting trim by digging out the rot. Fill with epoxy or other fillers, caulk and repaint. (Go to thefamilyhandyman.com and search for "epoxy wood repair.")

(Go to thefamilyhandyman.com and search for "epoxy wood repair.")

PRO TIP

Get connected

New windows as part of a remodel can become the focal point of a room, making it feel bright, warm and much larger. You'll feel connected to your yard and neighborhood.

If you can't repair the rotted area, you'll end up having to replace the window. Be vigilant and check on your windows even if your windows have maintenance-free exteriors (if aluminum or vinyl-covered). Stains running down the siding below your windows can indicate a seal failure and the start of rot behind the cladding. Look for open joints and flaking or peeling caulk. Clean bad joints and then recaulk.

C. TOO MUCH MAINTENANCE

If you're sick and tired of scraping and painting wood windows every few years, it may be time for a change. New windows with maintenance-free exteriors will eliminate those tiring, time-consuming chores. All-vinyl or composite windows and windows with vinyl or aluminum exterior cladding won't rot and don't need painting. The double-pane glass eliminates the need for storm windows. And new window mechanisms allow you to rotate the sashes and wash your windows from the inside; no more climbing ladders.

If your old windows are basically in good condition and you're not up for all those maintenance chores, hire a professional painter or home

D.

High-efficiency glass reduces energy loss and will make your home more comfortable. It's a good investment when it comes time to buy new windows.

E.

If you're just not pleased with how your windows look, consider replacing them. New windows add value to your home, and they can make you much happier with its appearance.

maintenance pro to service and clean your windows annually. It'll take about a day every year.

Don't fret about the cost, either. While, yes, it would be cheaper to complete these tasks yourself, if you want to keep your old windows in working order for as long as possible, having your windows serviced and cleaned is a worthwhile investment.

D. YOUR OLD WINDOWS WASTE ENERGY AND MONEY

New high-efficiency windows will cut your heating and cooling costs, which is a benefit many homeowners certainly appreciate. But unfortunately (and maybe even surprisingly), this alone is generally not a good reason to replace your windows.

Stopping any air leaks, especially by thorough exterior caulking and sealing attic bypasses, is the most important step toward energy efficiency. (Go to thefamilyhandyman.com and search for "attic air leaks.") The energy savings from new windows alone is unlikely to cover their costs, even with a federal tax credit. An energy audit will show you the most cost-effective improvements,

and the auditor can assess your windows at the same time.

However, if you have to replace your windows anyway, buy the most energy efficient ones you can afford. They'll cost a little (10 to 20 percent) more, but the additional savings will usually pay you back in the long run.

OTHER GOOD OPTIONS FOR SAVING ENERGY

Many less-expensive strategies will bring significant savings. For example, to tighten drafty double-hung and slider windows, you can add exterior storms ($100 to $200).

Another lower-cost option is to mount storms on the inside. (To help you locate this option, search online for "interior storm windows.") Or you can simply cover windows with heavy drapes at night to cut drafts and reduce heat loss.

E. YOUR OLD WINDOWS JUST PLAIN LOOK BAD

If your existing windows look shabby, whether it's from many layers of paint, permanent water stains, or general wear and tear, consider new windows. New windows will improve the appearance

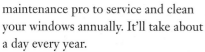

PRO TIP

Take it slow

Don't assume you have to replace all your windows at the same time. Windows sheltered from sun and rain or those on the north side of your home may be in far better shape than your home's unsheltered, south-facing windows.

of a room and add to the market value of your home—and make you happier in your house, too.

It's possible to refurbish old windows. You can chemically strip and refinish both sash and trim, restain or paint, reputty, install new glass and/ or replace hardware—but it's time consuming and usually notably more expensive than replacement.

Exceptions are windows that have historic value or windows that are unique and can't be duplicated at a reasonable price. In those cases, trying a self-refurbishment is probably not a good idea; you wouldn't want to damage anything you can't fix. Instead, it might be worth calling a pro.

Stop patio door drafts

Put your blanket away and pick up your hammer— it's time to block the breeze.

Patio door weather-strip seals slowly degrade and wear, letting in small drafts that are barely noticeable. If you spent the winter kicking up the thermostat (or grabbing a blanket) just to be comfortable near the door, you've already wasted enough money on heat to buy several sets of weather-strip seals. If you open your patio door frequently or the door is exposed to sunlight, it pays to replace the weather stripping every 10 years. Spring is the perfect time to do this.

Replacing the seals is a one-person job, but be sure to enlist a friend to help lift the heavy door in and out of the track. The tools for the job are simple and inexpensive (and you probably already have them lying around). You need a screwdriver, a hammer, hooks and picks, and a putty knife. The entire job takes just a few hours. Here's the process.

FIND THE MAKE AND MODEL

Some patio door manufacturers engrave their logos on the door pull lock hardware, but others hide the branding and model information. If you can't find a manufacturer logo or model label, look along the door edges or jamb for an AAMA Gold Label sticker from the Fenestration & Glazing Industry Alliance (FGIA). If you find the label, take a photo and go to fgiaonline.org. Once you're there, click on "product directory" to decipher the codes and get the correct brand and model information.

If you can't locate the label, copy the numbers on the metal strip between the panes of glass. Then go to igcc.org to decipher the codes. If neither approach works, or the manufacturer no longer sells replacement weather-strip seals, you'll have to use off-the-shelf weather stripping and come up with a custom fix.

Next, measure the stationary and movable sections. Take a digital photo of the entire door, track and jamb. Then contact the manufacturer's customer service/parts department to order replacement parts.

REMOVE THE DOOR

Most sliding patio doors tilt into the room from the top and then lift off the bottom track. The door is usually held in place with a removable header strip, which has to come off first. Brace the door or have a helper hold the door upright while you remove the header retaining screws **(Photo 1)**. Lean the door against a wall in a safe place after you lift it out

Removing the door can be tricky; be sure you tilt the top out far enough to clear the frame. Get help if you need it, since patio doors are often quite heavy.

WHAT IT TAKES		
TIME 3 hours	**COST** $50-$100	**SKILL LEVEL** Beginner

TOOLS & MATERIALS
Drill, hook or pick, scissors

1 Unscrew and remove the header. Open the patio door so the sliding door is in front of the stationary section. Start removing the header screws from that end. As you reach the open part of the door, have a friend brace the movable door so it doesn't tip out. Then remove the header strip. Door trim overlapping the header strip? Remove it.

2 Tilt and lift. Tilt the top of the sliding door out far enough to clear the frame. Then lift the door up and off the bottom track (get help—it's heavy). Set the door on a drop cloth and lean the door against a wall.

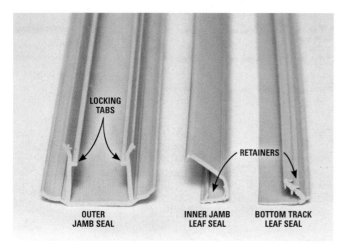

3 Identify and locate the seals. The outer jamb seal is hard plastic with locking tabs and rubber sealing wings. The inner and track leaf seals are made from a softer flexible material and are held in place with retainers.

4 Remove the jamb seals. Grab the outer jamb seal at the top and pull it off. Then pull the leaf seal out of the inner part of the jamb.

5 Remove the header seal. Starting at one side, slide a hook or pick behind the header seal and pry it away from the wood. Then slide the pick along the header as you pull off the entire header seal.

6 Cut the new seals. Using the old seals as templates, mark and cut the seals to the proper length. Cut with a scissors, utility knife or hacksaw.

7 Install the new seals. Spread the locking tabs and snap the outer and header jamb seals into place. Push the inner leaf seal into the groove. Then slide the bottom seal into the track.

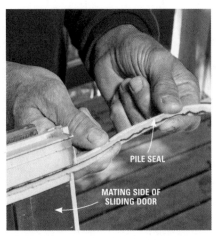

PILE SEAL

MATING SIDE OF SLIDING DOOR

8 Install new mating seal. Slide the new pile seal into the groove on the mating side of the sliding door. Then attach new self-adhesive pile strips at the top and bottom of the stationary door.

9 Lubricate the rollers. Clean the bottom rollers with a grease-cutting household cleaner. Then apply a few drops of oil to the roller axles. Wipe off the excess before installing the door.

of the track (**Photo 2**). The bottom rollers are usually dirty and the door latch can be greasy, so spread a drop cloth over carpeting to prevent stains.

REMOVE AND REPLACE JAMB, HEADER, TRACK AND PILE SEALS

Although weather-strip styles vary among manufacturers, this Marvin patio door is pretty common. The jamb has two seals: a hard plastic outer seal with locking tabs that snap into grooves on the jamb and a flexible leaf seal that's wedged into a groove on the inside part of the doorjamb (**Photo 3**).

Remove both jamb seals (**Photo 4**) and the header seal (**Photo 5**). Next, cut the new seals to length and install them (**Photos 6 and 7**). Then replace the pile seal on the stationary and sliding doors (**Photo 8**).

Clean and lubricate the bottom rollers using an all-purpose oil (**Photo 9**). Thoroughly clean the plastic or metal track that the rollers ride on. Then reinstall the sliding door and retaining header piece.

Finally, store your blanket in the linen closet—thanks to your hard work, you won't be needing it all the time anymore.

PRO TIP

Tip for replacing a shutoff valve

When you replace a compression-style shutoff valve, it's always best to use a new compression sleeve. Sawing through the sleeve without cutting into the copper tubing can be tricky, and sometimes you just don't have enough room to use a saw.

That's where a compression sleeve puller earns its keep (one choice is the Pasco No. 4661; $25 at certain supply stores). Crank out the screw and slide the jaw behind the compression nut. Then turn the screw until the pilot fits into the copper tubing. Continue turning until the sleeve slides off. That's it. Just slide on the new compression nut, sleeve and valve, and then tighten.

If you can't find factory parts

If you can't locate manufacturer weather-strip seals in stores, try these sources:

- amweatherguard.com
- biltbestwindowparts.com
- strybuc.com
- swisco.com

If you've checked all online sources and still can't find an exact match, you'll have to improvise with off-the-shelf materials. V-seal can be used in place of factory jamb, header and track leaf seals. Just fold along the score line to form a "V," remove the backing and stick it in place. Place EPDM foam rubber on the jamb and adjust the latch to accommodate the thickness. Use entry door seal strips to replace the factory pile strips in mating areas.

Mask pet claw scratches

It's so easy to hide those marks in your wood, you won't even mind when your pet tries to open the door.

Dogs and cats still haven't figured out how to open closed doors, but as any pet owner knows all too well, that's never stopped them from trying. Painted doors can be spackled and repainted to hide the damage, but natural wood doors can be more of a problem. However, if the scratches aren't too deep, you can usually mask the damage with stain and varnish.

Sand the damaged area lightly **(Photo 1)**, feathering the sanding into the surrounding undamaged area. Wipe off all dust. If you don't have the original stain or finish, find a matching stain at a paint store.

Gel stains (available at home centers and paint stores) work best. Buy a small piece of matching wood and experiment with it first, or bring a photo of the door to the paint store for help. Start with a lighter stain—it can always be darkened. You can also buy a few different colors and blend them or streak them together.

Wipe the scratched area with a rag dipped in thinner to keep the stain from looking blotchy. Put a small amount of the gel stain on a rag, then dab a little on a dry brush. Wipe excess stain on the rag. Drag the brush lightly along one edge and quickly wipe it dry to see how the color looks. Leave the stain on longer, apply additional coats or blend in other colors to darken it **(Photo 2)**.

If the stained area looks too dull after it dries, lightly spray the area with clear finish, feathering it into the surrounding area. This should solve the problem, and your doors will bear no marks of Fido's attempts to open them.

WHAT IT TAKES		
TIME 2 hours	**COST** Under $50	**SKILL LEVEL** Beginner
TOOLS & MATERIALS Sandpaper, brush, rags		

CLAW MARKS

FINE SANDING BLOCK

1 Lightly sand the scratches and the area around them.

2 Brush the stain over the sanded area with a dry brush, mixing colors to match the old finish.

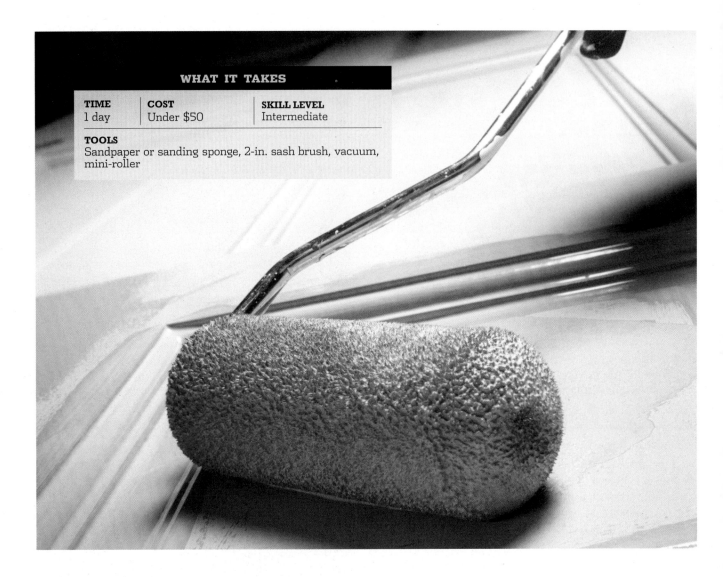

WHAT IT TAKES

TIME	COST	SKILL LEVEL
1 day	Under $50	Intermediate

TOOLS
Sandpaper or sanding sponge, 2-in. sash brush, vacuum, mini-roller

Paint a panel door

Every second counts in this tricky, but rewarding, weekend project.

Paneled doors are the ultimate painter's challenge. A large area broken up by shaped surfaces is just plain tough to cover before the paint becomes sticky and unworkable. And since doors are a prominent feature, ugly mistakes like brush marks or drips are noticeable.

BEFORE YOU START

The actual work involved in painting a door typically amounts to three to five hours, depending on the condition of the door and how fussy you are. But add in the drying time and it's a full-day project. If you're painting a door you can't live without—like a bathroom or exterior door—get started first thing in the morning so it can be back in service by day's end. While you're picking a paint color, also think about sheen: With a flat finish, scuff marks and handprints are hard to wipe away. High gloss is easy to clean but accentuates every little flaw, so your prep and paint job have to be perfect. Satin and semigloss are good compromise choices. Also check the operation of the door. If it rubs against the jamb or drags on the carpet, now's the time to sand or plane the edges. If you have several doors that need painting, start with the least prominent one. It's better to make learning mistakes on the inside of a closet door than on your entry door.

PREP TIPS

Pros often paint doors in place. But from prep to painting, you'll get better results if you remove the door. Working in your garage, shop or basement, you can better control lighting and drying conditions. And laying the door flat minimizes runs in the paint job.

Here's what to do after you remove the door:

- Clean the door with a regular household cleaner.
- Almost any cleaner will do, as long as it cuts grease. Areas around doorknobs are especially prone to greasy buildup.
- Remove all the door hardware to get a neater paint job and save time. If you're dealing with more than one door, avoid hardware mix-ups by labeling plastic bags that will hold the hardware for each door.
- Fill dents and holes with a sandable filler. You'll probably have to fill deep dents twice to compensate for shrinkage.
- Remove old paint from the door's hardware. Start with a product intended to remove paint splatter. You can use paint strippers, but they may also remove clear coatings from the hardware or damage some types of finishes.

SANDING TIPS

If your door is in good shape, all it needs is a light sanding with sandpaper or a sanding sponge (180 or 220 grit). That will roughen the surface a little and allow the primer to adhere better. But, most likely, you'll also need to smooth out chipped paint and imperfections from previous paint jobs. This is usually the most time-consuming, tedious part of the project. Here are tips for faster, better results:

- Paint often sticks to sandpaper, making it useless. Be sure to check the label and buy sandpaper intended for paint. You may still get some clogging, but you'll get less. This goes for sponges and other abrasives you use, too.

CAUTIONARY INSTRUCTIONS
If your home was built before 1978, check the paint for lead before you sand. For more information, go to epa.gov/lead.

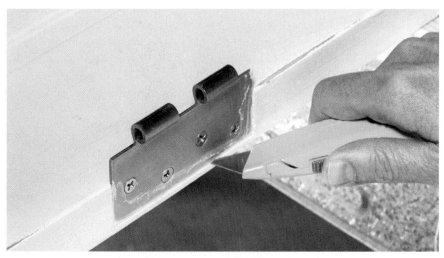

1 Remove all the hardware. Slice through paint buildup around hinges and latches. Otherwise, you might splinter surrounding wood as you remove hardware.

HARD RUBBER SANDING BLOCK

2 Sand it smooth. On flat areas, level out old runs and brush marks with a hard sanding block. For the shaped profiles, you'll need a combination of sanding pads, sponges and scraps of sandpaper.

3 Remove the sanding dust. A vacuum with a brush attachment removes most of the dust. Wipe off the rest with a damp rag.

4 Sand after priming. Sand out any imperfections in the coat. Shine a light on the surface to accentuate imperfections, and mark them with tabs of masking tape.

- Start with 120 or 150 grit. You can switch to coarser paper (such as 80 grit) on problem areas, but be sure to follow up with finer grit to smooth out the sanding scratches.
- On flat areas, a hard sanding block will smooth the surface much better than sponges or other soft-backed abrasives **(Photo 2)**.
- Try a finishing or random-orbit sander on flat areas. It might save you tons of time. Then again, the sandpaper may clog immediately from heat buildup. It depends on the type and age of the paint.
- Buy a collection of sanding sponges and pads for shaped areas. Through trial and error, you'll find that some work better than others on your door's profiles.
- Inspect your work with low-angle lighting **(see Photo 4)**.

TIPS FOR A PERFECT WORKSPACE

After the messy job of sanding is done, set the door aside and prep your workspace. For priming and painting, you want a work zone that's well lit and clean. Sawdust on your workbench ends up on brushes; airborne dust will create whiskers on the paint. The conditions in your work area should allow paint to dry slowly. Slower drying means more time for you to smooth the paint before it becomes gummy and more time for the paint to level itself. Here's how to prep your space:

- Clean everything. Vacuum work surfaces and sweep the floor.
- Minimize air movement for less airborne dust and slower drying. Close doors and windows. Turn off forced-air heating or cooling.
- Don't rely on overhead lighting. Instead, position a work light 4 to 5 ft. above the floor. This low-angle light will accentuate drips or ridges.
- Have all your tools and supplies ready, including a pail of water to dunk your paint tools in as soon as you're done.

- If you're working in the garage, unplug the garage door opener so it can't be opened while you work. An opening door raises dust. Also, wet the floor to keep dust down.

PRIMING TIPS

You can "spot-prime" a door, coating only patched dents or areas you sanded through to bare wood, but priming the whole door is best. The new paint will stick better and you'll get a more uniform finish. Here are some tips for this critical step:

- Your choice of primer is just as important as your choice of paint. At the paint store, ask for a primer that is compatible with your paint, levels out well and sands smoothly.
- Have the primer tinted, based on the color of your paint.
- Apply the primer with just as much care as the paint, following the same steps **(see Photos 5 – 9)**. Also, check out the painting tips in the next section.
- For an ultra-smooth paint job, apply two coats of primer. With a thick build of primer, you can sand the prime coat glassy-smooth without sanding through to the old paint.
- Lightly sand primer with 220 grit, inspecting as you go **(Photo 4)**. A couple of quick passes is all it takes. If you're not in a rush to get the door back in service, let the primer dry overnight before sanding. The longer it dries, the better it will sand.

PAINTING TIPS

Painting a door is a race against time. You have to lay down the paint and smooth it out before it becomes too sticky to work with or so stiff that brush marks won't level out and disappear. Be sure that you win that race by following these steps. And you'll want to keep moving, too. Don't stop to answer the phone or get coffee. In this situation, minutes count. In warm, dry conditions, even seconds really do end up mattering,

5 Paint the edges and wipe off the slop. Brush or roll paint onto all four edges. Immediately wipe any paint that slops onto the face of the door with a rag or foam brush. You don't have to completely remove the paint, but you do have to flatten it to prevent any ridges.

6 Brush around the panels. Work the paint into the corners and grooves, then drag the brush over the paint to smooth it. Wipe away any slop around the panel as shown in Photo 5.

7 Roll, then brush the panels. Coat the panels quickly with a roller. Then smooth the paint with a brush. Be careful not to touch the profiles surrounding the panel.

8 Roll the rails and stiles. Roll the door in sections, coating no more than one-quarter of the door at a time. Then brush out the paint. Be careful not to slop paint over the edges around the panels.

9 Brush with the grain. Brush across the joints where door parts meet. Then drag your brush in a straight line along the intersection. That way, any visible brush marks will look more like a wood grain pattern and less like sloppy brushwork.

Water-based alkyd is best

If you want a smooth finish, choose a smooth paint. You'll know them by their cost—they often cost as much for a quart as cheap paints do for a gallon! But it's worth it for first-class results.

One category stands out for smoothness: water-based alkyds. These paints dry slowly and level out almost as well as traditional alkyds. After applying them with a roller, you can skip the brush-out step shown in Photos 7 and 9 and still get perfect results.

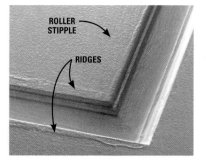

The wrong paint. Some paints show brush marks, ridges and roller stipple no matter how skillful or careful you are. Others go on smoothly and then level out beautifully, even if you're not a master painter.

so make sure you use every one to your advantage.

- Consider a paint additive to slow down drying and improve leveling. Your paint dealer can recommend one compatible with your paint.
- Start with a dust-free door; wipe it down with a damp rag just before you start painting.
- Spend the extra money to get a quality brush for a smoother finish. Pro painters disagree about the size and type to use, but a 2-in. sash brush generally works well.
- Don't use cheap roller sleeves or you'll get fibers in the finish. Use a mini roller and get good results with microfiber, mohair and foam sleeves. Foam sleeves leave a smooth finish, but they hold very little paint, which slows you down.
- Paint all four edges of the door first **(Photo 5)**. Here's why: When painting edges, some paint inevitably slops onto the faces of the door. It's better to have that happen before the faces are painted.
- Brush on a light coat. A heavy coat of paint covers better and sometimes levels out better, but runs are more likely and brush marks are deeper. Start out light, then lay it on a little thicker as your brush skills improve.
- Roll on the paint where you can. Rollers lay on paint much faster than a brush, giving you a few more precious minutes to work the paint before it begins to stiffen.
- Brush out rolled paint. Brushed paint usually levels out better than rolled paint, and any brush marks are less noticeable than roller stipple. But you might be able to skip the brush-out step altogether. With top-quality enamel and roller sleeves, roller results can be super smooth. It depends in part on drying conditions, so try it on a closet door or a primed scrap of wood first.
- Plan to apply at least two coats. Lightly sand between coats with 220 grit to remove any dust nubs.

Beef up entry door security

Preventing burglars takes about an hour with this quick fix.

You can spend hundreds on a fancy "pick-proof" dead bolt, but that won't stop most burglars; they gain entry with one well-placed kick or body slam that splits the doorjamb. Stop them in their tracks by beefing up your door and jamb with reinforcing hardware. Here's how to do it.

Start by measuring the entry door thickness and the spacing between the entry knob and the dead bolt cylinder. Then buy either a single or double wrap-around door reinforcement plate kit (less than $20 at any home center or hardware store) and four 1-1/2-in.-long stainless steel wood screws. Then get a doorjamb reinforcement kit.

Remove the entry knob and dead bolt cylinder. Then take off the dead bolt and latch, and toss the short screws. Install the wrap-around door reinforcement plate, and reinstall the latch and dead bolt plates using the longer stainless steel screws **(Photo 1)**.

Next, mark both the latch and the dead bolt "centers" on the strike side of the jamb **(Photo 2)**. Remove the latch and strike plates and the weather stripping from the jamb. Leave any weather stripping that's attached to the doorstop. Then align the jamb reinforcement plate, predrill a few mounting holes and add the screws **(Photo 3)**. Check the reinforcement plate alignment before snugging the screws by hand, and do not overtighten.

If the prescored dead bolt knockout lines up with the marking along the jamb, remove it and then finish by installing the remaining screws. If it doesn't line up, drill a new dead bolt hole with a 3/8-in. bimetal hole saw. Replace two screws in each hinge with the longer screws provided in the kit.

WHAT IT TAKES		
TIME 1 hour	**COST** $100-$250	**SKILL LEVEL** Beginner
TOOLS Drill		

1 Reinforce the door. Slide reinforcement plate onto the door and insert the dead bolt and dead latch. Secure them with 1-1/2-in.-long stainless steel screws. Then secure the plate to the door with the matching screws from the kit.

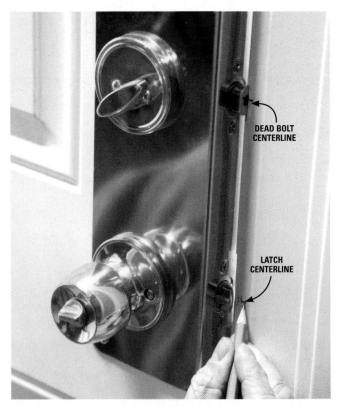

DEAD BOLT CENTERLINE

LATCH CENTERLINE

2 Mark the latch and bolt centers. Extend the dead bolt slightly and close the door. Mark the center of the bolt on the edge of the doorjamb with a pencil. Then mark the center of the latch on the jamb.

LATCH
ALIGNMENT
HOLE

CENTERLINE
MARK

3 Attach a jamb reinforcement plate. Extend the pencil marks to the doorstop. Then line up the center of the latch alignment hole on the reinforcement plate with the centerline mark. Slide the plate into place. Predrill two holes and run the supplied screws almost all the way into the jamb with your drill. Stop before they're seated or you'll bow the door frame.

Great Goofs®

Laughs and lessons from our readers

HONEY, SOMEONE'S AT THE FURNACE!

We needed a new doorbell, so my brother-in-law helped us install one. Early in the morning a few days later, the doorbell rang. We got up to check the door, but nobody was there. About a half hour later, it rang again, yet no one was there. Convinced it was a practical joke, we waited by the door. The bell rang again, and this time we could see there was no one even ringing it. We remembered that a doorbell uses low voltage supplied by a transformer. We traced the wires and found they were connected to a transformer that was also hooked to the furnace thermostat. As a result, whenever the furnace came on, the doorbell rang. We bought a dedicated transformer for the new doorbell, and now we are sleeping in.

BOB SCHWINDT

SUNROOF DISASTER

I finally got around to replacing the flashing on one of our dormers. My extension ladder was too short to let me work comfortably at the peak of the dormer, so I drove my pickup into the front yard and placed the ladder in the bed, propping the bottom against the tailgate. It worked perfectly, giving me the extra height I needed.

I climbed the ladder and went to work. I had just gotten down to business when the hammer slipped out of my hand, ricocheted off the ladder rungs and smashed through the sunroof of my truck—a one in a million shot. To look on the bright side, at least it didn't go through my windshield. But from now on, I'll use scaffolding to tackle the high points of my house.

RON BENDER

LAUNDRY WASHOUT

While folding laundry one rainy Saturday, I noticed water seeping from the sill of a window in the basement. Figuring the window had not shut properly because of a dirty seal, I got a small rag and started to open the window to wipe it out.

When I turned the latch, a tidal wave washed over the laundry room, completely soaking me and everything else. I hadn't realized that the entire window well was full of water. I went upstairs to change and told my wife the laundry was still a little damp.

TERRY JOBKE

PAINT-BUCKET BOMB

I was painting some windows high above my deck and needed to hang a paint bucket from my ladder. I'd fashioned a hook from some aluminum wire the day before to hold my tool bucket, so I figured that would do. As I was painting, the hook came unbent, sending the bucket plummeting and the paint exploding all over the deck below. The deck was in need of sprucing up, but this wasn't exactly what I'd had in mind.

STAN DICKERSON

CHAPTER TWO

BACKYARD

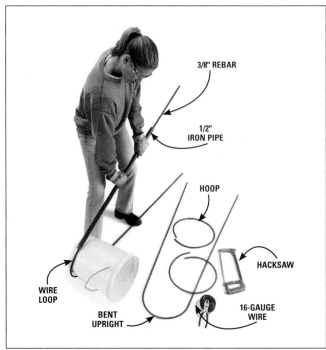

1 Bend 10-ft. lengths of 3/8-in. rebar around a 5-gallon bucket to form two arches as shown. Drill two holes in the side of the bucket, and loop a wire through the holes and around the rebar to hold it in place. Slip a 3-ft. length of 1/2-in. pipe over the rebar for leverage. Bend the hoops the same way, but wrap the rebar around the bucket to form a circle. Then cut the straight section off with a hacksaw, leaving the hoop and a few inches of overlap. Wrap and twist-tie wire around the overlap to form the two hoops.

Rebar plant cage

This rustic metal plant cage makes an attractive addition to your flower garden.

This cage is a perfect support for peppers or tomatoes. It is built from concrete reinforcing steel (rebar) connected by twisted wire. You'll need three 10-ft. lengths of 3/8-in. (No. 3) rebar and 20 ft. of 16- or 18-gauge wire. Ask the supplier to cut standard 20-ft. lengths in half to make it easier to haul.

WHAT IT TAKES		
TIME 1 - 2 hours	**COST** Less than $50	**SKILL LEVEL** Beginner
TOOLS Hacksaw, 1/2-in. pipe, pliers, 5-gallon bucket		

2 Stack the two hoops on the ground. Poke the ends of the arches a few inches into the ground inside the hoops. Twist a 12-in. length of wire around the intersection of the two arches, then cut off the extra wire. Slide the first loop up to about 16-in. from the top, and wire it in place. Stand back and eyeball the hoop to make sure it's level and the uprights are evenly spaced before you tighten the tie wires. Repeat this process for the second hoop, leaving about 16 in. between hoops.

Classic backyard bench

Need outdoor seating in a hurry? This simple bench, based on author and ecologist Aldo Leopold's classic design, can be constructed in a couple of hours. All it takes is two boards, some glue and 18 screws.

Cut the legs from a 2x8 x 10-ft. piece of rot-resistant wood **(Photo 1)**. Cut the seat and backrest from an 8-ft. 2x8.

Lay out and assemble the sides as mirror images, using the seat and back pieces for alignment **(Photo 2)**. Join the legs with three 2-1/2-in. deck screws and construction adhesive. Predrill all the screw holes with a countersink bit to avoid splitting the wood. Finally, set the sides parallel to each other, and glue and screw the seat and back into place. Finish the bench with a coat of exterior oil or stain.

WHAT IT TAKES		
TIME 2 - 3 hours	**COST** Less than $50	**SKILL LEVEL** Beginner
TOOLS Speed square, circular saw, drill/driver		

1 Starting at one end of a 10-ft. board, make the same 22-1/2 degree cut five times to create the four legs.

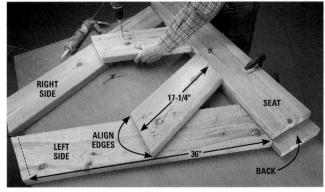

2 Clamp the seat and back to the workbench as a stop, then predrill, glue and screw the rear legs to the front legs.

Cutting List

KEY	PART
A	Rear legs: 2x8 x 17-1/4" (22-1/2° cuts)
B	Front legs: 2x8 x 36" (22-1/2° cuts)
C	Seat: 2x8 x 42"
D	Back: 2x8 x 45"

Plant markers

Unique, simple and cheap, these markers make your favorite plants stand out in the garden.

Your beloved blooms deserve more recognition than sticks with scribbled names! Instead, make these unique plant markers that hold a label or a seed packet with bent copper wire set in a decorative base. They're easy to assemble, so let your creativity flow. Decorate them with rocks, glass beads or even seashells. They're delightful gifts for friends and relatives, and you can make dozens of them for cheap. Best of all, you probably already have all the tools you'll need.

To make these markers, grab your 2-gallon bucket and a wooden spoon for mixing the mortar. A 4- x 8- x 2-in. disposable plastic container works as a form, but you could also try using a cut-off milk carton or a bread pan. Round up a pair of pliers, wire cutters and a utility knife for working with the wire. For supplies, you'll need a bag of mortar mix (60 lbs. is plenty), a dust mask, a can of nonstick cooking spray and 12-gauge copper wire (sold by the foot at home

centers). For decoration, use about 1/3 lb. of rocks, glass beads or seashells per holder. Craft stores are overflowing with materials.

For the markers shown, a latex bonding agent was added to the mortar. It's not absolutely necessary, but it'll make the mortar stick better to smooth rocks and glass. Buy it from a masonry supplier and follow the directions for mixing.

WHAT IT TAKES		
TIME	**COST**	**SKILL LEVEL**
1 - 2 hours	Less than $50	Beginner
TOOLS		
Wooden spoon, pliers, wire cutters, utility knife		

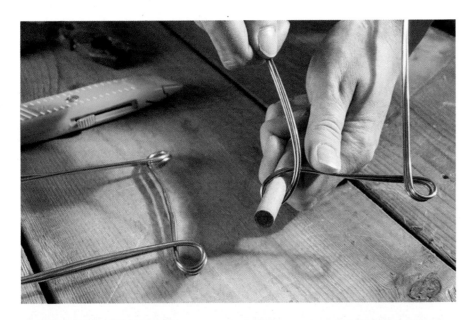

1 Bend the copper wire. Hold a dowel 8 in. from the end of a 5-ft. piece of wire folded in half. Wrap the wire around dowel as shown, forming a loop. Move the dowel over 3-1/2 in. (or the width needed to fit your seed packet) and wrap it again, making a second loop in the opposite direction. Cut the wire off even with the first leg, and bend a 1/2-in. 90-degree turn at the bottom of each leg to anchor it in the mortar.

2 Add the mortar. Mix up the mortar to the consistency of cookie dough, slowly adding water to the dry mix as needed. Mix thoroughly; let it sit for about 3 minutes, then remix, adding a dash more water if needed. Coat the plastic form with cooking spray. After filling the form, give it a few quick shakes to settle the mortar. Form a mound using a spoon or small trowel so it resembles a loaf of baked banana bread.

3 Push the copper marker into the mortar so the 90-degree bends are about 1/2-in. up from the bottom and centered. If the mortar is too wet to support the wire, take a quick coffee break and let it stiffen a bit. Now arrange the rocks or beads to your liking. When arranging the rocks, it's best to start at the edges and work toward the center. Embed the decorations at least halfway into the mortar so they're held tight. If you don't like how a rock looks, remove it, rinse it off and reposition it. Once you're done with the arrangement, let the marker set for at least 24 hours before removing it from the form.

WHAT IT TAKES

TIME	COST	SKILL LEVEL
2 - 3 hours	$100-$250	Beginner

TOOLS
Drill/driver, circular saw, hand tools
Optional: Router, random orbital sander

Simple timber bench

We knew what we wanted in a bench, and this one has it all.

Building this bench happens surprisingly fast. If you have some experience with power tools, you'll have it built in just a few hours, though staining it may add a couple more. You can build it with just a drill/driver, circular saw and basic hand tools, but you'll get faster, better results if you also have a router and a random orbit sander.

All the materials are available at home centers. When you're choosing timbers, take the time to pick through the pile for the straightest ones. They'll twist a little after you build the bench (see "One year later..." on p. 51), but they need to be nice and straight when you're cutting the joints and assembling the bench.

CUT THE PARTS TO SIZE

Three of the landscape timbers will become the beams for the bench's seat. The timbers are slightly longer than 8 ft. when you buy them, so you'll need to cut a little off each end to make them exactly 96-in. long.

Set each timber on a pair of sawhorses and use a Speed square to draw a pencil line on all four sides **(Photo 1)**. Set your circular saw blade for a full-depth cut. Then, using your

4X6
TIMBERS

This bench is made entirely from pressure-treated landscape timbers and a few galvanized lag screws and washers. Add black spray paint and exterior stain and you'll have a beautiful, low-maintenance bench. The hardest part of the project is picking through the pile of heavy landscape timbers at the home center to find the best ones.

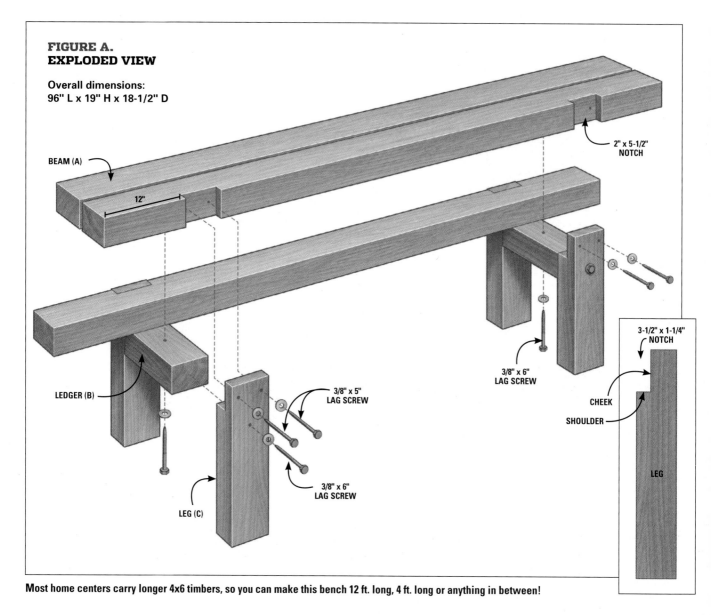

**FIGURE A.
EXPLODED VIEW**

Overall dimensions:
96" L x 19" H x 18-1/2" D

BEAM (A)

12"

2" x 5-1/2"
NOTCH

LEDGER (B)

3/8" x 5"
LAG SCREW

3/8" x 6"
LAG SCREW

LEG (C)

3/8" x 6"
LAG SCREW

3-1/2" x 1-1/4"
NOTCH

CHEEK

SHOULDER

LEG

Most home centers carry longer 4x6 timbers, so you can make this bench 12 ft. long, 4 ft. long or anything in between!

Materials List

ITEM	QTY.
4x6 x 8' pressure-treated landscape timbers	5
3/8" x 5" galvanized lag screws	8
3/8" x 6" galvanized lag screws	6
3/8" galvanized washers	14
Exterior stain and black spray paint	

Cutting List

KEY	PART	QTY.
A	4x6 x 96" beams	3
B	4x6 x 11-1/2" ledgers	2
C	4x6 x 19" legs	4

square as a guide, make the first cut on one of the wide "faces" of the timber. You're not going to be able to cut all the way through in one pass, but doing three passes works well **(Photo 2)**.

When you finish the first cut, rotate the timber on edge, start the saw and slip your saw's blade partway into the "kerf" (slit) you just made to align the blade for your second cut.

Guide the saw with your square again, finish the second cut, rotate the timber one more time, and do the same thing to make the third and final cut. Now cut the rest of the parts to length the same way, and use a random orbit sander to remove any saw marks left behind **(Photo 3)**.

CUT THE NOTCHES

The joinery that connects the legs to the seat beams looks complicated, but it's really simple. The outside beams of the bench's seat are supported by L-shape notches in the legs. U-shape notches are also cut into the seat beams so the leg's faces can sit about 1/4-in. proud of the beams. The notches are all formed the same way using a circular saw, a square and a sharp wood chisel.

Tip each of the outside beams on end. Using a pencil and your square, mark layout lines for the sides and bottoms of the notches **(Photo 4)**. Set your circular saw blade to the proper depth. Then, using the square as a guide (clamp it down if needed), make a perfectly

1 MARK THE LENGTHS OF THE PARTS. For each part, mark with a square and pencil where you'll be cutting. Draw lines on all four sides of each timber to help align your cuts.

2 CUT THREE TIMES. A 4x6 timber is too thick to cut in one pass; it's easy in three. Guide your saw with a square and rotate the timber 90 degrees in between cuts. To align the second cut, slip the saw blade partway into the kerf you made on the first. Repeat this for the third cut.

3 SAND OFF SAW MARKS. Remove any saw marks left behind with a random orbit sander and 60-grit sandpaper.

4 MARK THE NOTCHES. Draw layout lines for the notches in the legs and beams (Figure A). Make X's to remind yourself where to cut.

5 MAKE THE SHOULDER CUTS. Guide your saw with the square to make dead-straight "shoulder" cuts that will define the outsides of the notches in the legs and beams (Figure A). The beams get two shoulder cuts per notch. The legs get one shoulder cut per notch.

6 MAKE THE KERF CUTS. Cut a series of freehand kerfs between the shoulder cuts you made for the notches in the beams. The legs have only one shoulder cut per notch, so start your kerf cuts at the ends and work toward the shoulder cuts.

7 KNOCK AWAY THE SLIVERS. Remove the thin slivers of wood left behind with the claw of a hammer.

8 CHISEL THE NOTCHES SMOOTH. Smooth the "cheek" of each notch (Figure A) with a sharp wood chisel.

ROUND-OVER BIT

9 ROUND OVER THE EDGES. Remove the sharp edges from the beams and legs with a router and 1/4-in. round-over bit.

LEDGER

10 DRILL PILOT HOLES. Temporarily clamp together all the bench parts and drill 5/16-in. pilot holes for lag screws.

11 PAINT THE LAG SCREWS AND WASHERS. Coat the heads of the lag screws and washers with black spray paint. Save the can for future touch-ups.

IMPACT DRIVER

6" LAG SCREWS

5" LAG SCREWS

12 DRIVE THE LAG SCREWS. Drive lag screws with washers through the pilot holes you drilled earlier. An impact driver with a socket works great for this, but you can also use a wrench or ratchet. Touch up any scuffs on the lag screws with black paint.

straight cut on each side of the notch **(Photo 5)**. Then make a series of freehand kerf cuts between the two outside cuts you made **(Photo 6)**. The notches for the legs are made nearly the same way.

When you're done cutting, knock out the thin slivers of wood with the claw of your hammer **(Photo 7)**. Use a sharp wood chisel to smooth and flatten the bottoms of the notches **(Photo 8)**.

ROUND OVER THE SHARP EDGES

The edges of the seat beams and legs are sharp and can give you splinters, so deal with them before you assemble the bench. Lay the beams and legs on sawhorses. Knock off all sharp edges with a router and 1/4-in. round-over bit **(Photo 9)**. With the router, be sure to go counterclockwise. If you don't have a router, you can do the job with a block plane, a sanding block or a random orbit sander. Don't round over the edges of the notches.

ASSEMBLE THE BENCH

If you're planning to stain your bench, do it now before you assemble all the parts. You might need to let the wood dry out a bit before staining, because pressure-treated lumber is very wet when you buy it. Be sure to read the directions on the can.

Set the outside beams for the seat upside down across your sawhorses with the U-shape notches facing out, and fit the L-shape notches of the legs into each of the U-shape notches. The L-shape notches should fit snugly into the U-shape notches, and the tops of the legs should be flush with the tops of the seat beams. The faces of the legs will sit a little proud of the seat beams—about 1/4 in. If the joints won't go together by hand, knock them together with a rubber mallet or dead blow hammer. If they still won't go together, you might have to fine-tune the fit of each joint with your chisel.

Set the third beam (the one without notches) between the other two beams, making sure the spaces are even—about 1/2 in. Now set the ledgers between the legs, pull it all together tightly and use long clamps to hold it temporarily.

Drill pilot holes through the tops of the legs for lag screws **(Photo 10)**, with two through each L-shape notch and one below each notch's shoulder **(Figure A)**. Drill one hole in the center of each ledger.

Next, spray-paint the heads of the lag screws and washers, and let them dry before driving **(Photo 11)**. Once they're dry, drive the lag screws with washers through all the pilot holes you drilled **(Photo 12)**. Touch up the tops of the lag screws with more paint if they get scuffed up (spray a little paint on a disposable brush).

PRO TIP

One year later ...

This bench sat outside, completely unsheltered, through a hot summer and a hard Minnesota winter, and it still looks fantastic! The timbers twisted a little, but that just adds to the rustic look. The joints loosened a bit from wood shrinkage, but that was easily fixed by tightening the lag screws.

LIMESTONE
STEPPING-
STONES

DRYWALL
KEYHOLE SAW

1 Space the stepping-stones along the path to match your stride. Using the stones as patterns, cut through the sod around each stone with a drywall saw or a bread knife.

Stepping-stone path

Fast, simple and attractive.

Stepping-stone paths offer many of the same advantages as concrete sidewalks and paver stones but without all the work and mess. You can save wear and tear on your lawn or take a trip to the garden without getting your feet wet from dew. Since you remove only enough sod to place the stones, you can lay this path without tearing up your lawn. And if you pile the dirt and sod on a tarp as you work, cleanup can be easy.

Almost any type of flat stones will work as long as they're about 2-in. thick. We picked these limestone stepping-stones from a pile at the local landscape supply center. You'll also need one 60-lb. bag of playground sand for every 10 stones.

WHAT IT TAKES		
TIME	**COST**	**SKILL LEVEL**
1 day	Varies	Beginner
TOOLS		
Drywall saw or bread knife, trowel		

2 Move the stone to the side and dig out the sod with a trowel. Dig the hole 1 in. deeper than the thickness of the stone to allow for the sand base.

1" LAYER
OF SAND

3 Roughly level a 1-in. layer of sand in the hole. Set the stone on the sand and wiggle it until it's flush with the surrounding sod. Add or remove sand as necessary.

Fold-up grill table

This handy companion for your barbecue collapses for easy storage.

After using this collapsible cedar table, your family members will wonder how they ever grilled without it. The legs nest under the top for quick storage or for carrying to all kinds of other jobs. All you need to build it is a drill, a saw, basic hand tools, a short stack of cedar boards and half an afternoon.

The table is made entirely from 1x4 cedar boards. Wood quality varies, so pick over the lumber for flat, straight boards

WHAT IT TAKES		
TIME	**COST**	**SKILL LEVEL**
2 - 3 hours	$100-$250	Beginner
TOOLS		
Drill, saw, basic hand tools		

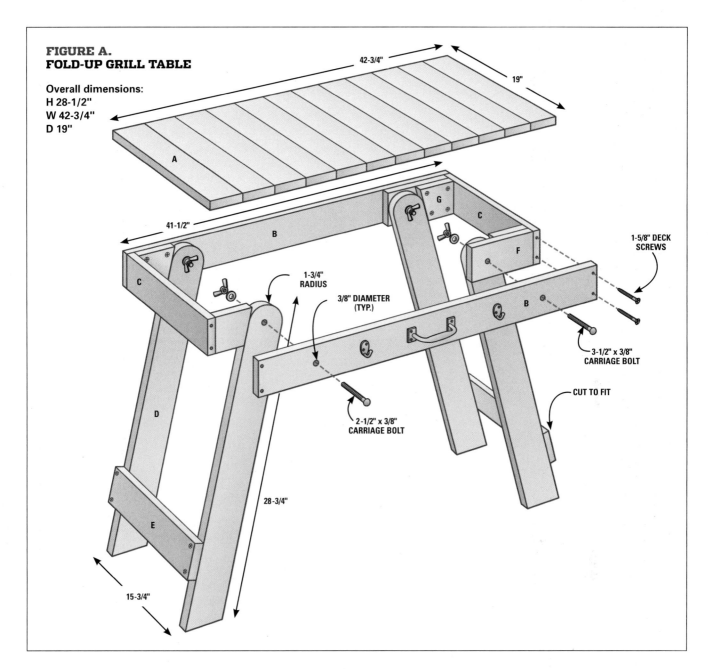

FIGURE A.
FOLD-UP GRILL TABLE

Overall dimensions:
H 28-1/2"
W 42-3/4"
D 19"

42-3/4"

19"

A

41-1/2"

B

C

G

C

F

1-5/8" DECK
SCREWS

1-3/4"
RADIUS

3/8" DIAMETER
(TYP.)

B

B

3-1/2" x 3/8"
CARRIAGE BOLT

D

2-1/2" x 3/8"
CARRIAGE BOLT

CUT TO FIT

28-3/4"

E

15-3/4"

that are free of large or loose knots. You can make the table from eight 6-ft. boards, but buy 10 to allow for possible miscuts and to give yourself more choices for the top slats.

CUT THE PARTS

You can use a handsaw to cut the parts, but an electric jigsaw speeds up the job significantly. Use a square to help make straight cuts **(Photo 1, p. 56)**. To ensure matching legs and frame parts, clamp two boards together and mark and cut them at the same time **(Photo 2)**. Cut slats one or two at a

time. You'll cut the stretchers after bolting on the legs.

To assemble the frame, drill two holes in the ends of the longer frame boards and add a countersink hole for the screwheads to nestle into. Cut slats and place them top-side up on a flat surface **(Photo 3)**. Center the frame on

Materials List

ITEM	QTY.
2-1/2" x 3/8" carriage bolts	2
3-1/2" x 3/8" carriage bolts	2
3/8" wing nuts and flat washers	4
1-5/8" deck screws	1 box
Penofin wood finish	1 pint
Drill with countersink	1

Cutting List

KEY	PART	QTY.
A	1x4 x 19" top slats	12
B	1x4 x 41-1/2" long sides	2
C	1x4 x 15-3/4" short sides	2
D	1x4 x 28-3/4" legs (15° angled end cut)	4
E	1x4 x 15-3/4" leg stretchers (cut to fit)	2
F	1x4 x 6-3/4" leg spacers	2
G	1x4 x 4-3/8" leg stop blocks (15° angled end cut)	4

(Note: All parts cut from 1x4 S3S cedar, so each board is a "fat" 3/4" thick and 3-1/2" wide, with two smooth edges, one smooth side and one rough side.)

1 Cut the boards for the top and the frame using a jigsaw or handsaw and a square.

SQUARE

2 Clamp the leg boards together (rough side in) and cut both of them at once to create identical leg pairs. Drill the 3/8-in. bolt hole in the upper end before unclamping.

FRAME
3/4" OVERHANG
TOP BOARDS

3 Lay the frame on the top boards and lightly trace the frame shape so it's easy to see where to drill holes. Space the top boards with about 1/16-in. gaps between them.

8d NAIL
DRILL BIT WITH COUNTERSINK

4 Drill two holes in each top board end with a countersink bit and screw it to the frame. A nail is really handy for creating even spacing.

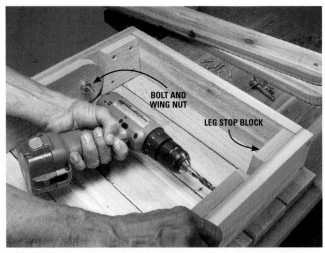

BOLT AND WING NUT
LEG STOP BLOCK

5 Screw a pair of angled leg stop blocks in one end of the frame, then butt the rounded ends of the legs against the blocks. Drill through the frame, and bolt on the legs.

SPACER BLOCK
3-1/2"
2-3/8"
LEG STOP BLOCK

6 Screw spacer blocks in the other frame end. These allow the other pair of legs to nest inside the first pair. Then drill and bolt on the second pair of legs and the leg stop blocks.

7 Screw stretchers across each pair of legs. For the best fit and overall results, mark and cut the stretchers based on the actual spacing between the legs.

8 Test the fit of the legs in the frame by pulling the legs up from the frame. If they bind and scrape, sand the sides for a smoother fit.

the slats to create a 3/4 in. overhang on all four sides. Lightly trace the frame shape on the slats with a pencil.

Lift off the frame, and drill and countersink screw holes in the slats using the traced lines as a guide. Then screw the slats to the frame **(Photo 4)**. Lightly tap a couple of nails between the slats while screwing them to the frame in order to create the approximate 1/16-in. spacing between the slats. The end slats will overhang the frame approximately 3/4 in. to match the slat overhang along the frame sides.

ATTACH THE LEGS

Flip the tabletop upside down and screw the pair of angled leg stop blocks to the corners of one end **(Photo 5)**. Butt the rounded leg ends against the blocks, then drill and bolt on the outer leg pair with the shorter 2-1/2-in. carriage bolts, washers and wing nuts. Attach the inner leg pair to the other frame, first screwing in the spacer blocks to allow the legs to nest inside the other pair **(Photo 6)**. Add the angled leg stop blocks, then drill and bolt on the second leg pair with the longer 3-1/2-in. carriage bolts.

With the legs flat on the underside of the table, measure for the stretchers, cut, drill and fasten them to the legs **(Photo 7)**. To pull out the legs, lift the more widely spaced pair first so the second pair can be raised without catching on the first pair's stretcher **(Photo 8)**.

SAND, FINISH, GRILL!

Sand the table with 100-grit paper, and with a sanding block or rasp, slightly round the top edges of the slats. Put on your favorite finish; we used two coats of Penofin penetrating oil finish (in the cedar color). Pull out the legs, tighten the wing nuts and throw some rib eye steaks on the grill—just in time for dinner! You'll enjoy this table for years to come, and friends and family will appreciate how often you want to grill.

This majestic fountain mimics the majesty of national parks, right in your own backyard.

Backyard spring

Build this beautiful bubbling fountain in an afternoon.

If you've ever been to Yellowstone, you probably remember the magic of the natural springs. In less than half a day, you can build your own small spring to enjoy at home. You can tuck this spring fountain in the corner of a patio where you can easily see and hear the water. It'll go anywhere in your yard or garden, but you'll need to make sure you have an outdoor outlet nearby. Here's what you need:

- A large sturdy tub or bucket (about a 15-gallon size).
- A piece of pond liner large enough to line the bucket with an additional foot on each side.
- A small fountain pump (this moves 210 gallons per hour).
- A piece of flexible braided plastic tubing the diameter of the pump outlet, cut to the length of the bucket height.
- A hose clamp to connect the tubing to the pump.

- A brick to rest the pump on.
- A square piece of heavy-gauge, galvanized hardware cloth with a 1/4-in. grid, cut 6 to 8 in. larger than the diameter of the bucket.
- About 40 lbs. of round rocks 1-1/2 to 3 in. in diameter. Mexican beach pebbles were used here.

WHAT IT TAKES		
TIME 5 - 6 hours	**COST** $100-$250	**SKILL LEVEL** Intermediate
TOOLS Shovel, utility knife, tin snips		

DIG IT IN

Dig a hole the size of your bucket, but slightly deeper. Place the top lip of the bucket 2-1/2 in. below the surface of the patio or ground.

Place the bucket in the hole and backfill around it, then line the inside of the bucket with your pond liner. Extend the liner out at least 8 in. beyond the diameter of the bucket, more if you want your spring to shoot higher.

You want the liner to catch any water splashing on the rocks and to direct the runoff back into the bucket. Curl up the edge of the liner to create a ledge for that purpose. Then, create a ledge for the pond by wedging the liner between two bricks.

RUN THE CORD AND PLACE THE STONES

Place the brick and the pump in the center of the bucket. Connect the tubing to the pump outlet with a hose clamp.

Follow the manufacturer's instructions for running the cord, and don't bury it. Place the hardware cloth over the bucket and then snip a small hole in the center to allow the tubing through.

The hardware cloth should be larger than the diameter of the bucket. Place stones and brick on top of the hardware cloth and fill the bucket with water.

Turn the pump on and adjust the tubing, wedging it between the rocks to get the desired effect. You can restrict the flow of the water by pinching the pipe with wire or buying a flow restricter from your pump supplier. The diameter of the pipe will determine how high the water bubbles up.

CAUTIONARY INSTRUCTIONS
Plug the cord into a GFCI-protected outlet.

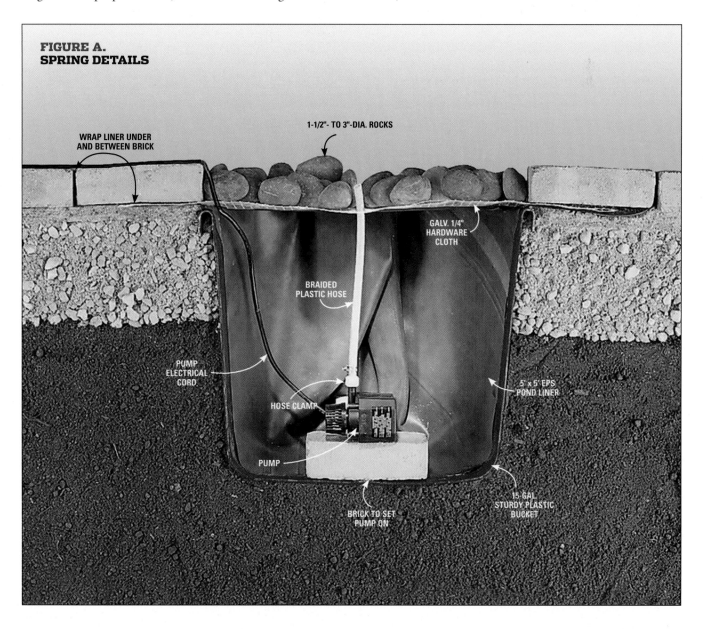

FIGURE A.
SPRING DETAILS

WRAP LINER UNDER AND BETWEEN BRICK

1-1/2"- TO 3"-DIA. ROCKS

GALV. 1/4" HARDWARE CLOTH

BRAIDED PLASTIC HOSE

PUMP ELECTRICAL CORD

HOSE CLAMP

5' x 5' EPS POND LINER

PUMP

BRICK TO SET PUMP ON

15-GAL STURDY PLASTIC BUCKET

ABOVE: Pavers, sand and glue can take your patio from gloomy to gorgeous. INSET: This project revived the tired concrete on this DIYer's patio.

Concrete patio cover-up

No need to tear out an ugly slab—just hide it!

A concrete patio is made for practicality—not beauty. It starts out looking plain and goes downhill from there. As craters, cracks and stains accumulate, it can go from dull to downright ugly in just a few years. But there's a simple solution, whether you want to dress up a bland patio or hide one's signs of aging. Covering concrete with paver bricks is easier than pouring new concrete or laying pavers. It requires less skill and less time, and it's a whole lot easier on your back.

BEFORE

AFTER

WHAT IT TAKES		
TIME 2 days	**COST** $5 per square foot	**SKILL LEVEL** Intermediate
TOOLS Plate compactor, chalk, utility knife, broom, screed pipe, screed board, caulk gun, rubber mallet		

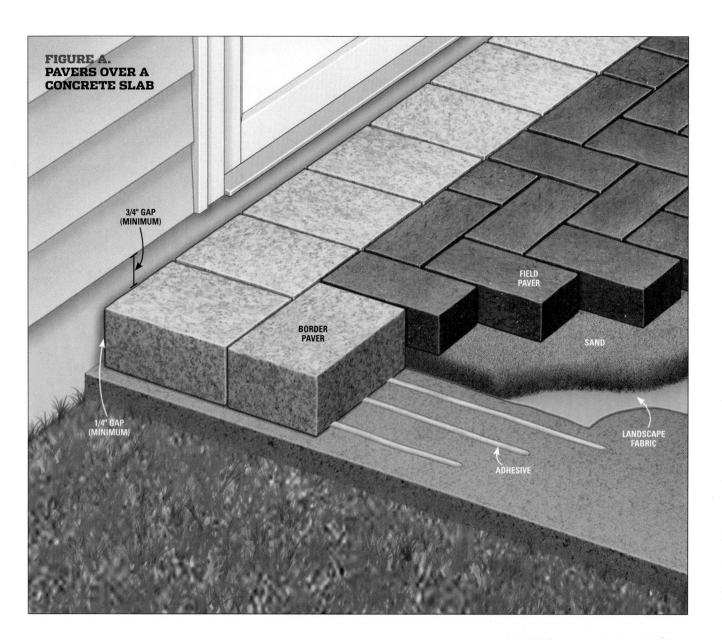

**FIGURE A.
PAVERS OVER A
CONCRETE SLAB**

3/4" GAP
(MINIMUM)

1/4" GAP
(MINIMUM)

BORDER
PAVER

FIELD
PAVER

SAND

LANDSCAPE
FABRIC

ADHESIVE

ASSESS YOUR SLAB

This project will work with most patios. Surface damage like flaking, chips and craters is no problem, but a few conditions make this method a no-go:

- A too-low threshold. Thresholds have to be high enough above the existing patio to allow for the thickness of the border pavers, plus an extra 3/4 in. to allow for "frost heave"—rising of the slab when the soil freezes.
- Expanding cracks. This method will work over most cracks—which grow and shrink with seasonal ground movement. But if you have a crack that has noticeably grown in recent

years, this method is risky. The crack may "telegraph" through the pavers.

MONEY AND MATERIALS

The materials for this 12 x 14-ft. patio cost approximately $5 per sq. ft. Using less expensive pavers, you could cut the cost by almost half. Most landscape suppliers and home centers stock all the materials, but you may have to do a little hunting for the right combination of pavers.

The pavers used for the border must be at least 3/4-in. thicker than the "field" pavers, which cover the area between the borders. That thickness

PRO TIP

Save 12 tons of toil

A standard paver patio rests on a thick base of compacted gravel. This patio cover-up will save you the cost of that gravel. More important, it eliminates the backbreaking drudgery of breaking up concrete, digging up soil, hauling it all away and hauling in gravel. On this 12 x 14-ft. patio, a patio tear-out and new gravel base would have meant more than 12 extra tons of wheelbarrow work.

1 Scrub the perimeter. Clean the edges of the patio where you'll later glue down the border pavers. Clean concrete means a stronger glue bond.

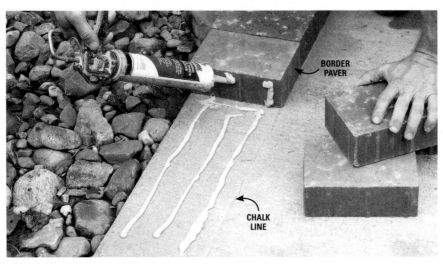

BORDER PAVER

CHALK LINE

2 Glue down the border pavers. After setting each paver, run a bead of construction adhesive up the side. That will keep the sand from washing out between pavers.

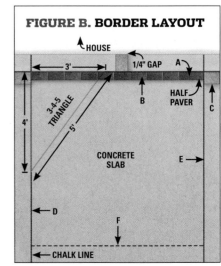

FIGURE B. BORDER LAYOUT

HOUSE

3'

1/4" GAP A

3-4-5 TRIANGLE

5'

4'

B

HALF PAVER

C

CONCRETE SLAB

E

D

F

CHALK LINE

A. Snap a chalk line parallel to the house to mark the location of the border pavers. Remember to leave a gap of at least 1/4 in. between the border pavers and the house.

B. Lay field pavers to locate the side borders. A simple row of pavers will work even if you plan to lay them later in a herringbone pattern as we did. The goal is to establish a field width that allows each course to end with a full or half paver, but not smaller pieces. That means less cutting, less waste and a neater look.

C. Position the border pavers and mark their locations. It's OK if the border pavers don't quite reach the edge of the patio, but do not let them overhang. Nudge one border outward by 1/4 in. to allow a little extra space for the field pavers.

D. Snap a chalk line to mark one side border. To make this line square with the line along the house, use the 3-4-5 method.

E. Mark the other side border. Measure from the first side to make sure the two sides are parallel.

F. Leave the final border unmarked, and install the border after the field is complete. That open end makes screeding off the excess sand easier and lets you position the final border perfectly.

difference will allow for a bed of sand under the field. A difference of more than 3/4 in. is fine; you'll just need a little more sand. If you can't find thick pavers you like, consider retaining wall cap blocks for the border.

To estimate how much sand you'll need, grab your calculator. Determine the square footage of the sand bed, then divide that number by 12 for a 1-in. bed or 18 for a 3/4-in. bed. That will tell you how many cubic feet of sand to

get. Aside from pavers and sand, you'll need one 10-oz. tube of adhesive for every 8 ft. of border, concrete cleaner or muriatic acid, a 2x6, landscape fabric and a screed pipe. To tamp the pavers, you'll need to rent a plate compactor.

LAY THE BORDER FIRST

To get started, scrub the border area **(Photo 1)** with a concrete cleaner or muriatic acid mixed with water

(check the label for mixing and safety instructions). Any stiff brush will do, but a deck-stripping brush on a broom handle makes it easier. Hose down the patio when you're done scrubbing the border.

While the concrete is drying, grab a tape measure and a chalk line, and carefully plan locations for the borders **(see Figure B)**. Using the chalk lines as a guide, glue down the border pavers along the house and two sides of the

3 Spread fabric, then sand. Lay down landscape fabric to keep the sand from washing down into cracks. Then position the screed pipe and spread the sand.

SCREED PIPE

LANDSCAPE FABRIC

4 Flatten the sand. Notch one end of a 2x6 to match the depth of the field pavers. The other end rides on the screed pipe. Screed both halves of the field, moving your screed pipe as you go.

SCREED PIPE

NOTCH

5 Lay the pavers. Cover the sand with field pavers. When the field is complete, glue down the final border pavers. Then tamp the field with a plate compactor, and sweep sand over the pavers to fill in the gaps.

patio (**Photo 2**). If adhesive squishes up between pavers, don't try to wipe it off. Just let it harden, then trim it off with a utility knife.

A FLAT BED OF SAND

If the field area is more than 10 ft. wide, you'll need a screed pipe in the center of the patio (**Photo 3**). A 10-ft. section of black or galvanized steel plumbing pipe works best. For a 1-in. bed, use a 3/4-in. pipe; for a 3/4-in. bed, use a 1/2-in. pipe.

Keep in mind that each pipe size is listed by its inner diameter, but the outer diameter is what matters here: 3/4-in. pipe has an outer diameter of about 1-1/8 in.; 1/2-in. pipe, about 5/8 in. In both cases, you'll get an extra 1/8 in. of sand bed thickness, and the field pavers will stand about 1/8 in. above the border pavers. Then, when you "tamp" the field with a plate compactor, the sand will compact and the field pavers will settle flush with the border.

"Screed" the sand flat with a notched 2x6 (**Photo 4**). The depth of the notch should be 1/8 in. less than the thickness of the field pavers. If the field is less than 10-ft. wide, notch both ends of the screed board and skip the pipe. Screeding is hard work, and it's best to have a helper.

LAY THE PAVERS AND FINISH THE BORDER

From here, this is mostly a standard, everyday paver job. First, lay the field pavers as you would on any paver patio. Then scrape away the excess sand and cut off the excess landscape fabric with a utility knife. Finally, glue down the last border.

Let the glue dry for a few hours before you tamp the field pavers and sweep sand across the patio to fill the joints. Then step back and admire your new, nicer patio. Whether you're reading a book or firing up the grill, you'll be far happier spending time on your patio in the future.

PRO TIP

Keep a spare blade

The store will probably be closed when you need it!

WHAT IT TAKES

TIME	COST	SKILL LEVEL
10 minutes	Less than $50	Beginner

TOOLS
2x4, breaker bar or long-handle wrench, hand file

Sharper mower blades, made easy

This simple job will keep your lawn healthy all summer long.

One of the best ways to encourage a greener, fuller and healthier lawn is to sharpen your lawn mower blade. A dull blade rips and pulls the grass, leaving ragged tears that both weaken the plant and promote fungal growth and other grass diseases. A sharp blade, on the other hand, cuts cleanly, allowing the plant to heal and recover quickly. Sharp blades also let you complete your lawn-cutting chore faster and with less stress on the mower.

Sharpening is a simple task, even for a novice. It'll take a few sharpenings to master the technique. After that, the chore will take less than 10 minutes. Plan to do it twice every mowing season. Shown here are the steps that will work for just about any walk-behind mower.

PLAY IT SAFE WHEN REMOVING THE BLADE

Always remove the spark plug wire **(Photo 1)** when working on the blade. If the position happens to be at the top of the compression stroke, a little bump to the blade could force the piston into the power stroke. If that happens, the blade could spin around and hit your hand.

Then, look for the carburetor and air filter. The carburetor is easy to recognize because it has throttle cables running to it. If you keep this side up when you tip your mower over to get at the blade **(Photo 2)**, you won't get a smoke cloud from leaking oil the next time you start it. Some mowers have gas caps with air holes that could leak a little gas onto your garage floor, so work outside or keep a rag handy to clean drips. Once the blade is off, set the mower back onto all four wheels until you're ready to reinstall your blade.

You'll usually find a single bolt or nut holding the blade on. It's usually very tight, and you'll need to clamp the blade to loosen it. The 2x4 method shown **(Photo 3)** is simple,

1 Pull the spark plug wire from the spark plug, and remove the spark plug to prevent the motor from accidentally starting.

AIR FILTER

2 Turn the mower onto its side with the air filter and carburetor side up. This keeps oil and gas from dripping into the air filter.

Mark your blade

Mark your blade with spray paint before you remove it so you know which way to reinstall it. Mower repair pros say that the biggest mistake homeowners make is reinstalling a blade upside down after sharpening it. The blade won't cut—and they go nuts trying to figure out why!

SPRAY PAINT

BLADE WEDGED

3 Wedge a short 2x4 between the blade and the deck to clamp the blade. Loosen the bolt (or nut) with a long-handled wrench. Turn counterclockwise. Remove the bolt and blade.

quick and safe. Don't use your foot! A good tool to keep handy to loosen the bolt is a breaker bar or long-handle wrench with a socket to match the bolt. It'll give you plenty of leverage to loosen extremely tight bolts, and you can keep your knuckles well away from the blade when bearing down. Use a squirt of penetrating oil on really rusted, stuck bolts. Wait 10 minutes to give the oil time to work.

SHARPEN IT WITH A FILE

Once you remove the blade, examine it to determine whether to sharpen or replace it. Sharpen it with a hand file **(Photo 4)**. Mower blades are made from fairly soft steel. You can sharpen most with fewer than 50 strokes of a clean, sharp "mill bastard" file that's at least 10-in. long. Grinders also work, and much more quickly, but they're more difficult to control and you might overheat and ruin the blade.

Always sharpen from the top side of the cutting edge; this will give you the longest-lasting edge on the blade. The file cuts in one direction only, on the push stroke; you'll feel it bite into the steel on the blade. If you don't feel that cutting action, your file is probably dull or you're not pressing down hard enough. Don't try to make your blade razor sharp; it'll dull more quickly. "Butter knife" sharp will do.

Sharpening mulching blades is sometimes more difficult. Mulching

Do you need a new blade?

Examine your blade when you remove it and look for the problems shown. If you're unsure of the condition of the blade, take it to a hardware store or home center and compare it with a new one.

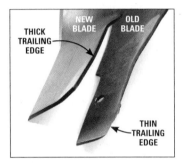

THIN TRAILING EDGE. The trailing edge, or fin, is the edge opposite the cutting edge. This fin is often slanted upward, which creates an updraft to lift grass and grass clippings. Dust and sand will wear this fin down. When it's thin, replace the blade.

BENT. Set your old blade on your workbench and check for bends. If you're unsure, compare it with a new blade.

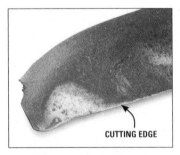

DENTS IN CUTTING EDGE. Replace a blade that has deep dents you can't file out and that shows erosion. Also replace any blade that has cracked.

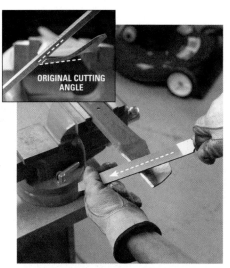

ORIGINAL CUTTING ANGLE

NAIL

4 Clamp the blade in a vise and sharpen the cutting edge with a mill bastard file, held at the original cutting angle. File until the blade is "butter knife" sharp.

5 Hang the blade on a nail to check the balance. If one side dips, file a bit more off that side until the blade remains continually horizontal.

6 Reinstall the blade and screw in the bolt. Then wedge the 2x4 back in and tighten the bolt firmly with your socket and breaker bar.

blades may have longer or curved cutting edges, and you could need several types of files to sharpen them. In some cases, you may have to resort to a 4-1/2-in. angle grinder. If your blade is difficult, take it to a hardware store or sharpening service.

BALANCE THE BLADE BEFORE YOU REINSTALL

Before reinstalling, be sure to balance the blade. Unbalanced blades cause vibration and could ruin the shaft or bearings. To check the balance, simply

drive a nail into a stud and set the blade onto it like an airplane propeller **(Photo 5)**. If one side falls, it's heavier and you have to file more metal off it. Keep filing until the blade stays level.

Reinstall the blade and hand-tighten the bolt. Insert the 2x4 in the reverse direction so you can bear down on the breaker bar to tighten the bolt. It's pretty difficult to overtighten the bolt. Mower sharpening pros often say that the second most common mistake they see is undertightening the bolt. A loose blade throws off the engine timing and makes the mower hard to start.

No excuses!

To get in the habit of keeping your blade sharp, dedicate a set of tools for sharpening only. Hang them nearby so they're ready to go. And keep a second, sharp blade handy, too. You can slip it on and sharpen the dull one later.

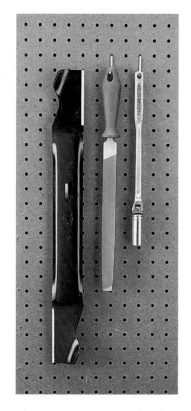

PRO TIP

Buying a brand-new blade

Always replace your blade with an exact replacement or the blade in your owner's manual. Resist the temptation to convert your regular straight-blade mower to a mulching mower by changing the blade. It won't work differently than before, and it may not work as well. The deck on a straight-blade mower is shallow and has a side discharge to eject the grass clippings quickly. A mulching mower has a deeper deck without a side discharge; the grass is chopped three or four times before it drops to the ground. The design is as important as the blade.

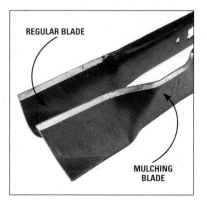

REGULAR BLADE

MULCHING BLADE

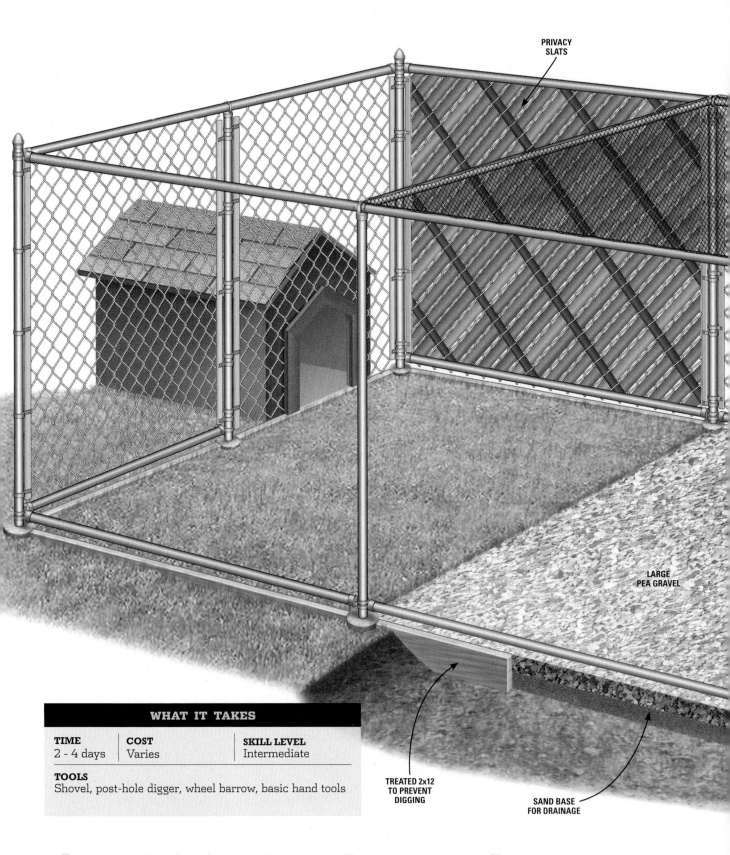

PRIVACY
SLATS

LARGE
PEA GRAVEL

TREATED 2x12
TO PREVENT
DIGGING

SAND BASE
FOR DRAINAGE

WHAT IT TAKES

TIME	COST	SKILL LEVEL
2 - 4 days	Varies	Intermediate

TOOLS
Shovel, post-hole digger, wheel barrow, basic hand tools

Outdoor dog kennel

**Outfit your outdoor kennel with the proper flooring and drainage,
a shady area and a windbreak.**

LANDSCAPE FABRIC ROOF

LOCKING LATCH

PATH

room you have to spare. If your dog is going to be outside all day, he needs a larger kennel so he can run and exercise. If you make it too small, he'll take every opportunity to "get even" with you and your neighbors with nonstop barking and other bad behaviors. So, if you were wondering, larger is truly better.

For walls and doors, chain link fencing is your best bet (4 ft. tall minimum, and taller if you have a larger dog). It's affordable and easy to assemble, and you can buy premade wall and door sections at any home center. To secure the swing-down latch (some dogs can figure out how to open those latches and escape), buy a spring-loaded "snap clip."

If your dog is a digger, you'll have to embed a "direct burial" treated 2x12 below the fence. Or bury the fence itself about 1 ft. into the soil. Those methods aren't foolproof, but they'll usually prevent a great escape. Screen off any sides that face streets or sidewalks by sliding privacy slats through the fencing. That'll cut down on barking and overall stress.

When it comes to flooring material, concrete may seem like the best choice because you can slope it for drainage and it's easy to clean. But it's actually a mistake. The hard floor will, over time, cause calluses, worn pads, splayed toes and painful joints. Instead, the Kennel Club recommends either large pea gravel (some dogs eat smaller gravel) or large flat stones (flagstone). The irregular shapes actually help your dog develop stronger paws. But before you throw down gravel or set the stones, take the time to install a sand base for drainage, at least 6-in. deep if you're building on clay. Then lay down landscaping fabric to prevent weed growth. You'll probably scoop out gravel along with the poop, so it'll need replenishing every year. If you have enough space, the ultimate dog oasis is a grassy area within the kennel.

Several companies offer composite flooring materials for dog kennels. It definitely looks better than gravel and is easy to clean. But if your dog likes to chew things, it's not a good choice. Plan on a surfaced path to the kennel. If you have just grass, you'll soon have a muddy path, and all that mud will get tracked into the house.

Finally, dogs need protection from the elements. A doghouse isn't mandatory, but if you don't provide one, you should at least install a small roof and a windbreak. Dogs can withstand cold, but not cold and wind or rain. An elevated cot will get them off a freezing cold or searing hot floor. Even if you include a doghouse, provide other shaded areas in the kennel (landscape fabric stretched across the top works well).

When placing a doghouse, avoid the common DIY mistake of setting it in a corner (the roof is a perfect launching pad for a jump-over). Instead, locate it outside the kennel with an entrance hole cut through the fence.

Or, if necessary, place the doghouse in the center of the kennel. If you're stuck with a corner location, make the fence higher in that area to prevent jump-outs.

We reached out to the experts at the American Kennel Club for design advice and size guidelines for an outdoor kennel. We were hoping to get a sizing formula, but it turns out there's no such thing. Kennel sizing is based on how much time your dog will be spending in the kennel and how much

Self-watering raised plant bed

Build this planting bed and have tonight's salad at your fingertips.

Growing veggies during high summer means daily watering, which becomes a problem if you go away for vacation. You could hire the neighbor kid—and maybe he'll remember or maybe you'll come home to withered veggies.

The solution is self-watering veggie planters that you can leave for a week. The planter boxes themselves are gorgeous, they keep rabbits and other critters away from the greens, and

you can be gone for weeks on end without having to water. We watered just three times all summer long—no kidding—and had garden-fresh salads until frost. Here we'll show you how to build one for yourself. (The secret is in the perforated drain pipe, shown in the photo at right.)

Self-watering planters are sometimes called sub-irrigated planters, or SIPs, because your plants get to "sip" water

WHAT IT TAKES

TIME	COST	SKILL LEVEL
1 day	Over $500	Intermediate

TOOLS
Drill, circular saw, clamps, staple gun, utility knife

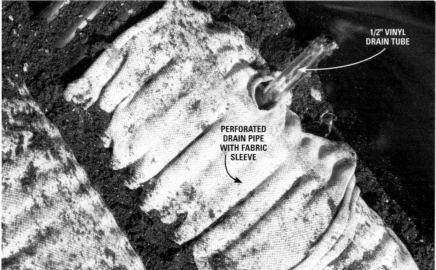

1/2" VINYL
DRAIN TUBE

PERFORATED
DRAIN PIPE
WITH FABRIC
SLEEVE

Top 8 reasons to build this planter

1. It will save your back and your knees.
2. You'll have fewer weeds.
3. It will water your plants while you're away.
4. It will save water.
5. You'll have fresh veggies steps from your back door.
6. It will create perfect soil.
7. It will protect your veggies from hungry critters.
8. It'll look great on your patio.

Self-watering planter basics

- Choose a spot that gets at least six hours of sun. If your planter is against a wall, you can get by with less sun because of reflected heat.
- A 4-ft.-wide planter is ideal for harvesting from both sides. Keep it to 3 ft. wide if you're placing your planter against a wall or fence.
- Line your planter with a "fish-safe" rubber membrane. It will prolong the life of the wood without leaching chemicals into the soil (and your food). You can buy fish-safe pond liners in different thicknesses and materials at home centers, garden centers and various online retailers.
- Don't use garden soil or a heavy potting soil in your raised garden. Use a light, fluffy "soilless" blend that will retain moisture without compacting or becoming waterlogged. You can also buy potting soil formulated for self-watering planters.
- Mulch your containers to keep weeds down and to slow evaporation.
- For more great ideas for building these planters, visit insideurbangreen.org.

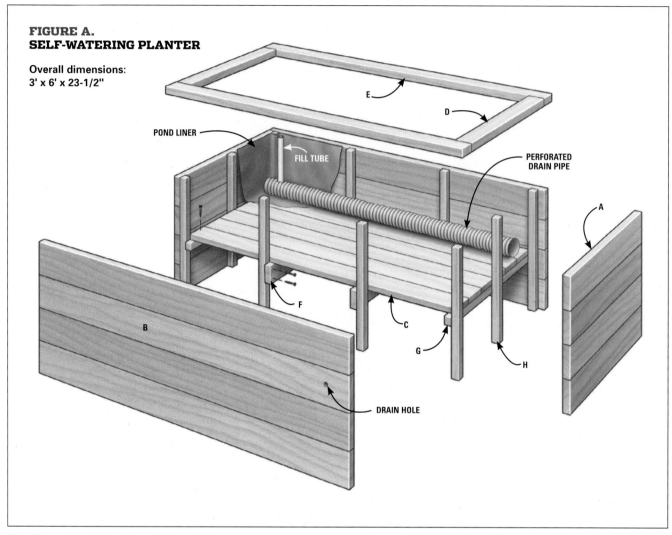

FIGURE A.
SELF-WATERING PLANTER

Overall dimensions:
3' x 6' x 23-1/2"

POND LINER

FILL TUBE

PERFORATED
DRAIN PIPE

E

D

A

B

F

C

G

H

DRAIN HOLE

Note: We notched the flooring to fit (Photo 5). You can also fit the floor within the 2x2s as shown and let the liner span the gap.

Materials List

ITEM	QTY.
12' cedar 2x6s (sides and ends)	6
12' cedar deck boards	3
10' 2x4s (top cap)	2
8' 2x4 (joists)	1
8' 2x2s (cleats)	4
24' of 4" diameter perforated drain pipe with sleeve	
Pond liner (rubber or poly)	
Exterior screws	
Soilless potting mix	
1/2" vinyl tubing (drainage)	
1" CPVC (fill tube)	

Cutting List

KEY	PART	QTY.
A	1-1/2" x 5-1/2" x 33" (ends)	8
B	1-1/2" x 5-1/2" x 72" (sides)	8
C	1" x 5-1/2", cut to fit (floor)	6
D	1-1/2" x 3-1/2" x 30" (end cap)	2
E	1-1/2" x 3-1/2" x 73" (side cap)	2
F	1-1/2" x 3-1/2" x 33" (joists)	2
G	1-1/2" x 1-1/2" x 33" (horizontal cleats)	2
H	1-1/2" x 1-1/2" x 22" (vertical cleats)	10

whenever they want. Our version uses inexpensive perforated drain pipe with a fabric sleeve in the bottom of the planter. Once you fill the drain pipe reservoirs, they allow air to circulate and water to wick up to your plants' roots whenever they need it.

When plants are watered from below, the roots stay consistently moist, there's less evaporation and you don't need to water as much. The vinyl tubing allows any overflow water to drain. There are many commercial self-watering planters available—the EarthBox is one. But you can easily make one.

BUILD YOUR PLANTING BOX

Photos 1 – 6 show you how to build a handsome wood planter box. We used

cedar (you can save money by using treated wood) and a thick EPDM pond liner (thinner versions at home centers are a lot less). To give the box a nice finished look, we routed the boards and sanded the faces and cap. We left the cedar unfinished, but you could seal yours. After we built the basic box, we moved the planter to its final position and then added the self-watering system, soil and plants. Even without soil and plants, this planter is heavy!

Photos 7 and 8 show you how to construct the self-watering system. Once you're ready to plant, add a soilless mix to just below the top of the planter.

Once your plants are in, fill the drain pipe reservoirs through the fill tube until water runs out the drainage hole

1 Screw the box ends together. Pick the straightest 2x2s for the corner cleats. Align the parts with the corner of your worktable to keep the assembly square.

2x2 VERTICAL CLEAT

2x6

2 Construct the box sides. Straighten bowed boards with a clamp. The top boards need to be straight so the cap will go on straight and tight.

3 Screw the box together. Clamp the edges together and press firmly with the other hand when screwing each plank so everything comes together tightly.

FLOORING DEPTH GUIDE

TOP OF DECKING JOIST

4 Mark location for the decking joists. Determine the floor depth (see "Building tips," p. 74), and cut a block that length to mark the locations for the horizontal cleats and joists.

2x2 HORIZONTAL CLEAT

2x4 JOISTS

5 Attach the joists and lay the floor. Screw the horizontal end cleats in place first and then the center joists. Notch your deck boards to fit around the vertical supports.

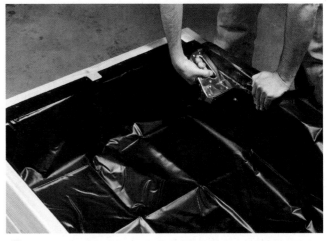

6 Staple the rubber membrane in place. Fold the pond liner at the corners and staple it around the perimeter. Trim the excess.

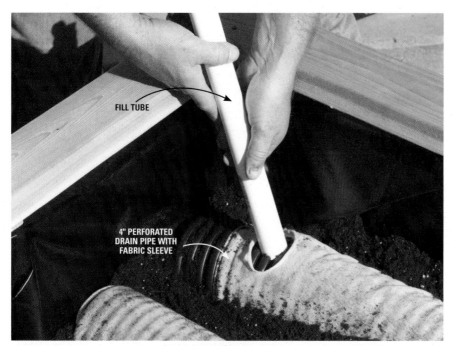

FILL TUBE

4" PERFORATED
DRAIN PIPE WITH
FABRIC SLEEVE

7 Position the drain pipe and the fill tube. Space the drain pipes evenly along the deck floor, wedging the ends tightly against the short sides of the planter. Pack potting mix around the pipes to keep them straight. Stick a fill tube in the top end of one of the outside drain pipes.

1/2" VINYL TUBE

8 Drill a drain hole and fit the tubing. In the end of the planter opposite your fill tube, drill a drainage hole just above the height of the pipe. Run vinyl tubing from the drain pipe to the drainage hole.

(this can take a while). The water will wick out of the perforated pipes into the potting mix packed around them and up into the mix and roots above.

You'll have to experiment to see how long your planter will stay moist.

Fill the drain pipes whenever the soil feels dry 2- or 3-in. down. When we set up this planter, we filled the drain pipes, gave the plants an initial surface watering and then mulched all the way around them.

After that, and despite a record hot, sweltering summer, we refilled the pipes only three times throughout the season. And even better, we had plenty of herbs and greens growing right up until the first frost!

Building tips

- When assembling the box ends **(Photo 1)** and sides **(Photo 2)**, leave gaps between planks to allow for expansion and contraction. We used 1/16-in. washers as spacers.
- To determine where to put your planter floor **(Photo 4)**, add together your soil depth, the flooring thickness, the height of the drain pipe and another inch so that the soil level will sit an inch below the top of the box.
- For greater strength, use 2x2 horizontal cleats for each end (33 in. long for our planter) and 2x4s for the center two joists.
- Don't miter the top cap. Miter joints open with changes in humidity. Butt joints will look neater than miter joints over time.
- Cut the perforated drain pipe into 6-ft. lengths and lay them in rows across the bottom of the planter. Wedging them in place against the sides prevents potting mix from getting into the pipes, so you don't need to cap the ends.
- Wedge the CPVC fill tube tightly into the top of the drain pipe. It should be long enough to poke out of the top of your soil once your container is planted **(Photo 7)**. You need only one fill tube in the planter because the water will flow through the perforations of the pipe section with the fill tube and then into the surrounding soilless potting mix and through the perforations of all the other drain pipes.
- You can buy perforated drain pipe with an attached sleeve at home centers and landscape centers.

One-day patio pond

If you can build a box, you can build this.

WHAT IT TAKES

TIME	COST	SKILL LEVEL
2 - 3 days	$250-$500	Intermediate

TOOLS
Drill/driver, basic hand tools, clamps, caulk gun

A simple box with a rubber lining

We wanted a super-easy-to-build water feature, so we designed this wooden box that anyone can build with basic tools. What makes it work as a pond is a paint-on rubber lining. There are a few different brands of liquid rubber available at home centers and online. It's ultra-stretchy and UV-stable, and it can be used on lots of materials, including wood, metal and concrete. It's amazing stuff, though expensive.

You can use liquid rubber to fix leaky gutters and metal roofs, to seal RVs and trailers, and for many other applications. Ranchers love it for sealing leaks in metal water tanks. And we love it because it can turn just about anything, even a simple wooden box, into a water feature.

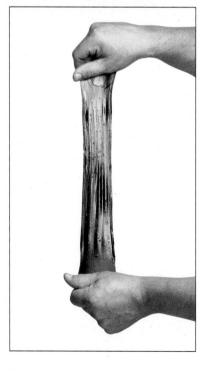

This patio pond is simple to build, and it holds both water plants and regular plants. It's a fabulous way to dress up your deck or patio.

JOIN THE BOTTOM BOARDS

Cut the two bottom boards (A and E; see **Figure A**, p. 79) to length. Cuts made at the lumber mill are usually rough, so trim the ends of all the boards before measuring.

Join all the components with both trim-head screws and construction adhesive. Adhesive works better than wood glue on rough-sawn lumber and is more forgiving on joints that aren't super tight. Apply a bead of adhesive and clamp the two bottom boards together. Scrape off the excess adhesive with a putty knife, and clean the rest with mineral spirits.

Install temporary cleats on the smooth side of the boards, which will be the inside of the container (**Photo 1**). Hold them in place with 1-1/4-in. screws. We used cabinet screws, but other types of screws would work fine.

Don't worry about the screw holes left behind when you remove the cleats; the liquid rubber will fill them in.

CUT THE BOARDS TO SIZE

The width of 1x12s can vary slightly, so double-check the width of the bottom before you cut the ends and dividers (B and C) to length. The rough-sawn cedar we used was 7/8-in. thick. If you are working with material that's only 3/4-in. thick, you'll have to adjust the length of the sides.

All of the trim parts are made from 1x6s ripped in half. A few home centers sell 1x3 boards, so you wouldn't have to bother with ripping at all.

ASSEMBLE THE CONTAINER

Mark guidelines for the dividers with a framing square 14-in. in from the ends of the bottom. Transfer that line to the

1 Build the bottom. Glue the bottom boards together with construction adhesive, and install three temporary cleats to hold them together until the project has been assembled.

2 Install the dividers. Fasten dividers to the bottom, and then add the sides. Join all the parts with both adhesive and trim-head screws. Scrape any excess adhesive with a putty knife.

3 Add corner brackets. Cut aluminum angle stock to create corner brackets. Drill four holes in each bracket, and secure them with adhesive and screws.

inside of the sides (D). Face the smooth sides of the dividers toward the center compartment. That will ensure even coverage of the liquid rubber in the compartment where it matters most.

Attach ends and dividers to bottom with adhesive and three 1-1/2-in. exterior-grade trim-head screws **(Photo 2)**. Join the sides with adhesive and screws, three in each side of each end and divider. Space the screws about 10-in. apart along the bottom. The end caps hide the end grain and strengthen the corners. Secure them with four screws and adhesive. Cedar isn't quite as prone to splitting as harder woods, so predrill holes for screws only in the areas where a knot is in the way.

Install four aluminum angle brackets **(Photo 3)**. Cut these brackets to size with a hacksaw or a jigsaw fitted with a bimetal blade. Drill two holes in each side, and secure them with adhesive and 3/4-in. screws.

Assemble the base with two 3-in. screws into each joint. It's easier to center the base when the container is upside down. Hold it in place by driving in four screws at an angle. Flip the whole thing over and secure the base to the container with 3-in. screws driven down through the bottom of the container.

After removing the temporary cleats, drill four 1/2-in. drainage holes in the corners of the outside compartments and one in the middle. If you plan to install a water pump, drill a 1-1/2-in.hole for the cord with a hole saw. Figure out which side of the container has the best-looking wood grain and drill the hole on the opposite side, about 3/8 in. down from top edge.

POOR MAN'S POCKET HOLE

If you're a weekend woodworker, you really ought to get yourself a pocket hole jig. But if you don't have one, here's a quick and easy trick that works well on soft woods like cedar: Start by laying out the face frame, rough side down, and marking two guidelines at each joint. Then drill 1/8-in. holes through the end grain at an angle so the drill bit pops out about 3/4-in. to 7/8-in. down from the end of the board **(Photo 4)**. At that length, a 1-1/2-in. trim-head screw will travel about 3/4-in. into the adjoining frame section. If you mess up and drill at a funky angle, you can always drill another hole a little bit over, and no one will be the wiser because it's on the underside of the face frame.

BUILD THE FACE FRAME

Assemble the sides and ends of the face frame with two 1-1/2-in. trim-head screws and adhesive **(Photo 4)**. Keep downward pressure on both trim boards while driving in the first screw. A wood clamp on the seam works well as a third hand. Before installing the face frame dividers, measure diagonally from one corner to the other both ways to make sure the frame is square. If the frame is a little out of whack, adjust the frame until it's square, and clamp it to your workbench to hold it square.

APPLY THE LIQUID RUBBER AND WOOD FINISH

Tape off the top edge of the container, the power cord hole and the drainage holes on the bottom. Brush the rubber on thick into the corners, seams, screw holes and defects in the wood **(Photo 5)**. It takes three heavy coats to make a watertight seal and at least three hours between coats. You can get away with only one coat in the two outside compartments because they'll be filled with soil rather than water. Also apply just one coat on the very top edge of the container. Avoid blocking the drainage and cord holes with rubber by mopping out the excess with a cotton swab or rolled-up paper towel. The rubber needs to dry for a few days before it's ready for water. Rough-sawn cedar isn't supposed to

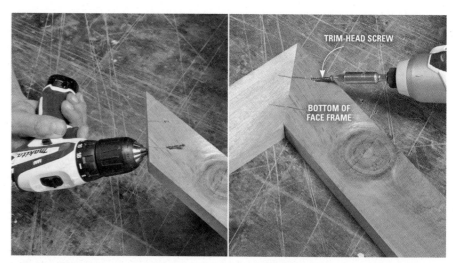

4 Build the face frame. Join the face-frame parts so that the new screws will be invisible. First, drill pilot holes through the end of one part (left photo). Then just hold the parts together and drive in screws (right photo).

5 Apply the liquid rubber. Glob a thick coat of the liquid rubber into all the seams, corners and defects in the wood. Apply one coat on the outside compartments and three on the middle.

6 Secure the face frame. Clamp the face frame into place, and hold it down with adhesive and trim-head screws. Leave the screw heads flush with the surface to avoid pockets where water can pool and penetrate the wood.

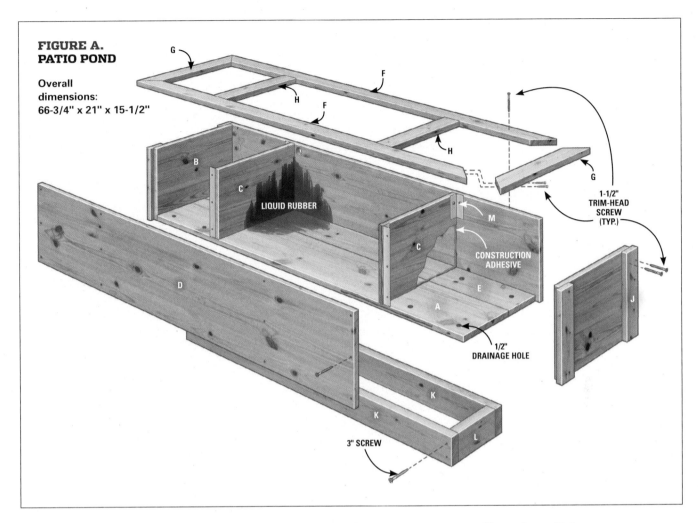

**FIGURE A.
PATIO POND**

Overall
dimensions:
66-3/4" x 21" x 15-1/2"

G

F

H

F

B

C

LIQUID RUBBER

H

M

CONSTRUCTION
ADHESIVE

C

E

A

1/2"
DRAINAGE HOLE

D

G

1-1/2"
TRIM-HEAD
SCREW
(TYP.)

J

K

K

L

3" SCREW

be smooth, hence the name. So resist the urge to sand, and embrace the imperfections. We applied a cedar-tinted wood finish, but any exterior stain or clear finish would work.

FINISH UP AND ADD WATER

Once the finishes are dry, clamp the face to the container and fasten it with adhesive and 1-1/2-in. trim-head screws spaced every 10-in. or so **(Photo 6)**. Set the screws flush with the surface of the wood to keep water from pooling.

A water pump isn't necessary, but it does help the water stay fresh. Some pumps have suction cups to hold them to the bottom, but the rubber-coated wood may not be smooth enough for them to stick.

Instead, lay down a small chunk of Plexiglas at the bottom and stick the

pump's suction cups to that. Floating water plants with exposed roots will clog the pump filter, so use only potted plants, or plan to build some sort of additional screen or filtration system. A pump that moves 120 gallons per hour is plenty big enough for this particular situation. Now it's time to fill your new creation with water and plants. If the local nursery doesn't carry water plants, you can order them online.

Materials List

ITEM	QTY.
1x12 x 12' rough-sawn cedar	2
1x6 x 8' rough-sawn cedar	3
2x4 x 12' cedar-tone pressure-treated lumber	1
1-1/4" x 1/16" x 4' aluminum angle stock	1
Small box of 1-1/2" exterior trim-head screws	1
Small box of 1-1/4" drywall or cabinet screws	1
Small box of 3" screws compatible with pressure-treated lumber	1
Small box of 3/4" screws	1
Tube of construction adhesive	1
Gallon of liquid rubber	1

Cutting List

KEY	PART	QTY.
Cut from rough-sawn 1x12 cedar		
A	62-1/4" x 11-1/4" x 7/8" (bottom)	1
B	16-3/4" x 11-1/4" x 7/8" (ends)	2
C	16-3/4" x 10-3/8" x 7/8" (dividers)	2
D	64" x 11-1/4" x 7/8" (sides)	2
(Note: widths may vary)		
Cut from 1x6 rough-sawn cedar		
E	62-1/4" x 11-1/4" x 7/8" (bottom)	1
F	2-11/16" x 66-3/4" x 7/8" (face frame sides)	2
G	2-1/16" x 21" x 7/8" (face frame ends)	2
H	2-11/16" x 15-9/16" (face frame dividers)	2
J	2-11/16" x 11-1/4" (end caps)	4
Cedar-tone pressure-treated 2x4		
K	54" x 3-1/2" x 1-1/2" (base sides)	2
L	8-1/2" x 3-1/2" x 1-1/2" (base ends)	2
Aluminum angle stock		
M	10-1/4" x 1-1/4" x 1/16" (corner bracket)	4

Build a compost bin

This folksy "log cabin" bin will keep your compost pile from becoming an eyesore.

Why not turn your yard waste into yard gold by building this compost bin? Build it now, then start your compost pile with leaves, garden plants and some grass clippings. (Leave most of the clippings on the lawn to return nitrogen to the grass as they decompose.)

You probably already own all the tools you'll need. Round up a circular saw, a coping saw, a tape measure, a drill/driver, 1/16-in.-dia. and 3/8-in.-dia. drill bits, a carpenter's square, two pipe clamps and a wood chisel. The bin is constructed from "five-quarter" (5/4) rounded-edge decking boards. (Although the name implies that these are 1-1/4-in. boards, they're actually only about 1 in. thick.) The boards are pressure-treated, which makes the bin resistant to rot and insects. There's very little hardware because the pieces fit together like classic Lincoln Logs.

CUTTING THE PIECES

The 5/4 decking needs to be cut to 42-in. lengths—you'll get four 42-in. boards from each 14-ft. board. (Hauling 14-ft. boards can be a hassle, so have the lumberyard cut each one into two 7 footers.) The 42-in. boards, when assembled, give you a compost bin that's approximately a 3-ft. cube.

WHAT IT TAKES		
TIME 1 day	**COST** $100-$250	**SKILL LEVEL** Beginner
TOOLS Circular saw, coping saw, tape measure, carpenter's square, drill/driver and drill bits, two pipe clamps, wood chisel		

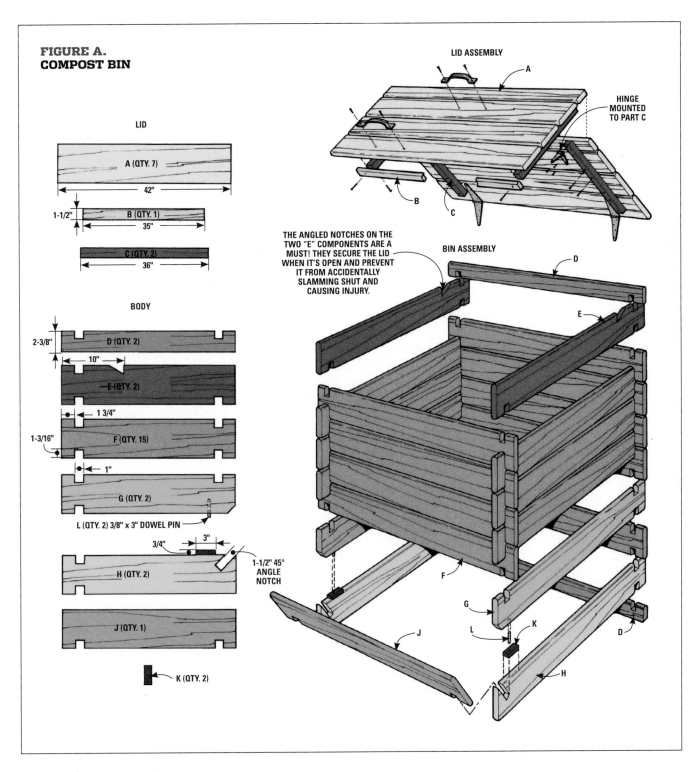

**FIGURE A.
COMPOST BIN**

LID ASSEMBLY

HINGE
MOUNTED
TO PART C

THE ANGLED NOTCHES ON THE TWO "E" COMPONENTS ARE A MUST! THEY SECURE THE LID WHEN IT'S OPEN AND PREVENT IT FROM ACCIDENTALLY SLAMMING SHUT AND CAUSING INJURY.

BIN ASSEMBLY

LID

A (QTY. 7)
42"

1-1/2"
B (QTY. 1)
35"

C (QTY. 2)
36"

BODY

2-3/8"
D (QTY. 2)

10"
E (QTY. 2)

1 3/4"
1-3/16"
F (QTY. 15)

1"
G (QTY. 2)

L (QTY. 2) 3/8" x 3" DOWEL PIN

3/4"   3"
H (QTY. 2)   1-1/2" 45° ANGLE NOTCH

J (QTY. 1)

K (QTY. 2)

Two of the 42-in. boards will need to be ripped in half (cut down their length). Two of the ripped pieces (D) need to be cut to 2-3/8-in. wide and then notched **(see Figure A)**. One of the pieces should be cut to 1-1/2-in. wide (C). The remaining piece is scrap, which you'll use later. Cutting treated lumber requires you to take several special precautions. Here's what you'll need to be sure you do:

■ Wear a dust mask to avoid inhaling the sawdust.
■ Do the cutting outdoors.
■ Clean up scraps and throw them in the trash.
■ DO NOT burn treated lumber. It gives off toxic fumes!

Materials List

ITEM	QTY.
5/4 x 6" x 14' decking boards	8
2" x 2" x 4' treated (for cleat boards)	2
4" galv. steel strap hinges	2
6" galv. steel strap hinges	2
Large galv. steel handles	2
2-1/4" galv. wood screws	32
3/8" wooden dowel rod	1
(Note: All lumber is pressure-treated except the dowel rod.)	

1 Clamp the like components together with pipe clamps on both ends. Use a circular saw to cut 1/4-in.-wide slices to make the 1-in.-wide, 1-3/16-in.-deep notches.

2 Remove the slices with a wood chisel. Use a coping saw to square the corners of the notches to make a tight-fitting joint.

■ Wash any exposed skin after cutting the lumber.

NOTCHING THE BOARDS

Interlocking, 1-3/16-in. deep notches hold the bin together. Notches cut to this depth leave about a 3/4-in. space between each pair of boards when interlocked. The exact width of the notches depends on the thickness of the lumber.

HOW TO CUT THE NOTCHES:

■ Clamp the like components together with pipe clamps. Then stand them on edge on a solid work surface **(Photo 1)**. Not all the pieces require the same number of notches; check **Figure A** for the number required for each component.

■ Measure in from the edge of the boards 1-3/4 in. and draw a line at this distance on all of the boards. Now, measure from this line 1 in. (or the thickness of your lumber) toward the center of the boards and draw a second line.

■ Set your circular saw to cut at a depth of 1-3/16-in. and cut along the entire length of both lines. Now make a series of 1/4-in.-wide cuts or slices **(Photo 1)**.

■ Remove the slices with a wood

chisel **(Photo 2)**. Square the bottom corners of each notch with a chisel for tight-fitting corners.

After you finish the interlocking notches, cut the 45-degree diagonal notches in the two bottom side boards (H). The cuts can be started with the circular saw, but finish them with a coping saw.

Next, cut two 3/4-in.-thick, 3-in.-long spacer blocks (K) from the scrap lumber. Drill a 1/16-in.-dia. hole through each end of each spacer and a 3/8-in.-dia. hole in the center of the spacer. Then nail the spacers to the bottom side boards (H).

Measure from the front edge of parts H to the center of the 3/8-in. hole in the spacer. Mark this measurement on the bottom front of the part G boards and drill a 1-1/4-in. deep, 3/8-in.-dia. hole for the dowel (L).

Cut two, 3-in. lengths of 3/8-in.-dia. dowel and tap them into the holes through the spacers.

Now you're ready to assemble the other components Lincoln Log style. First, move all of the components to the bin site before you start; you'll want to have everything within reach.

CONSTRUCTING THE TOP

Building the lid is quick. Here's how:
■ Lay out the seven remaining 42-in.

What to compost
■ Green plant material (the nitrogen supply) with brown materials such as fall leaves (the carbon supply).
■ Any plant materials (except weeds with seeds and poisonous plants such as poison ivy), straw, coffee grounds, eggshells (not the whole egg), and raw fruit and vegetable scraps. Do NOT compost meat, dairy products or pet feces.

Starting the pile
The pile needs to be built in layers. The bottom should be 8 to 10 in. of an even mix of grass and plant trimmings.
■ Water this layer so that it's moist. Add a 1-in. layer of soil over the nitrogen-rich plant matter to increase the number of decomposing microorganisms.
■ Repeat these layers until the pile fills the bin.

boards, making sure they're tight together, edge to edge.
■ Measure in 3-1/2 in. from both ends and mark. This is where you'll attach the 2 x 2-in. cleats (C). Use 2-1/4-in. galvanized wood screws.
■ Don't put screws into the cleat board that's directly over the center of the top's middle board. Now rip the center board in half to form the two lid sections. Cut completely through the cleat board when you rip the center board.
■ Connect the lid sections with 4-in. strap hinges using the screws that come with the hinges.
■ Mount one leaf of the 6-in. strap hinges (they secure the lid to the bin) just inside the cleat boards. Mount the other leaf on the outside of the back of the bin.
■ Finally, attach the handles as shown in the illustration on p. 81. And now you're done—enjoy your brand-new compost bin.

1 Pry up the paver with a thin screwdriver, pounding on adjoined pavers to vibrate loose packed sand.

Fix sunken patio pavers

Stop tripping in the low spots on your patio.

Paver block patios and walkways often develop low spots, but these areas can be brought back up to grade. First, remove the pavers from the low area. If they're packed in tight, use a screwdriver to lever the first paver out, levering each end a little at a time and tapping on surrounding pavers until you can pull out the paver **(Photo 1)**.

Make a screed board long enough to rest on the level pavers around it. Then notch the ends 1/8 in. less than the depth of the pavers. If the area is large, set a screed pipe along one side and level it against the pavers you're matching. If you're trying to match a sloping walk, shim the level at the downhill end to match the slope **(Photo 2)**.

Fill the low area with coarse, all-purpose sand, and then screed it level **(Photo 3)**. Use a trowel like a spatula to go around the edges and scrape away any excess sand.

Brush any old sand off the sides of the pavers. Set them back into place and drive them down until they're flush with the other pavers **(Photo 4)**. Spread dry sand over the pavers, tamping and sweeping until all of the the joints are completely full.

WHAT IT TAKES		
TIME	**COST**	**SKILL LEVEL**
1 day	Under $50	Beginner

TOOLS
Screed board, screed pipe, rubber mallet, screwdriver

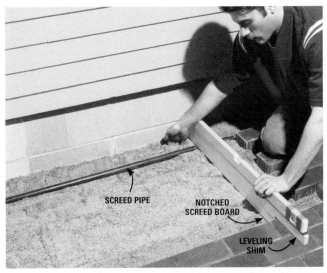

2 Level a screed pipe using a screed board with a notch at one end 1/8 in. shallower than the depth of the pavers.

3 Add sand to the low area, then level it by pulling the screed board along the pipe and the pavers.

4 Remove the screed pipe and set the pavers back, tapping them down level with a board.

Install a large valve to quickly fill watering cans and a smaller valve for a garden hose. Secure the valves to the cross brace with J-brackets.

Build a rain barrel

Don't pay top dollar for a rain barrel! Build your own using these simple steps.

Rain barrels are expensive, but it's pretty easy to build your own from plastic drums or trash cans. Check online for an "open head" plastic 55-gallon drum with a cover. Or find a used barrel by talking to car wash managers (they buy soap and wax by the barrel). If you can't find a container you like, buy a large, heavy-duty garbage can at a home center. All the other materials will be available there, too.

Place the drum near a downspout, drill a hole in the side near the bottom and screw in a drain valve. That's an OK installation if you plan to run a soaker hose to your garden. If you want to use a wand or a spray nozzle, you'll need to elevate the barrel on a stand for more water pressure. Water is heavy (55 gallons weighs 440 lbs.), so use 4x4 treated lumber for the legs and secure everything with construction screws or stainless steel lags. And don't place the stand on soft ground. You could kill somebody if the rig toppled over. If you have large gardens and want to store more water, double the size of the stand and add a second barrel.

Cut holes in the bottoms of the barrels with a 2-1/4-in. hole saw. Then screw in a 2-in. male threaded electrical

(gray PVC) conduit adapter (electrical adapters aren't tapered like plumbing adapters, so you can tighten them down all the way). Squirt a thin bead of silicone caulk around the opening and screw on a threaded electrical PVC coupler to cinch the barrel between the two fittings **(Figure A)**. Next, glue together sections of 2-in. PVC pipe, unions (to make winter disassembly easier), reducers and valves. As long as you're at it, install an overflow pipe so you can direct the excess where you want it.

Finally, cut a hole in one of the covers and mount a screen to filter out leaves and debris. Then just wait for the next big rain.

WHAT IT TAKES		
TIME	**COST**	**SKILL LEVEL**
1 day	$100-$250	Intermediate
TOOLS		
Drill, 2-1/4" hole saw, basic hand tools		

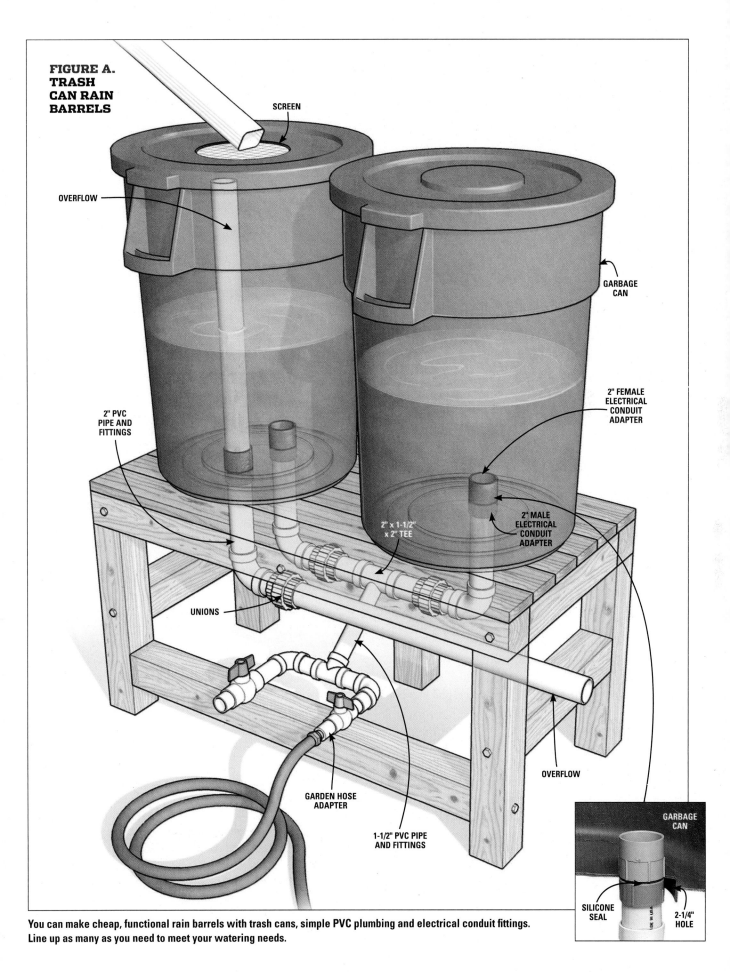

FIGURE A. TRASH CAN RAIN BARRELS

SCREEN

OVERFLOW

GARBAGE CAN

2" FEMALE ELECTRICAL CONDUIT ADAPTER

2" PVC PIPE AND FITTINGS

2" x 1-1/2" x 2" TEE

2" MALE ELECTRICAL CONDUIT ADAPTER

UNIONS

OVERFLOW

GARDEN HOSE ADAPTER

1-1/2" PVC PIPE AND FITTINGS

GARBAGE CAN

SILICONE SEAL

2-1/4" HOLE

You can make cheap, functional rain barrels with trash cans, simple PVC plumbing and electrical conduit fittings. Line up as many as you need to meet your watering needs.

Build this spiffy backyard feature and add some interest to your garden.

Raised-bed border

This eye-catching feature really makes your garden rock, and it doesn't require any fancy skills, just a strong back.

A stone wall does more than make a clean border along your lawn. It's a handsome visual statement in itself and a great way to add depth and texture to a flat, featureless yard. It's practical, too. If you have poor or clay soil, just fill the interior with topsoil and compost to have a raised planting bed. It also provides good drainage, making it a super solution for low-lying, soggy gardens. And it's a good way to terrace a sloped yard and create nice, flat gardens.

To reduce maintenance, we added a 4-in.-deep trench that we lined with plastic edging and filled with mulch. The edging keeps grass roots from creeping into the stone wall, and the mulch provides a mowing track for the lawn mower wheels. With taller types of grass, you can mow right over the plastic border and cut the lawn edge cleanly. There's no need to trim the grass.

This project doesn't require any special skills, just a strong back. Besides a good shovel and a wheelbarrow, you'll need a cold chisel and a 2-lb. maul for breaking stones and driving edging stakes.

Design your raised bed to blend into the contours of your yard like a natural feature. You can handle slopes in one of two ways: Either let your wall follow the slope of the yard for an informal look or level the stones as we did and step the wall up or down as the slope requires to maintain approximately the same height.

The exact size of stacking stone for walls varies by region. Visit a local landscape supplier to check types. (Shown is Chilton limestone.) For lawn edging, limit the height of your wall to two courses so you won't have stones falling out. Measure your wall length and make a sketch. The

WHAT IT TAKES		
TIME 2 - 3 days	**COST** $250-$500	**SKILL LEVEL** Intermediate
TOOLS Shovel, wheelbarrow, cold chisel, 2-lb. maul, level		

1 Mark the path of the border with paint, then dig a 4-in.-deep trench along the line. Make the width the stone width plus 6 in.

2 Pack in and level a bed of gravel. Keep the height at or below soil level. If necessary on slopes, plan to step the stone up or down.

3 Lay the first row of stones about 4 in. back from the grass edge. Push in more gravel or dig it out to align and level the stones. Wear goggles when chipping stones.

4 Stack the second row of stones onto the first, overlapping the joints. Test several stones to find the most stable fit.

5 Lay a strip of landscape fabric against the back of the stones and fill the planting bed with topsoil. Trim off excess fabric later.

LANDSCAPE FABRIC

6 Scoop out 4 in. of gravel in front of the wall and install plastic lawn edging. Pack mulch into the gap between the plastic and stone.

PLASTIC EDGING

stone dealer will help you figure out the quantities of all the materials you need. The stone will probably be sold by the ton or pallet, and it's heavy. Have it delivered and dropped as close to the wall location as possible. And have gravel or sand delivered to use as a setting bed for the stone **(Photo 2)** as well as topsoil to fill behind the wall **(Photo 5)**. The stone or landscaping dealer will help you calculate how much of these you need.

Follow the photos for step-by-step installation instructions. Get started by laying out the border with a garden hose or paint. We drew a curve by setting a string at a center point and marking an arc with paint **(Photo 1)**. The trench width will vary depending on the width of the stone. Add 6 in. to the stone width (2 in. for the mowing edge plus 4 in. extra).

It's usually best to keep the bottom row of stone an inch or so below the original soil level, but this will vary if you keep the stones level and the yard isn't level (what yard is?). At some point, you may have to step the stones up or down or use thinner or thicker stones. There's no rule here. Experiment when you lay the stones for the best appearance.

Lay the stones that have the most irregular faces in the first row so you can place the irregular face down in the gravel and level the top **(Photo 3)**. Vary the sizes and colors for the best look. Chip off irregularities with the maul and chisel. Then add the second row **(Photo 4)**. Make this row as stable as possible so the stones won't rock and fall off. As a last resort, stabilize the stones by shoving stone chips into the gaps.

Lay landscape fabric against the back of the wall before backfilling in order to keep dirt from washing out through the stone **(Photo 5)**. Then move on to the next step: install the plastic edging in front. Finally, add your organic mulch to finish up the mowing edge **(Photo 6)**.

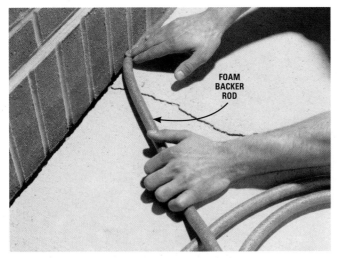

1 Push foam backer rod into the gap with your fingers. Set the rod 1/4 in. lower than the surface of the concrete.

Caulk cracked concrete

Preventing this common problem is as easy as picking up a tube of caulk.

Cracks and gaps in concrete are more than just an eyesore. Water can get into the joints, freeze and then expand, making the cracks even larger. Gaps against a house can direct water against the foundation, leading to more problems. Once a year, go around your home and fill these gaps and joints with urethane caulk to prevent problems. The caulk is available at contractor supply stores, well-stocked home centers and hardware stores. For gaps and joints more than 1/4-in. wide, install foam backer rod to support the caulk. You want the rod to fit tight in the joint, so buy it one size larger than the gap.

Keep the urethane caulk off your bare hands and clothes; it's the stickiest stuff you'll ever touch. Wear disposable gloves when you're tooling the joints. If you get some on your skin, quickly wipe it off with a paint thinner–dampened cloth.

WHAT IT TAKES		
TIME	**COST**	**SKILL LEVEL**
2 - 4 hours	Under $50	Beginner
TOOLS		
Caulk gun		

2 Fill the crack with urethane caulk. Snip the opening of the tube at a 30-degree angle, making the opening the same size as your gap. Use a smooth, even motion, filling the crack flush with the surface, beveling it if it's against the house. Smooth the caulk in wide joints with the back of an old spoon. Wipe the spoon clean as needed with a rag and mineral spirits.

3 Caulk cracks 1/4-in. wide or less without using backer rod. Draw the gun down the crack, smoothing the caulk as you go.

WATERLINE

SLIP COUPLING

BAND CLAMP

A.

SLIP COUPLING

ABOVE: Cut out the damaged section of line and replace it with a slip coupling. Secure the coupling with band clamps. INSET: A slip coupling easily expands and contracts to replace a damaged section of line.

Sprinkler system fixes

Repairing your sprinkler system on the weekend? It doesn't have to be a guessing game—here are some easy solutions.

PROBLEM: LOW WATER PRESSURE

Solution A: Find and repair leaks

Check for leaks in the waterline. Look for a series of sprinkler heads that aren't watering properly. The waterline problem is always located between the last working head and the first nonworking head.

Look for signs of leaking water, such as water bubbling up from the soil when the sprinklers are running, a depression

in the ground or a very wet area. If you find running water, follow the water to the highest point to find the source.

Once you locate the approximate leak site, dig straight down to the waterline. Then enlarge the hole along the line, following the flow of the leaking water until you find the break or crack. Before making the repair, make sure the system is turned off at the controller. Use a slip coupling to repair the leak. This coupling contracts to make insertion

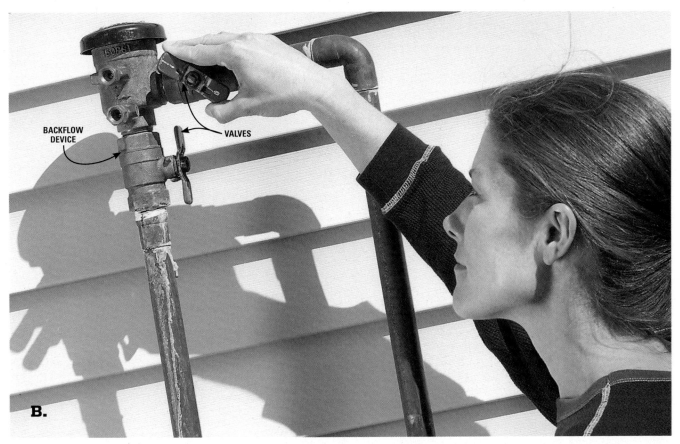

BACKFLOW DEVICE

VALVES

B.

Check the valves on the backflow device to make sure they're open. Turn the valve on the horizontal pipe first, then the vertical pipe valve.

easy. To fix the leak, use a hacksaw to cut out a 4-in. section of line at the leak. Place a clamp on one of the line ends, insert the coupling, then tighten the clamp.

Place a clamp on the second pipe end, expand the coupling while inserting the nipple into the pipe and then tighten the clamp. Backfill the hole with dirt and replace the sod.

Solution B: Turn on valves at backflow device

Low water pressure results in sprinkler heads barely shooting water. In extreme cases, many of the heads won't even pop up. Start with the easiest solution. Make sure the valves at the backflow device are open.

The backflow device is located above ground, with the valve at least 12 in. above the highest sprinkler head in the yard. Most backflow devices have a valve on the horizontal and vertical pipes. Turn the valves to their open positions

as shown. The valve is open when the handle and pipe are parallel.

Solution C: Look for crushed pipes

If you can't locate a leak, the waterline could be crushed or obstructed. Sometimes roots wrap around the line and squeeze it closed, or vehicles may have compressed the soil and collapsed the line. These problems are harder to find and often require a lot of digging. Again, look for the problem after the last working head. Dig along the waterline until you find the damaged section. If the line runs near a tree, start your digging there.

Once you locate the damaged section, cut it out with a hacksaw. If the line was damaged by tree roots, reroute the line by digging a new trench away from the tree. Cut a new section of pipe to replace the damaged one. Then replace the section of pipe, connecting it at each end with regular couplings and band clamps.

TREE ROOT

CRUSHED LINE

COUPLING

DAMAGED LINE

C.

Cut out damaged section of line. Replace it with a new section of line, making connections with standard couplings and band clamps.

PRO TIP

Note:

In areas of the country that experience freezing temperatures, polyethylene (poly) pipe is used for the irrigation waterlines. PVC pipe is used in areas that don't typically freeze.

PROBLEM: SPRINKLER HEADS NOT WORKING

Solution: Clean the clogged sprinkler heads

Dirt sometimes gets inside sprinkler heads, causing them to clog up. Clogged heads may rise but fail to spray, not lower after watering or produce an erratic spray pattern.

To clean a head, dig it out and remove it from the riser. Take the head apart by holding the bottom of the canister and turning the top of the head counterclockwise. Once it's unscrewed, lift it out of the canister **(Photo 1)**.

Remove the plastic screen basket, which serves as a filter, at the base of the head. If you can't pop the basket out with your fingers, pry it out with a flat-head screwdriver or pull it free with pliers.

Rinse the basket in a bucket of clean water, washing out the debris **(Photo 2)**. Clean the rest of the sprinkler head by rinsing it with water. Replace the head on the riser. If it still doesn't work, replace it with a new head. Reset the spray pattern

When putting on a new sprinkler head or using the same head after cleaning, you may need to adjust it to water a specific area. Adjustment methods vary.

You can adjust some head types by turning a slot at the top with a screwdriver. Others require a special key that you insert into the head and turn **(Photo 3)**. Some heads allow you to adjust the spray pattern by turning a tiny screw located next to the nozzle.

1 Disassemble the sprinkler head by unscrewing the top from the canister. Rinse away soil and debris in a bucket of water.

2 Remove the screen basket from the bottom of the head, then clean it with water.

3 Adjust the range of the sprinkler head before installing it. Place the head in the canister so the nozzle is at the edge of the area to be watered. Make final adjustments with the water running.

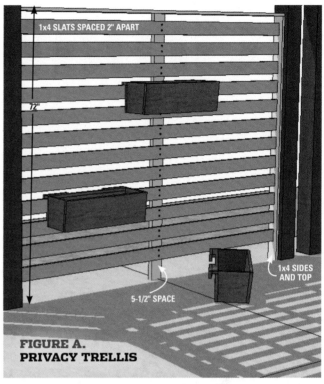

FIGURE A.
PRIVACY TRELLIS

1x4 SLATS SPACED 2" APART

72"

5-1/2" SPACE

1x4 SIDES AND TOP

Privacy trellis with planters

This versatile box looks great anywhere in your yard, and it's incredibly easy to build.

For privacy and more greenery during the warm summer months, build a trellis with removeable planter boxes. You can adapt this design to fencing (or a section of fencing), the side of a deck, an arbor or a pergola. Or make a stand-alone trellis in your yard. The possibilities are endless, and it looks wonderful anywhere.

The trellis shown here is adapted to an existing pergola and is built from 1x4s and a center 2x4. The boards are screwed to the 2x4 and the sides with 1-5/8-in. deck screws. The planter boxes are sized to hold four 6-in. plastic pots. Build as many as you want and just hang them from the 1x4s.

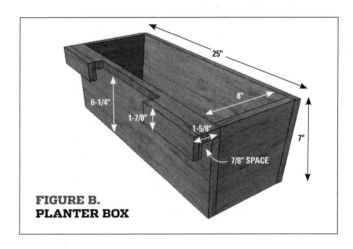

25"
8"
6-1/4"
1-7/8"
1-5/8"
7"
7/8" SPACE

FIGURE B.
PLANTER BOX

WHAT IT TAKES		
TIME 1 day	**COST** $100-$250	**SKILL LEVEL** Beginner

TOOLS
Circular saw, drill/driver, caulk gun

Materials List

ITEM	QTY.
1x4 x 8' treated pine	15
2x4 x 8' treated pine	1
1x8 x 10' cedar (per planter box)	1
No. 8 x 1-5/8" self-drilling exterior screws	50
1-3/4" galvanized nails (for planter box assembly)	1 box
Exterior construction adhesive (for planter assembly)	1 tube

Cutting List

KEY	PART	QTY.
A	3/4" x 3-1/2" x 71-1/4" (vertical sides)	2
B	3/4" x 3-1/2" x 92" (horizontal top)	1
C	1-1/2" x 3-1/2" x 71-1/4" (center support)	1
D	3/4" x 3-1/2" x 90-1/2" (horizontal slats)	12

Great Goofs®

Laughs and lessons from our readers

BRUSH-CUTTER BLUES

My friend Debby had a ton of brush cutting to do in the woods behind her house. "Debby, you have to borrow my commercial-grade brush cutter. It cuts brush like a razor cuts hair!" I bragged. Before she came to get it, I installed a new blade to really impress her.

The following week, she let me know that she wasn't at all impressed with my top-of-the-line tool. She had worked her tail off for three sweaty hours on a 90-degree day without getting much brush cleared. I was puzzled—until I noticed all the teeth were nearly ground off the brand-new blade. You guessed it. I'd installed the blade upside down and the teeth were facing backward. I couldn't let her buy me a new $30 blade, even though she offered.

TIM JOHNSON

MY PLAID LAWN

I bought a drop spreader to fertilize our malnourished lawn. I loaded up the hopper, set the drop rate and went to work. After spreading fertilizer down one row, I measured over to the next row and pulled the spreader backward across the lawn. I covered the entire yard this way—pushing the spreader in one direction, then pulling it back the other way. Then I spread fertilizer again, this time going perpendicular to my first pattern.

All seemed well and good until the lawn greened up a few days later. That's when my wife called me upstairs. From the second-story window, we could see an unmistakable plaid pattern over the whole lawn. It turns out that my spreader only drops fertilizer when you're pushing, not when you're pulling. Oops!

ERIC JONES

HOW NOT TO KILL WEEDS

In spring, I noticed my neighbor spot-spraying weeds that had invaded his lawn. He told me he'd bought a weed killer at our local hardware store to wipe them out. I had weeds in my lawn, too, so I decided to give his remedy a try. I went to the same hardware store, bought weed killer, and then came home and attacked the weeds.

After a few days, my sad lawn was as spotted as a leopard. The weeds were dead, but so was the grass around them. Turns out the product I had purchased was grass and weed killer. Now I'm the talk of the neighborhood for my goof.

I guess no one will be asking me for lawn care advice!

BRIAN UTHER

JUST ADD CONCENTRATE

I serve on our homeowners' association board and oversee the landscaping. Last spring, I decided to spot-spray the dandelions with weed killer. I poured 10 oz. of concentrate into a measuring cup, using up the last of the weed killer. I rinsed the bottle and put it in the recycling bin. Then I grabbed my 4-gallon backpack sprayer and passed the rest of the morning treating each and every dandelion in a four-block stretch.

When I got back to my garage with my empty sprayer, I saw the measuring cup with the 10 oz. of weed killer concentrate still sitting on the workbench. So I wound up spending my afternoon spraying the same weeds—this time with weed killer, not just water.

JOE ALBAUGH

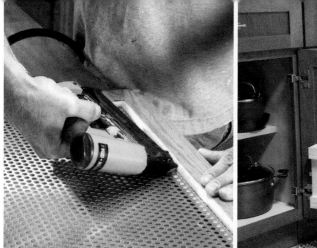

CHAPTER THREE

KITCHEN & BATHROOM

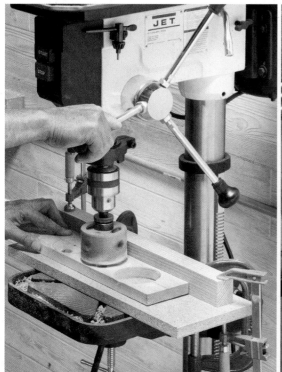

6 kitchen storage upgrades

Make space in your kitchen with these quick projects.

A. RACKS FOR CANNED GOODS

Use leftover closet racks as cabinet organizers. Trim the racks to length with a hacksaw and then mount screws to the back of the face frame to hold the racks in place. The back sides of the racks simply rest against the back of the cabinet.

B. THYME SAVER

If your spices are jammed into a drawer with only the tops visible, this rack that slips neatly into a drawer will solve the problem. Make it with scraps of 1/4-in. and 1/2-in. plywood. You'll never have to sort through countless identical spice lids again.

C. SPICE STORAGE

Small spice containers use shelf space inefficiently and are difficult to find when surrounded by taller bottles and items. Use a small spring-tension curtain rod as a simple shelf. It's easy to install and strong enough to support the spices.

D. WINE GLASS MOLDING

T-molding designed for wood floor transitions makes a perfect rack for stemware. Just cut it to length, predrill screw holes and screw it to the underside of a shelf. For a neater look, use brass screws and finish washers. Prefinished T-molding is available wherever wood flooring is sold.

E. PLASTIC BAG HOLDER

Don't throw out that empty rectangular tissue box — instead, use it as a place to store items you use every day, like garbage bags, plastic grocery bags and even small rags. Installation is a snap, too. You won't even need to go to your workshop; just thumbtack the box to the inside of a cabinet door. This is one of our favorite kitchen storage ideas!

F. MEASURING CUP HANG-UP

Free drawer space by hanging measuring cups inside a kitchen cabinet. Position and mount a wood strip so that the cups will hang between the shelves and allow the door to close completely. Mount a second strip for your measuring spoons, then screw in cup hooks on both strips.

CLOSET ORGANIZER RACKS

ATTACH SCREWS TO BACK SIDE OF FACE FRAME

A.

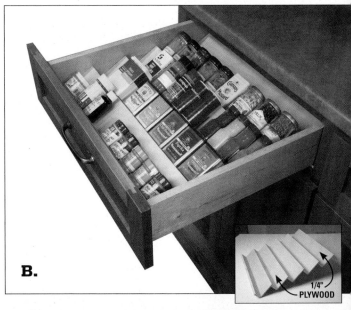

B.

1/4" PLYWOOD

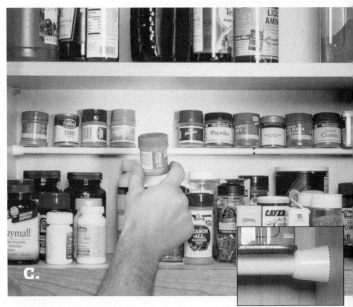

C.

T-MOLDING

FINISH WASHER

D.

E.

F.

WHAT IT TAKES

TIME	COST	SKILL LEVEL
1 day	$250-$500	Intermediate

TOOLS
Large slip-joint pliers, fine-tooth saw, set of open-end or two adjustable wrenches, hex head nut drivers

Install a new sink and faucet

It's less complicated than you think, and the results are well worth it.

Installing a new sink and faucet is easier than ever thanks to the simple-to-cut-and-assemble white plastic (PVC) drain parts **(Photo 7)** and nearly foolproof flexible water supply tubes **(Photo 6)**. Some plumbing experience would be helpful, but even without it you can replace your sink and faucet in less than a day using a few basic tools that you probably already own. You'll need large slip-joint pliers for the drain fittings **(Photo 1)**, a fine-tooth saw to cut the plastic pipe, a set of open-end wrenches or two adjustable wrenches to loosen and tighten the supply tubes, and hex

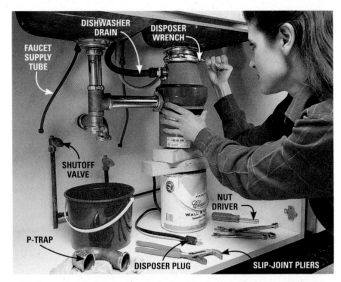

1 Remove the trap and other drain parts by loosening the slip-joint nuts with large slip-joint pliers or a pipe wrench. Disconnect the disposer by sticking a large screwdriver or disposer wrench into the ring near the drain and twisting it counterclockwise. You may have to tap it with a hammer to break it free. Close the water valves and disconnect the tubes leading to the faucet. Hold the shutoff valve steady with one wrench while you loosen the supply tube nut with a second wrench. Remove any clips holding the sink in and lift it out.

2 Mount the new faucet to the new sink. Follow the instructions provided with your faucet. Protect your countertop with some cardboard.

3 Set your new sink in the countertop to check the fit; trace around it with a pencil. Enlarge the hole if necessary. Remove the sink and apply a bead of mildew-resistant tub-and-tile caulk to the inside of the pencil line. Set the sink back in the hole and use a nut driver to tighten the clips that hold the sink down, enough to close the gap between the sink and countertop. Don't overtighten. Clean excess caulk with a damp cloth.

Materials List

ITEM	QTY.
Plumber's putty	1
12' cedar deck boards	1
Basket strainer assemblies (only one if you're installing a disposer)	2
You'll need the following 1-1/2-in. PVC drain parts:	
P-trap assembly	1
End or center outlet waste kit	1
Sink tailpieces—only one if you're installing a disposer. If you have a dishwasher and no disposer, get a special "dishwasher" tailpiece that has a tube to connect the dishwasher drain hose.	2
Special "disposer" waste arm, if you have a disposer	1
Flexible water supply tubes for kitchen sinks. Match the nuts on the ends to the threads on your faucet and shutoff valves. Also measure to determine the right length.	2

head nut drivers for the sink clips and the clamp on the dishwasher drain. If you have a plastic laminate countertop and need to enlarge the hole for the new sink, you'll also need a jigsaw.

THE KEY TO SIMPLICITY: BUY A NEW SINK THE SAME SIZE AS THE OLD

Measure your old sink. The standard size is 33 x 22 in. and about 7 in. deep. If yours is this size, you will have no problem finding a new one to fit the same hole. If you want to install a sink that's larger or deeper than your current one, first check the cabinet width below to make sure it'll fit. Then decide how to enlarge the hole. If your countertop is stone, tile, solid surface (Corian, for example) or metal, you may have to hire a pro to enlarge the hole. If it's wood or plastic laminate, enlarge the hole yourself with a jigsaw.

TIPS FOR REMOVING THE OLD SINK

Getting the old sink out is usually harder than putting the new one in. Old plumbing parts are likely to be corroded, and the sink may be glued to the counter with caulk or caked-on gunk. Sinks are mounted in several ways, but here are a few general tips for removing yours:

- Place a bucket under the trap to catch wastewater while you loosen the slip-joint nuts.
- Remove the disposer **(Photo 1)**.
- Use a pair of pipe wrenches to separate drain parts that won't yield to large slip-joint pliers. Don't worry about damaging pipes; you will be replacing them with new parts.
- Add shutoff valves if your hot and cold water supply pipes don't already have them.
- Working carefully, slice the caulk around the sink with a utility knife,

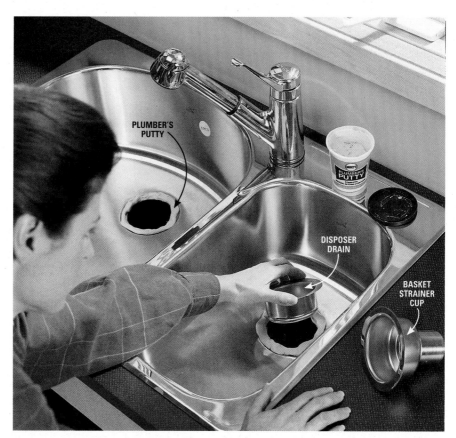

4 Roll plumber's putty into a 1/2-in.-dia. rope and form it around each drain opening. Press the top half of the basket strainer assembly down into the plumber's putty on one side. On the other, press the disposer drain down into the putty.

BASKET STRAINER CUP

DISPOSER DRAIN

BASKET STRAINER NUT

SINK DRAIN PLUGGED WITH RAG

5 Assemble the undersink half of the basket strainer assembly and tighten the large nut with slip-joint pliers. Hold the basket with your hand to keep it from spinning. Reassemble the disposer drain and tighten the three screws. Clean the excess plumber's putty from around the drain openings and polish the sink with a dry cloth.

then slip a stiff putty knife under the sink's lip and gently pry up to loosen it. On some old sinks, you must remove the mounting clips from under the sink before you lift it out.

■ Get help lifting out a cast-iron sink.

TIPS FOR INSTALLING THE NEW SINK

Follow the steps in **Photos 2 – 7** to assemble, install and connect your new sink and faucet. Some sinks, like the stainless steel model shown here, require clips tightened from below to hold them in place **(Photo 3)**. Most cast-iron sinks are held in place by their own weight and a bead of caulk. Follow the mounting instructions provided with your sink.

When you're finished with the installation, turn on the shutoff valves and check for leaks. Then run water in both bowls and check the drains for any leaks.

Most leaks can be fixed by tightening the connection. If this doesn't work, you'll have to take the leaky joint apart and inspect it carefully for any missing or misaligned parts.

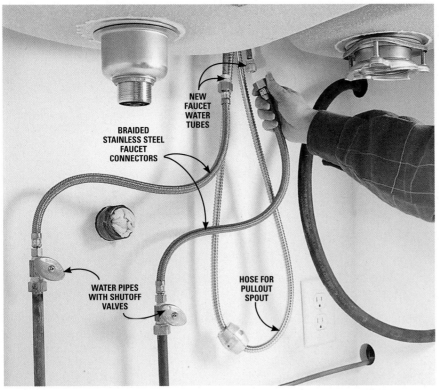

NEW FAUCET WATER TUBES

BRAIDED STAINLESS STEEL FAUCET CONNECTORS

WATER PIPES WITH SHUTOFF VALVES

HOSE FOR PULLOUT SPOUT

6 Connect the water supply valves to the new faucet with flexible braided stainless steel faucet connectors. Hand-tighten the connections. Then turn them an additional quarter turn with a wrench.

BACK-SAVING PLYWOOD LEDGE

Save your back

Prop up a scrap of plywood on some 1-qt. paint cans in front of the cabinet or grab a big bag of pet food. This will make working under the sink more comfortable. Otherwise, the edge of the cabinet will be digging into your back.

Replace a sink sprayer and hose

First, pick up a head and hose kit at a home center or hardware store. Then follow these steps:

A. Use an open-end or basin wrench to unscrew the sprayer hose from the hose nipple. Pull the old sprayer and hose out of the sink grommet. Slide the new hose through the grommet on top of the sink and reconnect it to the faucet.

B. Hold the base of the sprayer in your hand and then twist off the sprayer head. Screw on the brand-new head.

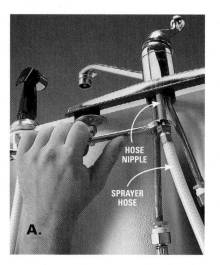

HOSE NIPPLE

SPRAYER HOSE

A.

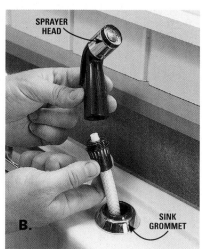

SPRAYER HEAD

SINK GROMMET

B.

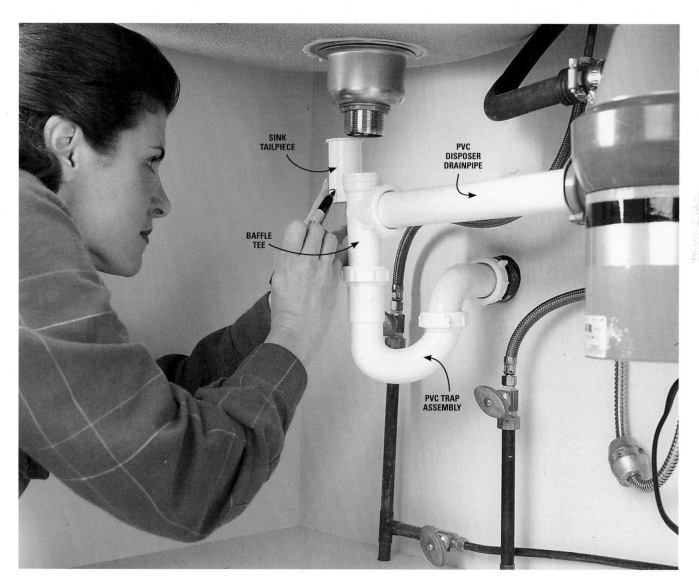

SINK TAILPIECE

PVC DISPOSER DRAINPIPE

BAFFLE TEE

PVC TRAP ASSEMBLY

7 Loosely assemble the new PVC drain fittings. Hold up and mark parts needing to be cut. Then saw them with a fine-tooth wood saw or hacksaw. Slope the horizontal pipes down slightly toward the drain in the wall. Hand-tighten all the fittings and turn the nuts an additional quarter turn with large slip-joint pliers.

1 Outline the inset medicine chest to fall against a stud on one side and cut out the opening with a drywall saw.

2 Cut the intermediate stud flush with the drywall on the back side. Push it sideways to release the drywall screws on the back side and remove the stud.

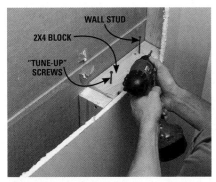

3 Screw blocking to adjacent studs at the top and bottom of the opening. Drive temporary "tune-up" screws into the block to help position it.

4 Cut and tap in vertical backing flush with the drywall edge, then toe-screw it to the blocking.

5 Slip the cabinet into the opening and anchor it with pairs of 2-in. screws. Add trim if needed.

One-morning medicine cabinet

Clear off your bathroom vanity with a medicine cabinet that tucks inside the wall.

The biggest challenge in installing a recessed cabinet is finding unobstructed stud cavities in an open wall. The wall behind the door is usually open, but make sure that pipes, ducts and wiring don't get in the way.

To choose the location for the cabinet, begin by finding the studs with a stud finder. Hold the cabinet to the wall at the best height and mark the cabinet near one side of a stud. Then find the exact location of that stud by sawing through the drywall until the blade is stopped **(Photo 1)**. Use the cuts to define one cabinet side, and then proceed to draw the cabinet outline.

Cut out the drywall and cut off the exposed stud **(Photo 2)**. Add the framing; screw the cabinet to the framing **(Photo 5)**. Add trim around the edges to conceal rough drywall edges.

WHAT IT TAKES		
TIME 4 hours	**COST** $100-$250	**SKILL LEVEL** Beginner

TOOLS
Stud finder, hammer, drill/driver, level, reciprocating saw

Simple bathroom shelf

Get more storage in a small space with this super-simple (and easy-on-the-wallet) project.

In a small bathroom, every single square inch counts. These shelves make the most of wall space by going vertical. The version shown here, made of cherry, cost about $100. But you can build one for $50 or less if you choose a more economical wood like oak or pine. All you need is a 6-ft. 1x4, a 6-ft. 1x6 and a 6-ft. 1x8.

Start by cutting the middle spacers and the shelves to be 12 in. long. Cut the bottom spacer 11 in. long to allow for a decorative 1-in. reveal. Cut the top spacer to fit (the one shown is 7-1/4 in.). Measure 1 in. from one edge of the backboard, and draw a guideline for the shelves and spacers along its length. Nail the bottom spacer in place, leaving a 1-in. reveal at the bottom edge. Center the first shelf by measuring 3-1/4 in. in from the edge of the backboard and nail it in place. Work your way up the backboard, alternating between spacers and shelves (**Photo 1**).

On the back side, use a 1/8-in. countersink bit to drill two holes, one at the top and one at the bottom of each spacer. Drill two holes spaced 1 in. from each side of the backboard into each shelf ledge. Drive 1-1/4-in. drywall screws into each hole (**Photo 2**).

Paint or stain the assembled unit. If you'd like to clearcoat it, use a wipe-on poly or spray lacquer—using a brush would be really tough. Mount the unit on the wall with two 2-1/2-in. screws and screw-in drywall anchors (E-Z Ancor is one brand). Drive the screws where they won't be seen: right below the bottom shelf and right above the top shelf.

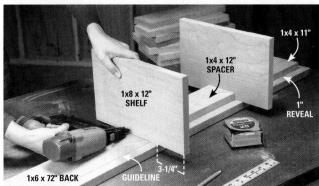

1 Nail the spacers and shelves in place, starting at the bottom and working your way up. Place the bottom spacer 1 in. from the lower edge of the backboard.

2 Strengthen the shelves by driving screws through the backboard into the shelves and spacers. Drill screw holes with a countersink bit.

WHAT IT TAKES		
TIME	**COST**	**SKILL LEVEL**
4 hours	$50-$100	Beginner

TOOLS
Drill/driver, circular saw

Vanity improvements

Help your vanity reach its full storage potential with this trio of projects that will benefit experts and beginners alike.

Most vanities are disappointing storage spaces because they're designed for the convenience of plumbers, not for you. While that big open box is nice for installing pipes, it leaves you with jumbled storage and wasted space. Convert that box into useful space by installing any or all of these three upgrades.

You'll expand the real estate under your sink and make it easy to find anything in seconds. Each of these projects is inexpensive and will help you organize your bathroom. And, best of all, even a beginning DIYer can put them together in just one day.

FIGURE A.
SWING-OUT SHELF

Cutting List

KEY	PART
A	1/2" x 11-3/4" x 12"
B	1/2" x 13" x 12"
C	1/2" x 11-3/4" radius
D	1/8" x 1-3/4" x 24"

Materials List

ITEM	QTY.
1/2" plywood (A–C)	3
1/8" hardboard (D)	2
No. 4 screws and No. 6 finish washers	
Piano hinge	1
Cabinet pull	

PRO TIP

Build it!

A homemade trammel is perfect for marking out the curved shelves.

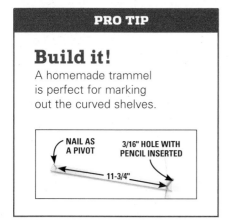

NAIL AS A PIVOT

3/16" HOLE WITH PENCIL INSERTED

11-3/4"

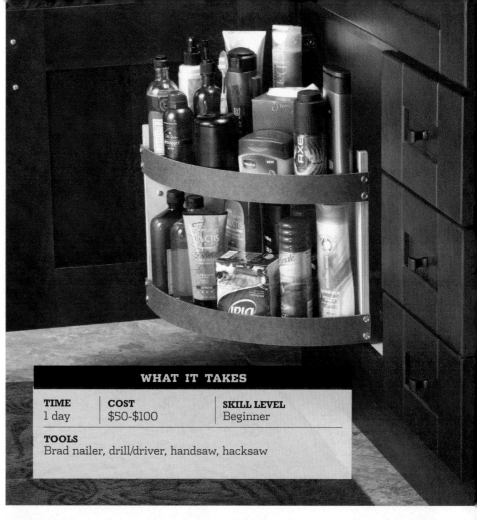

WHAT IT TAKES

TIME	COST	SKILL LEVEL
1 day	$50-$100	Beginner

TOOLS
Brad nailer, drill/driver, handsaw, hacksaw

HARDBOARD EDGING

NO. 4 SCREWS AND NO. 6 FINISH WASHERS

1 **INSTALL THE EDGING, THEN TRIM IT.**
Cut the hardboard edging a few inches too long, fasten it with screws and slice off the excess with a fine-tooth saw. Finish washers give the screws a neater look.

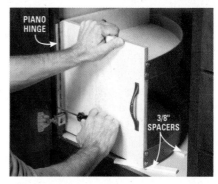

PIANO HINGE

3/8" SPACERS

2 **HANG IT ON A HINGE.** Raise shelf with spacers and align it with the inner edge of the face frame. Screw the piano hinge to the shelf back, then to the cabinet. Notch the shelf back to clear the door hinge if needed.

A. SWING-OUT SHELF

Here's the answer to all that inaccessible clutter on the floor of your vanity. With one pull, you can bring stored items out of the dark recesses and into easy reach.

Chances are the measurements given here won't be the best for your vanity. The best way to determine the right size for your shelf is to cut a quarter circle from cardboard and test the fit. If your vanity has double doors, you can still build this shelf, but you may need to open both doors to swing it out. Here are some tips for building your swing-out shelf:

■ To make the curved shelves, just mark a half circle and then cut it into two equal quarter circles.

■ A pneumatic brad nailer makes assembly a cinch. If you don't have a brad nailer, use trim screws. The awkward shape of the shelves makes hand nailing difficult. Whether you use nails or screws, also use glue.

■ You can finish your shelf with a couple of coats of polyurethane. A can of spray lacquer is another very good option.

■ Piano hinges come in various lengths, but you probably won't find exactly what you need for your shelf. That is OK; you can cut it to length with a hacksaw.

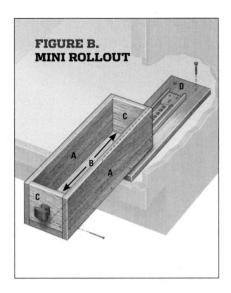

**FIGURE B.
MINI ROLLOUT**

Cutting List

KEY	PART
A	1/2" x 3-1/2" x 16"
B	1/2" x 3-1/2" x 16"
C	1/2" x 3-1/2" x 3"
D	1/2" x 3-1/2" x 16"

Materials List

ITEM	QTY.
1/2" plywood	1
14" full-extension drawer slide	1
Cabinet pull	1

B. MINI ROLLOUT

This super-handy little rollout has tall sides, fronts and backs to keep bottles and cleaners in place as you open it. Alter the dimensions given here to suit your needs. Here are some useful building tips:

■ Assemble the drawer boxes with glue plus trim screws, finish nails or brad nails.

■ Shown is a 14-in. "full-extension" drawer slide. This type of slide is typically mounted on the side of a drawer, but it also works well as a light-duty undermount slide. If your home center doesn't carry full-extension slides in the length you need, go to any online cabinet hardware supplier. You can use a standard undermount slide, but your tray won't extend fully.

■ Finish the rollout with two coats of polyurethane or spray lacquer.

■ If you add a cabinet pull as shown here, be sure to set the base back a bit so the vanity door can close.

WHAT IT TAKES

TIME	COST	SKILL LEVEL
2 - 4 hours	Under $50	Beginner

TOOLS
Table saw, drill/driver

1 MOUNT THE DRAWER SLIDES. Separate the two parts of the drawer slide. Screw them to the tray and the base, aligned flush at the fronts.

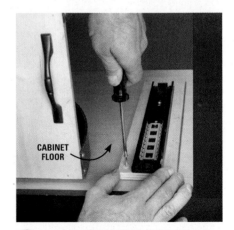

2 ELEVATE THE DRAWER SLIDE WITH A SEPARATE TRAY BASE. Fasten the base to the cabinet floor with No. 6 x 1-in. screws, then slide on the drawer.

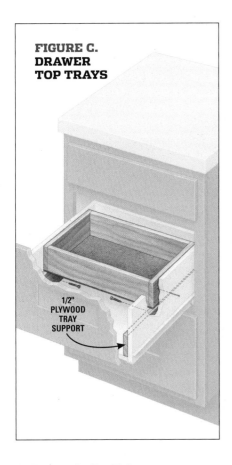

**FIGURE C.
DRAWER
TOP TRAYS**

1/2"
PLYWOOD
TRAY
SUPPORT

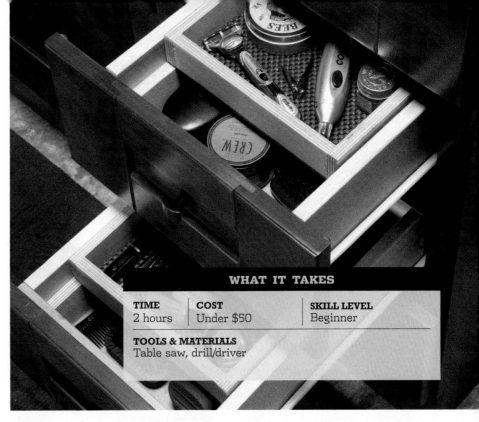

WHAT IT TAKES

TIME	COST	SKILL LEVEL
2 hours	Under $50	Beginner

TOOLS & MATERIALS
Table saw, drill/driver

Materials List

ITEM	QTY.
1/2" plywood	1
1/8" hardboard	1
Shelf liner	1

C. DRAWER TOP TRAYS

Drawers are often too deep for small bathroom stuff like razors, medicine and cosmetics. That means wasted space. These sliding trays reduce that waste and increase drawer real estate by 50 percent.

- Size the tray by measuring the drawer. Subtract 1/16 in. from the width of the drawer space and divide the length in half. Cut a piece of 1/8-in. hardboard this size.

- You can make the tray any depth you like. If the opening in the vanity is taller than the height of the drawer, your tray can protrude above the drawer sides.

- Finish the tray with a couple of coats of polyurethane or spray lacquer.

- Stored items tend to slide around in the trays, so add shelf liner (available at home centers and discount stores).

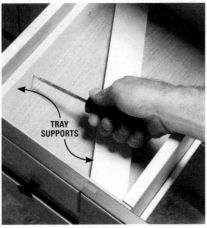

TRAY
SUPPORTS

1 **ADD TRAY SUPPORTS.** Fasten strips of plywood to the drawer to support the tray. You need only two screws per support.

SHELF
LINER

2 **LINE THE TRAYS.** Cut shelf liner to fit the trays. Liner helps stored items stay put when you slide the tray.

No vanity, no problem

If you can get by without a vanity, an awesome way to make a small bathroom feel bigger is to replace the vanity with a stylish wall-hung sink. Visit familyhandyman.com and search "wall hung sink" for complete how-to instructions.

WHAT IT TAKES		
TIME 1 hour	**COST** Under $50	**SKILL LEVEL** Beginner
TOOLS Circular saw or table saw, drill/driver		

Divider for upright storage

With this quick and inexpensive fix you can stop storing stuff in ways that make it hard to access.

Who knows why the pan or tray you need is always the one at the bottom of the pile, but there is a solution: Store large, flat stuff on edge rather than stacked up. That way, you can slide out whichever pan you need.

Cut 3/4-in. plywood to match the depth of the cabinet, but make it at least an inch taller than the opening so you can fasten it to the face frame as shown. Drill shelf support holes that match the existing holes inside the cabinet. Finally, cut the old shelf to fit the new space.

Fasten the divider with brackets. Screw two brackets to the cabinet floor, one to the face frame and one to the back wall of the cabinet.

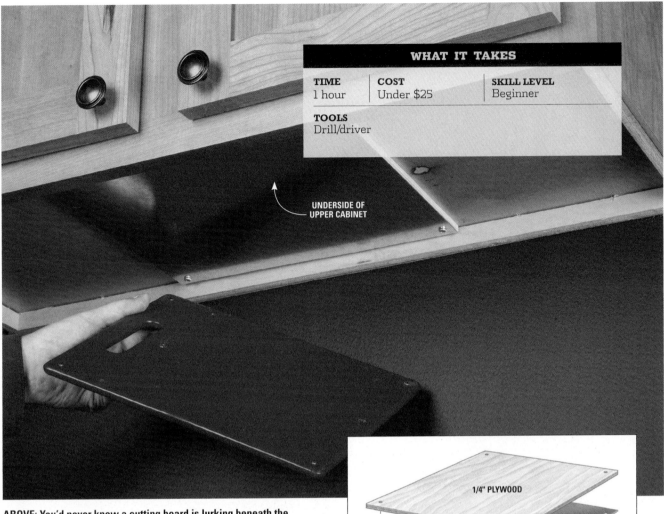

UNDERSIDE OF
UPPER CABINET

1/4" PLYWOOD

SHEET METAL (GLUE TO
PLYWOOD)

CUTTING
BOARD

ABOVE: You'd never know a cutting board is lurking beneath the cabinet. **BOTTOM RIGHT:** Magnetize your cutting board. First, drill holes sized for the magnets and drop in a dab of super glue. Then insert the magnets with a nail head, and slide the nail sideways to release the magnet.

Hidden
cutting board

Rare-earth magnets can save you plenty of kitchen space.

The secret to this project is rare-earth magnets. The ones we used are just 5/32 in. in diameter and 1/8 in. tall. Browse online to find lots of shapes and sizes. Implant magnets at the corners of your cutting board and add more if needed.

Make the metal plate under the cabinet larger than the cutting board so the board will be easy to put away. Glue the sheet metal to plywood with spray adhesive. Drill holes near the corners and screw it to the underside of a cabinet.

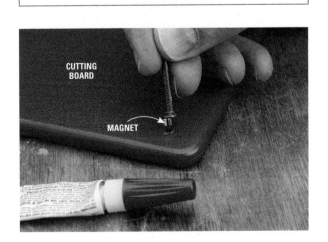

CUTTING
BOARD

MAGNET

Space-saving wine rack

It's easy to build with just three boards!

There's a lot of usable space below many upper kitchen cabinets, and it's the perfect place to store your favorite vintages. This easy-to-build wine rack requires just two 1x4s the length of the under-cabinet bay **(Photo 1)** and a strip of 3/4-in. plywood that same length and 8 in. wide **(Photo 7)**. If you have painted cabinets, poplar is a good choice for the 1x4s. Prime it and paint it to match the cabinets. If you have natural wood cabinets, select and finish the wood to match.

MODIFY THE WINE RACK TO FIT YOUR CABINETS

You can use any of the bays under the upper cabinets you wish. The wider the bay, the more wine you can store. Our instructions will work for any size cabinet bay. Most cabinets have a 3/4-in.-deep lip surrounding each bay so the plywood will be hidden. If you have lips that are deeper than 3/4 in., shim down the plywood. If your lips are shallower, use thinner plywood.

This wine rack will hold many of the most common bottle diameters, but not all. If you are a serious wine collector, take measurements of the diameters of the bottles in your collection. Select a hole saw at least 1/8 in. larger than the largest bottle. If you need to drill holes larger than 3-1/8 in., substitute 1x6s for the 1x4s.

HOLE-SAW SMARTS

- Running a 3-1/8 in. hole saw will tax all but the most powerful drills. If you have a drill press, use it instead of drilling by hand.
- For hand-held hole-saw work, use a corded drill instead of a battery-powered drill if you have one.
- Feel the motor housing as you drill. If it starts getting hot, let it cool down before continuing. Excess heat will destroy

WHAT IT TAKES		
TIME 1 hour	**COST** $10-$20	**SKILL LEVEL** Beginner

TOOLS & MATERIALS
Drill, 3-1/8-in. hole saw, any type of saw, 1-1/2-in. drum sander, clamps

Storing your wine has never been easier. And, best of all, you can customize the rack not only to fit your cabinet bay but also to match the cabinets themselves.

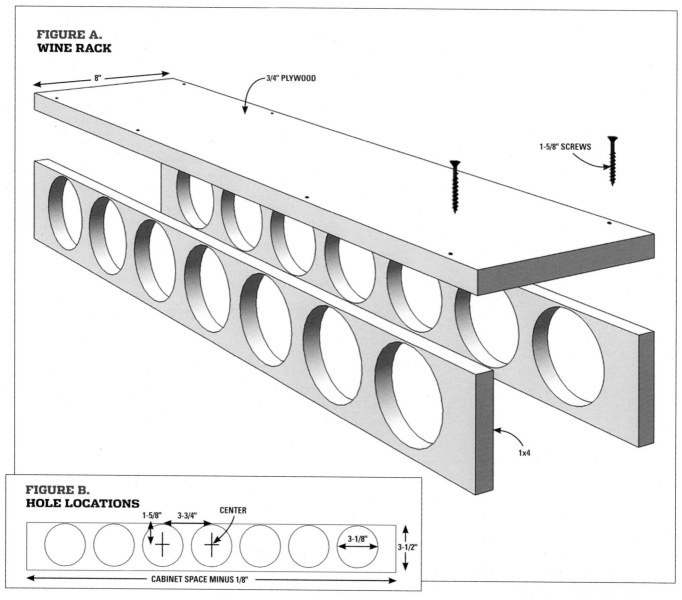

FIGURE A.
WINE RACK

8"

3/4" PLYWOOD

1-5/8" SCREWS

1x4

FIGURE B.
HOLE LOCATIONS

1-5/8"   3-3/4"   CENTER

3-1/8"

3-1/2"

CABINET SPACE MINUS 1/8"

the motor whether the drill is corded or battery-powered.

- Space the board up from the workbench on 2-by scraps to eliminate tear-out. Anchor it with two clamps or the board will spin free **(Photo 5)**.

- After you score each hole about 1/4 in. deep, drill a 1/2- to-3/4-in. clearance hole adjoining each score **(Photo 4)**. This will provide a place for sawdust to exit, which will keep

the hole saw cooler and speed up drilling.

- Take your time and let the hole saw cool off after about 15 seconds of cutting or you'll scorch the wood.

TOOLS & MATERIALS

- 1x4s: Select straight, knot-free boards for best results.

- 3/4-in. plywood: You'll find 2x4 partial sheets at the home center. Any type of plywood will work.

PRO TIP

Hammer tip
Tap or pry out plugs after each hole.

CAUTIONARY INSTRUCTIONS
Drill with the slow speed and use the auxiliary handle if you have one **(Photo 3)**. Don't force the cut, and never use the trigger lock. Hole saws can catch and cause bodily harm.

1 **MEASURE THE CABINET BAY.** Measure the bay opening on the underside of the cabinet. Subtract 1/8 in. and cut two 1x4s to that length. Also cut an 8-in.-wide piece of 3/4-in. plywood to the exact same length.

2 **LOCATE THE HOLES.** Mark a line 1-5/8 in. from the top edge of each board. Place the boards next to each other and mark the center of each hole. The centers should be at least 3-3/4 in. apart.

3 **START THE BOTTLE HOLES.** Clamp the wood over a 2x6 scrap or wider to protect your work surface from the hole saw. Then score each hole with the hole saw about 1/4 in. deep.

4 **DRILL CLEARANCE HOLES.** Using a spade bit, drill 1/2- to 3/4-in. clearance holes adjoining each hole-saw kerf.

5 **COMPLETE THE HOLES.** Finish cutting the wine bottle holes. Rock the drill slightly as you cut. That enlarges the kerf, reducing friction on the hole saw and speeding up cutting.

2x10 SCRAP

DRUM SANDER AND SLEEVE

CLAMP

6 **SAND BEFORE FINISHING.** Smooth holes with a drum sander and ease the edges around the holes by hand-sanding with 100-grit paper. Finish the boards before screwing them to the plywood.

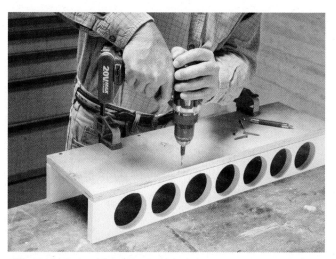

7 **ASSEMBLE THE RACK.** Drill pilot holes and fasten both boards to the plywood backer with 1-5/8-in. screws. Be sure to place the screws between the holes.

SUPPORT BOARD

8 **INSTALL THE RACK.** Clamp the rack to the cabinet; prop up the back with a support board. Drive 1-5/8-in. screws through the bottom into 1x4s. Position screws between holes so tips won't show.

- 3-1/8 in. hole saw: The hole saw itself will run you about $15. If you already have other hole saws, buy the same brand so your mandrel will work in the new one. Otherwise, you'll need to spend another $15 for a mandrel/pilot bit to operate it.
- If you don't have spade bits, be sure to pick up a 3/4-in. bit for drilling the clearance holes.
- A small box of 1-5/8-in. No. 8 screws for all fastening needs.
- 1-1/2-in. drum sander: For less than $10, you can get a drum sander kit that comes with several sandpaper sleeves of different grits.

Got a drill press? Use it!

Protect your hole saw from damage by clamping or bolting a sacrificial board over the cast-iron drill press table. Then clamp a fence to the board, positioned to exactly locate each hole from the edge without any guesswork. A speed of about 600 rpm is good for drilling the necessary holes.

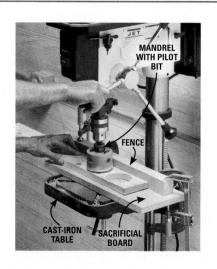

MANDREL WITH PILOT BIT

FENCE

CAST-IRON TABLE

SACRIFICIAL BOARD

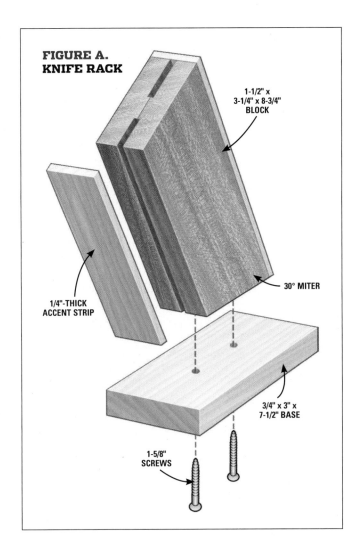

**FIGURE A.
KNIFE RACK**

1-1/2" x
3-1/4" x 8-3/4"
BLOCK

30° MITER

1/4"-THICK
ACCENT STRIP

3/4" x 3" x
7-1/2" BASE

1-5/8"
SCREWS

Space-saving knife rack

Keep your favorite knives handy with a block that doesn't take up much counter space.

Your knives will stay organized with this useful block made from walnut and maple. Start by gluing two 9-in.-long 1x4s together. (To hold four knives, glue three 1x4s together.) **Photos 1 – 3** show the rest!

WHAT IT TAKES		
TIME 1 - 2 hours	**COST** Under $50	**SKILL LEVEL** Beginner

TOOLS
Table saw, drill/driver

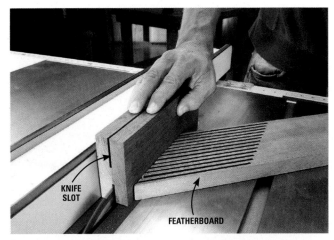

1 CUT KNIFE SLOTS. Set your table saw blade height to match the width of the knife blades, plus 1/8 in. Then cut slots in the block. A featherboard helps to keep the block tight against the fence. You have to remove the blade guard for these cuts—be extra careful!

KNIFE SLOT

FEATHERBOARD

2 CUT THE BLOCK. Glue strips to the block, covering the slots. Then cut a miter on one end of the block and square off the other end. Make these cuts with a miter saw or table saw. We removed the blade guard for photo clarity. Use yours!

FENCE

3 MOUNT THE BLOCK. Mark the position of the block with masking tape and glue it to the base. Then add screws for extra strength.

WHAT IT TAKES		
TIME 2 days	**COST** $100-$250	**SKILL LEVEL** Intermediate
TOOLS Basic tile tools, wet saw (optional)		

Mosaic tile adds interest to a kitchen at risk of being boring.

Mosaic backsplash

Spice up your kitchen with this eye-catching tile accent.

A WHOLE NEW LOOK IN JUST TWO MORNINGS

Nothing packs more style per square inch than mosaic tile. So if your kitchen's got the blahs, give it a quick infusion of pizzazz with a tile backsplash. Because the small tiles are mounted on 12 x 12-in. sheets, installation is fast. You can install the tile on Saturday and then grout it on Sunday.

Professionals charge by the sq. ft. for installing tile (plus materials), so you'll save big by installing it yourself. Tile styles and prices run the gamut from bargain basic to expensive elegance. Shown here are slate tiles. Other types of mosaic tile, especially ceramic tiles, are easier to cut.

Here you'll learn how to install tile sheets. You'll need basic tile tools, available at home centers and tile stores, including a 3/16-in. trowel and a grout float. You'll also need mastic adhesive, grout and grout sealer. You can rent a wet saw to cut the tiles.

PREPARE THE WALLS

Before installing the tile, clean up any grease splatters on the wall (mastic won't adhere to grease). Wipe the stains with a sponge dipped in a mixture of water and mild dishwashing liquid (like Dawn). If you have a lot of stains or they won't come off, wipe on a paint deglosser with a lint-free cloth or abrasive pad so the mastic will adhere. Deglosser is available at paint centers and home centers.

Then mask off the countertops and any upper cabinets that will have tile installed along the side. Leave a 1/4-in. gap

LABELS: VENT HOOD · TAPE · GAP BETWEEN TAPE AND WALL · LEDGER BOARD

1 Mark a centerline between the upper cabinets so the tiles will be centered under the vent hood. Screw a ledger board to the wall to support the tile.

LABELS: 3/16" TROWEL · CENTERLINE · OUTLET EXTENDER · MASTIC

2 Spread a thin layer of mastic adhesive on the wall, starting at the centerline. Spread just enough adhesive for two or three sheets at a time so the adhesive doesn't dry before you set the tile.

PRO TIP

Wide variety

Mosaic tile sheets make it easy to achieve a lovely backsplash. Layout is a cinch—you can simply cut the mesh backing on the sheets to fit the tile along counters and cabinets. In fact, the hardest part of this or any other tiling project may be choosing the look—the tiles come in a variety of shapes and materials, and many sheets have glass or metallic tiles built in for accents. To add to your options, strips of 4 x 12-in. tiles are available for borders. You can match the existing look of your kitchen— or try something new!

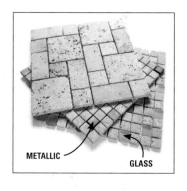

LABELS: METALLIC · GLASS

between the wall and the tape for the tile (**Photo 1**). Cover the countertops with newspaper or a drop cloth. Turn off power to the outlets in the wall and remove the cover plates. Make sure the power is off with a noncontact voltage detector. Place outlet extenders in the outlet boxes. The National Electrical Code requires extenders when the boxes are more than 1/4 in. behind the wall surface. It's easier to put in extenders now and cut tile to fit around them than to add them later if the tile opening isn't big enough. Set the extenders in place as a guide for placing the tile. You'll remove them later for the grouting step.

On the wall that backs your range, measure down from the top of the countertop backsplash a distance that's equal to three or four full rows of tile (to avoid cutting the tile) and make a mark. Screw a scrap piece of wood (the ledger board) to the wall at the mark between the cabinets.

The area between the range and the vent hood is usually the largest space on the wall—and certainly the most

seen by the cooks in the house—so it'll serve as your starting point for installing the tile. Make a centerline on the wall halfway between the cabinets and under the vent hood (**Photo 1**). Measure from the centerline to the cabinets. If you'll have to cut tile to fit, move the centerline slightly so you'll only have to cut the mesh backing (at least on one side).

INSTALL AND SEAL THE TILE

Using a 3/16-in. trowel, scoop some mastic adhesive out of the tub and put it on the wall. Spread the mastic along the centerline, cutting in along the ledger board, vent hood and upper cabinets (**Photo 2**). Then use broad strokes to fill in the middle. Hold the trowel at a 45-degree angle to the wall to spread the mastic thin—you should be able to see the layout lines where the points of the trowel touch the wall. Have a water bucket and sponge on hand to keep the trowel clean. Whenever the mastic starts to harden, wipe it off with the wet sponge.

Place plastic tile spacers on the ledger board and the countertop. This leaves a gap so tiles don't sit directly on the counter (you'll caulk the gap later).

Align the first tile sheet with the centerline, directly over the spacers. Press it onto the wall with your hand. If the sheet slides around and mastic comes through the joint lines, you're applying the mastic too thick (remove the sheet, scrape off some mastic and retrowel). Scrape out any mastic in the joints with a utility knife.

Eyeball a 1/16-in. joint between sheets of tile (you don't need spacers). After every two or three installed sheets, tap them into the mastic with a board and rubber mallet (**Photo 3**).

If tiles fall off the sheets, dab a little mastic on the back and stick them right back in place. The sheets aren't perfectly square, so you may need to move individual tiles to keep joints lined up. Move the tiles with your fingers or by sticking a utility knife blade in the joint and turning the blade. If an entire sheet is crooked, place a grout float over the tile and move the sheet. You'll have about 20 minutes after installing the tile to fine-tune it.

If you're lucky, you can fit the tile sheets under upper cabinets and around outlets by cutting the mesh backing with a utility knife. If not, you'll have to cut the tile with a wet saw. Nippers and grinders cause the slate tiles to shatter or crumble, although you can use these tools on ceramic tile. Slice the backing to the nearest full row of tile, install the sheet around the outlet or next to the cabinet, then cut tiles with a wet saw to fill the gaps **(Photo 4)**. Cut the tiles while they're attached to the sheet. Individual tiles are too small to cut (the blade can send them flying!).

Let the tile sit for at least 30 minutes, then apply a grout sealer if you're using natural stone (like slate) or unglazed quarry tile. The sealer keeps the grout from sticking to the tile (it's not needed for nonporous tiles such as ceramic). Pour the sealer on a sponge, then wipe on just enough to dampen the tiles.

GROUT AND CLEAN THE TILE

Wait 24 hours after installing the tile to add the grout. Use a premium grout that has a consistent color and resists stain. Since the backsplash will be subject to splatters and stains from cooking and food prep, spend the extra money for a premium grout. You can find or special order it at home centers or tile stores. One brand is Prism. Sanded grout will also work and will save you a few bucks.

Mix the grout with water until it reaches mashed potato consistency, then put some on the wall with a grout float. Work the grout into the joints by moving the float diagonally over the tiles **(Photo 5)**. Hold the grout float at a 45-degree angle to the tile. Scrape off excess grout with the float after the joints are filled.

Ten minutes after grouting, wipe the grout off the surface of the tiles with a damp sponge. If the grout pulls out of the joints, wait another 10 minutes for it to harden. Continually rinse the sponge in a bucket of water and wipe the tiles until they're clean.

These slate tiles have a lot of crevices that retain grout. While most of the grout comes off the tiles with the wet sponge, some won't. Most pro installers leave some grout in slate and other rough-surface tile—it's just part of the deal with some types of natural stone. But if you want the tile completely clean, remove the grout from individual tiles with a toothbrush.

After cleaning the wall, use a utility knife to rake the grout out of the joints along the bottom of the backsplash and in the inside corners **(Photo 6)**. These expansion joints allow the wall to move without cracking the grout.

Two hours after grouting, wipe the haze off the tiles with microfiber cloths. Then caulk the expansion joints with latex caulk. Use a colored caulk that closely matches the grout. After seven days, sponge on a grout sealer to protect the grout against stains.

That's it! Now when your family and friends gather around in the kitchen, they'll be impressed with your custom backsplash—be sure to tell them you didn't call a pro. You'll enjoy admiring your hard work (and handsome tile) right along with them.

Add under-cabinet lights

Good lighting allows you to make the best use of the space you have. Dimly lit or shadowy countertops are hard to utilize. Adding under-cabinet lights is a great way to make the countertops more useful while making a small kitchen feel larger.

It's easy to wire for under-cabinet lights with the rest of the wiring during a kitchen remodel. But adding them to an existing kitchen requires a little more ingenuity. Visit familyhandyman.com and search "under cabinet lighting" for step-by-step how-to. Otherwise, you can fish the electrical cables through the basement, crawl space or attic and pull them through the stud spaces to each light fixture. As a last resort, buy plug-in type under-cabinet lights. LED strip or tape lights are convenient, too.

3 Tap the tile into the mastic with a wood scrap and a rubber mallet. Stand back, look at the tiles and straighten any crooked ones.

SPACER

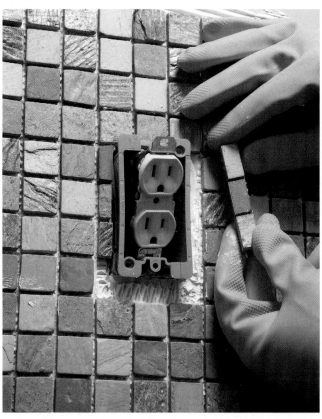

4 Cut tile sheets to the nearest full row to fit around outlets, then fill the gaps with tiles cut on a wet saw.

5 Force grout into the joints with a float. Scrape off excess grout by moving the float diagonally across the tile.

DULL SIDE

6 Rake the grout out of the joints at inside corners and along the bottom with a utility knife so you can fill them with caulk. Keep the dull side of the blade along the countertop.

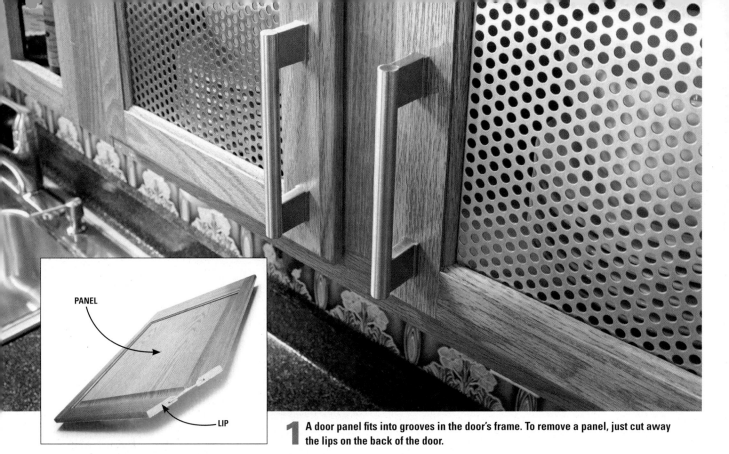

PANEL

LIP

1 A door panel fits into grooves in the door's frame. To remove a panel, just cut away the lips on the back of the door.

Metal panels for cabinet doors

Installing new panels in old cabinet doors can really dress up a kitchen—and they're cheaper than new cabinets!

Adding "feature" inserts to just one or two of your cabinet doors can be striking and inexpensive. Insert materials include glass, translucent plastic, copper and many others.

REMOVE THE PANELS

To cut away the lips that secure the door panel **(Photo 1)**, you'll need a pattern bit—a straight router bit with a bearing that's the same diameter as the cutting diameter. You can buy a pattern bit, but most are too long to use with a 3/4-in.-thick guide. You may have to shop online to find a shorter bit with a cutting depth of 1/2 in.

If you're working with just one or two cabinet doors, the only guide you'll need is a straight board. If you have a stack of doors to rout, a more elaborate guide will save you time **(Photo 2)**. The stops automatically position the guide without measuring, and you are able to rout two sides without repositioning.

Examine the back of the door before you rout. If you find any nails, pull them out so they don't chip your router bit. Before you start cutting, set your router depth so the bit just

touches the panel. After you cut away the lips, simply lift out the door panel. The router bit will leave rounded corners at each corner of the door frame; square them off with a chisel or utility knife.

INSTALL THE METAL INSERTS

Prefinish 1/4-in. quarter-round molding and use it to secure the inserts **(Photo 3)**. When you place the insert into the door frame, make sure the punched side is face up (the punched side will feel slightly raised around the holes). Fasten the quarter round with 5/8-in. nails or brads. If you don't have a brad nailer or pinner, you can use a hammer.

WHAT IT TAKES		
TIME 1 - 2 days	**COST** $100-$250	**SKILL LEVEL** Intermediate
TOOLS Router, pattern bit, brad nailer		

2 Run a pattern bit along a guide to remove the lips. Any straight board will work as a guide, but an L-shaped guide with stops speeds up the job.

3 Frame the back of the insert with quarter-round molding to hold the metal in place. If you use a nail gun, aim carefully so you don't shoot through the face of the door.

Buying metal inserts

Some home centers carry sheets of metal (including perforated) and will cut them for you for a small fee. But you'll find a much bigger selection online. Look for metal in the 16- to 20-gauge range. The metal inserts shown here were purchased directly from McNichols Co. (mcnichols.com) and were ordered over the phone. The website is full of information. Look at its "Products" drop-down menu and go from there.

Do your measuring after you remove the cabinet doors to get accurate insert measurements. Order inserts 1/8 in. shorter in both the length and the width so the inserts just fit in the opening. If stainless steel is out of your price range, consider aluminum or plain steel (called "mill finish"). You can spray-paint your metal any color you want.

No matter what finish you order, wash the metal with paint thinner to rinse off the manufacturing oils. If you choose not to paint the steel, spray it with a clear lacquer to prevent it from rusting.

FULL CLOVERLEAF

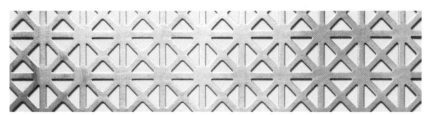

GRECIAN

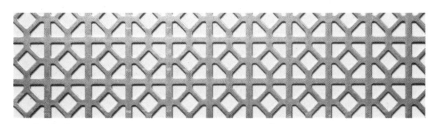

WINDSOR

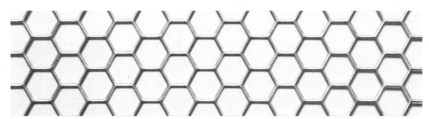

HEXAGONAL

SHELF
SUPPORT

Drawer in a drawer

Say farewell to jumbled silverware and rooting through drawers for the measuring cup you need.

Deep drawers often contain a pile of interlocking utensils. One solution is a sliding tray that creates two shallower spaces. Make it 1/8 in. narrower than the drawer box, about half the length and any depth you want (this one is 1-3/4-in. deep). When you position the holes for the adjustable shelf supports, don't rely on measurements and arithmetic. Instead, position the tray inside the drawer box at least 1/8 in. lower than the cabinet opening and make a mark on the tray. The shelf supports should fit tightly into the holes, but if not, dab in a little super glue.

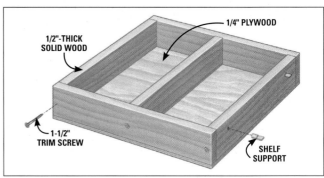

1/2"-THICK
SOLID WOOD

1/4" PLYWOOD

1-1/2"
TRIM SCREW

SHELF
SUPPORT

Gain storage space in your kitchen by adding a shallow drawer on top of the main drawer.

WHAT IT TAKES		
TIME	**COST**	**SKILL LEVEL**
2 hours	Under $50	Beginner
TOOLS		
Table saw, drill/driver		

Cutting board rack

Keep your boards out of sight and easy to find.

You can make this rack for less than $10 and mount it inside a cabinet door. It requires only a 6-ft. 1x2 and two L-brackets.

Measure between the door stiles to get the maximum width of your rack. Make sure the rack will be wide enough for your cutting board (or spring for a new one). You'll also need to mount the rack low enough so it doesn't bump into a cabinet shelf when the door closes. Cut the bottom and face rails to match the space between the cabinet door stiles.

Cut sides 7-1/4 in. long. Nail the sides to the base, then nail the two face pieces at the top and bottom to complete the rack (**Photo 1**). The easiest way to mount the rack is to take the cabinet door off its hinges and lay it down. Predrill the screw holes for the L-brackets and mount the rack to the cabinet door using a 1-in. L-bracket centered on each side of the rack (**Photo 2**).

WHAT IT TAKES		
TIME	**COST**	**SKILL LEVEL**
1 hour	Less than $10	Beginner
TOOLS		
Drill, basic hand tools		

1 Nail the bottom rail to the sides, then nail on the face rails. For a quick, clear finish, spray on two light coats of lacquer.

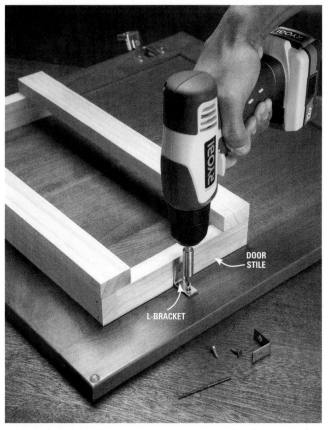

2 Mount the rack on the door with L-brackets. This is easiest if you remove the door. Be sure to predrill screw holes in the door stiles.

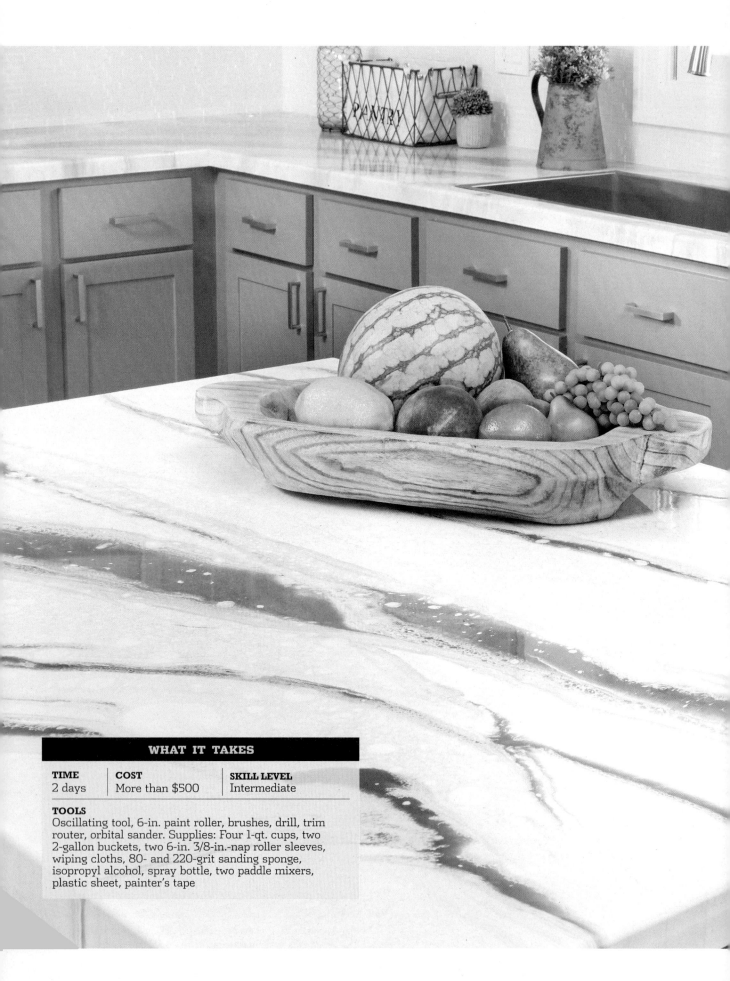

WHAT IT TAKES

TIME	COST	SKILL LEVEL
2 days	More than $500	Intermediate

TOOLS

Oscillating tool, 6-in. paint roller, brushes, drill, trim router, orbital sander. Supplies: Four 1-qt. cups, two 2-gallon buckets, two 6-in. 3/8-in.-nap roller sleeves, wiping cloths, 80- and 220-grit sanding sponge, isopropyl alcohol, spray bottle, two paddle mixers, plastic sheet, painter's tape

New life for old countertops

The look of marble at a fraction of the cost.

When imagining new countertops for a kitchen, it's clear that nothing looks as good as marble. But marble is soft and porous, making it prone to scratches, stains and chipping. It's also expensive. But this epoxy coating mimics the look of a marble slab—at a tenth of the cost.

Everyone will be amazed by the transformation. You'd have to look very closely to see mistakes that give it away: maybe a pair of drips down one edge or a slight orange peel texture in the corner from overworking the topcoat. The countertops are tough, too; we dragged heavy pots and pans across them without damage.

If your countertops are in need of a refresh, consider covering them with epoxy for a stunning new look.

Countertop coating kits

If you want to coat your countertops, you have several options. Kits cost anywhere from $90 to $600 or more. We used Rust-Oleum Countertop Transformations to create the black countertop shown below. You sprinkle decorative chips in the coating to get the look of granite. To see that project, search for "renew kitchen countertops" at familyhandyman.com. Other kits, like the one we used for this marble look, require a bit more artistry to mimic the beautiful veins of natural stone. At $550, it was more expensive than others we tried, but the results were stunning. It's available from Leggari Products (leggari.com).

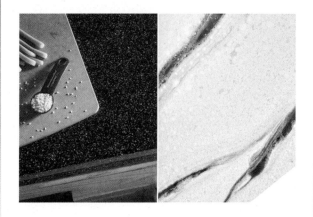

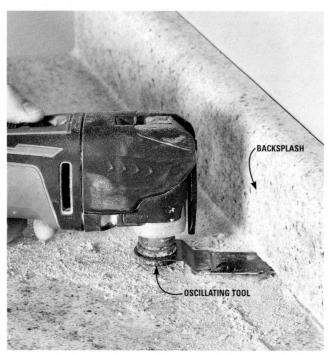

1 **CUT OFF THE BACKSPLASH.** Cutting off the backsplash isn't necessary and adds extra work, but if you want the genuine look of a marble slab, it's worth it. With an oscillating tool and a carbide blade, cut into the backsplash, flush with the rest of the counter. Once the backsplash is off, glue a piece of wood between the counter and the wall to fill the gap. Then sand it all flat. You'll also have to remove your sink before applying the epoxy.

2 **ROUT THE CORNERS.** Epoxy needs a rounded edge in order to bond well to the corner and to flow over it. On the ends, use a 1/8-in. round-over bit with the router positioned horizontally so the bit can follow the shape of the front edge. If the front edge isn't rounded over, use a 1/4-in. or 3/8-in. round-over bit.

3 **PATCH SEAMS.** Fill any gaps and seams with all-purpose body filler. This includes seams at miters, inside corners at the front edge, and the gap between the counter and the backsplash. Fill and smooth particleboard that's exposed after routing or cutting. Body filler is a two-part system that will harden in a few minutes once it's mixed together, so work in small sections and move quickly.

4 **SAND IT SMOOTH.** Once everything is patched, you'll find it easy to eliminate any high spots in the body filler using a paint scraper. Then sand the top, front edge and rounded corners with 60-grit sandpaper. Scuffing up the surface will help the epoxy bond with the old top.

PROTECT INSIDE

CATCH DRIPS WITH CARDBOARD

5 **MASK EVERYTHING.** The epoxy is really messy. Tape plastic to the floor beneath the counters. Then drape plastic over the cabinets, tape it underneath the front edge of the counter, tuck it into the toe-kick and tape it to the plastic on the floor. For the sink opening, tape plastic to the underside of the counter to catch the epoxy. Mask off the walls, leaving about a 1/8-in. gap above the counter. Finally, put cardboard under the counters to collect drips.

6 **PREPARE YOUR MATERIALS.** Once you start applying the primer coat to the counters, you're on the clock. If you have to stop to find something or run to the store, you'll be in trouble. So get organized and set everything you'll need from this point on within arm's reach.

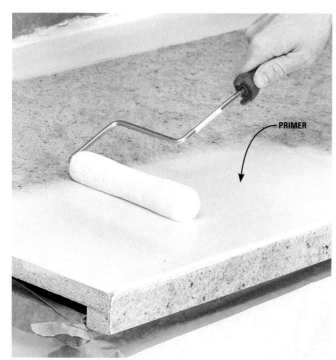

PRIMER

7 **APPLY PRIMER.** The primer creates a perfect surface for the epoxy to be applied. Mix the two-part primer in a small bucket, then cut it into the corners with a brush and roll it on the countertops. If you notice the old counter color showing through, roll on more primer while it's still wet.

8 **PREMIX THE HIGHLIGHTS.** The primer needs about an hour to become tacky. While you wait, mix the metallic powder into part A of the highlight epoxy. Don't mix part A with part B until you're ready; it will set up in as little as 15 minutes in a bucket. You'll also want to mix the metallic powder with isopropyl alcohol in a spray bottle to use later on.

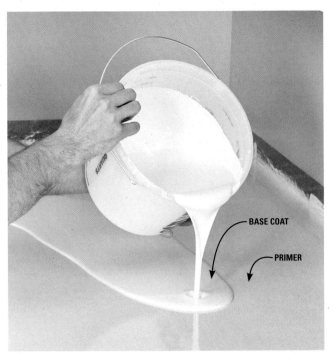

9 POUR THE BASE COAT. After an hour, mix your base coat of epoxy. The trick to getting the epoxy mixed is to use two buckets. Pour the two parts into one bucket, stir with the mixing paddle for a minute, then pour the mixed epoxy into a new bucket and mix for another minute. Pour it down the center of the countertop to cover the entire surface, then spread it around with a roller. Keep the epoxy puddle on top of the counter, but get it into the corners and near the edges.

10 ROLL THE EDGES. Pour a thin line of leftover epoxy along the edges of the counter. With the roller sleeve still saturated, roll the front edge of the counter, then lightly push the thin line of epoxy over the edge. Check that the base coat is an even thickness throughout the top; if it's not, move it around or pour more epoxy. Once the base coat is on, it's time to mix the highlights completely, just as you did with the base coat.

11 ADD HIGHLIGHTS. Drizzling the highlights is fun, but don't go overboard. You can always add more; you can't take them away. After mixing the highlights, use a combination of pouring from the mixing cup and dripping from a stir stick to create veins in the counter.

12 DRAG OVER THE HIGHLIGHTS. Feather the highlights into the base coat by dragging a brush lightly across the top. Follow the highlights and dab the brush to give them a natural look. If you overwork the epoxy, the highlights will blend into the base coat instead of jumping out. By waiting for the epoxy to set up slightly, you can feather without blending. It takes about an hour for the epoxy to set up.

13 SPRAY ON ALCOHOL. Spritz the counter with the isopropyl alcohol and metallic powder solution. It works like magic: The solution disperses the epoxy and gives a much more natural look. We did a few rounds of this, and also made sure to spray the front edges. You can always rework the epoxy and spray again.

14 SCRAPE OFF DRIPS. Wait a while after you think you're done. Look for divots starting to form and fill them with a few drops of leftover epoxy. As drips form underneath the front edge, scrape them off with a stir stick. Look for dust nibs or bugs that have fallen into the coating, and pick them out with a toothpick or tweezers. After about an hour of setting up, peel away the masking along the backsplash and wait a day for the epoxy to set.

15 SMOOTH THE TOP. The next day, prepare the counter for the protective topcoat; ideally this will be 20 hours after the pour so the topcoat will form a chemical bond with the not-yet-cured epoxy. Walk around the counters. Sand out any dust nibs you find with 220-grit sandpaper. Check the bottom edge for drips and sand them out with 80-grit paper. Dust the tops; wipe them down with denatured alcohol.

16 PROTECT YOUR COUNTERS. Mix the two-part topcoat in a container and apply a thick coat to the surface. Spread the topcoat on quickly; lightly reroll the surface in one direction. Start along the backsplash and pull the roller to the front edge, working your way around. It will take at least a week for the counters to cure, but once they do, they'll withstand dents and scratches from kitchen use.

Convert wood cabinet doors to glass

A pair of glass doors add a designer touch to any kitchen.

We recommend this alteration only for frame-and-panel cabinet doors **(see Figure A)**, where you can replace the inset wood panels with glass. Converting the two doors shown here took about two hours. To get started, remove the doors from the cabinets and remove all hardware from the doors. Examine the back side of each door; you might find a few tiny nails where the panel meets the frame. If so, gouge away wood with a utility knife to expose the nail heads and pull the nails with a pliers. Look carefully; just one leftover nail will chip your expensive router bit.

Cut away the lips using a router and a 1/2-in. pattern bit **(Photo 1)**. A pattern bit is simply a straight bit equipped with a bearing that rolls along a guide. Most home centers and hardware stores don't carry pattern bits, but you can find them online. Be sure to choose a bit that has the bearing on the top, not at the bottom.

Use any straight, smooth material to make two 3-1/2-in.-wide guides. To allow for the 1-in. cutting depth of our pattern bit, we nailed layers of plywood and MDF together to make 1-3/8-in.-thick guides. Position the guides 1/2 in. from the inner edges of the lips, and clamp them firmly in place over the door. Support the outer edges of the guides with strips of wood that match the thickness of the door to keep them level **(Photo 1)**. Before you start routing, make sure the door itself is clamped firmly in place.

Set the router on the guide and adjust the cutting depth so that the bit just touches the panel. Cut away the lips on two sides, then reposition the guides to cut away the other two lips. With the lips removed, lift the panel out of the

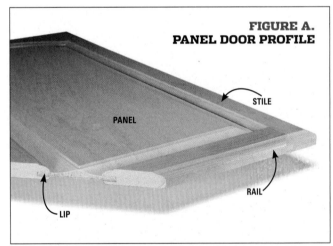

FIGURE A.
PANEL DOOR PROFILE

STILE

PANEL

RAIL

LIP

Most cabinet doors are made like this one: A raised or flat panel fits into grooves in the rails-and-stile frame. To remove the panel, just cut away the lips on the back side of the door.

frame. If the panel is stuck, it'll take only a few light hammer taps to free it.

If your door frame has a rectangular opening, it's now ready for glass. If it has an arched upper rail, cut a square recess above the arch **(Photo 2)**. This allows you to use a rectangular piece of glass rather than a curved piece (curved cuts are expensive). Then simply lay the glass in and anchor it with glass clips **(Photo 3)**. Clips are available from a glass supplier, at www.wwhardware.com or at a variety of other online retailers. If the glass rattles in the frame, add pea-sized blobs of hot-melt glue every 12 in.

WHAT IT TAKES		
TIME 1 day	**COST** $100-$250	**SKILL LEVEL** Intermediate

TOOLS & MATERIALS
Router, pattern bit, drill/driver

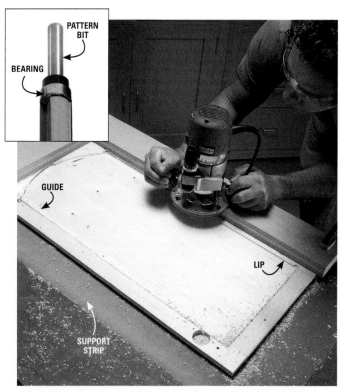

1 Clamp router guides to the back side of the door. Run a pattern bit along the guides to cut away the inside lips.

2 Lower the router bit and cut away the shoulders on the back side of the arched upper rail to create a square recess for the glass.

3 Set the glass into the frame and secure it with glass clips placed no more than 12 in. apart. Then reinstall the doors.

Great Goofs®

Laughs and lessons from our readers

BLINDSIDED BY THE LIGHT

My friend had installed a kitchen backsplash and asked me to help him change the wall outlets. Since I didn't have my voltage sniffer with me, I needed something to plug into the outlet so I'd know when the power was off. I found a clothes iron and plugged it in.

I changed the first two outlets and started on the third. I plugged in the iron—yup, the light was off. When I touched the wire, there was a flash of sparks and my arm went numb. I was floored—how could I get a shock when the iron showed the power was off? I learned the hard way that the light goes off when the iron reaches the right temperature.

SHAWN TOMBOLINI

MYSTERIOUS MEOW

I volunteered to install a handicap shower for my uncle, who was recovering from knee surgery. I framed in a corner of his bathroom. His cats were underfoot while I was working, so I carried them out of the room.

I finished the framing, installed the shower and even built a couple of shelves in the corner. Then I went home, ate and settled down to watch football. Right after kickoff, my uncle called. He'd heard meowing in the bathroom but couldn't figure out where it was coming from. You guessed it—one of the cats had somehow snuck back into the room and crawled into the space between the studs and the new shower just before I finished hanging the new drywall. I had to cut a hole in the wall to get Midnight out.

JASON ROUSH

TWO TIMES THE WATER DAMAGE

The toilet in the upstairs bathroom had been leaking for some time, which had rotted the floor. I removed the toilet, vanity and sink to replace the plywood. I laid the new vinyl floor and reinstalled the bathroom vanity, leaving off the sink to make it easier to solder on new shutoff valves.

With the main water supply to the house turned off, I installed the shutoff valves. Then I went downstairs to turn on the water supply and check the joints for leaks. As I walked back upstairs, fancying myself a master plumber, I heard the sound of gushing water. I had forgotten to turn off the shutoff valves! The bathroom was flooded. The ceiling below was ruined. But my soldering job held up perfectly.

GLENN MCCOMAS

KNOW WHEN TO PULL THE PLUG

When my garbage disposal went on the fritz, I went ahead and purchased and installed a new disposal. I turned it on and everything worked perfectly. Feeling proud of myself for conquering a problem without hiring a pro, I did a little victory dance.

That night, my dishwasher quit mid-wash and wouldn't drain. I called for help. When the service technician showed up and looked under the sink, he asked who installed the disposal. I hung my head and mumbled an expletive, then explained I'd followed the easy installation directions. "You're supposed to remove the factory plug from the drain line that runs to the dishwasher," he said. He unhooked the drain line, popped out the plug and solved the problem.

MARK BLAIR

CHAPTER **FOUR**

GARAGE & WORKSHOP

Organize your garage in one morning

There's no need to look around your garage and fret about the clutter. This simple project helps the area get, and stay, clean.

There are lots of ways to create more storage space in your garage, but you won't find another system that's this simple, inexpensive or versatile. It begins with a layer of plywood fastened over drywall or bare studs. Then you just screw on a variety of hooks, hangers, shelves and baskets to suit your needs. That's it. The plywood base lets you quickly mount any kind of storage hardware in any spot—no searching for studs. And because you can place hardware wherever you want (not only at studs), you can arrange items close together to make the most of your wall space. As your needs change, you'll appreciate the versatility of this storage wall, too; just unscrew shelves or hooks to rearrange the whole system.

Shown here are three types of storage supplies: wire shelves, wire baskets, and a variety of hooks, hangers and brackets (see p. 139). Selecting and arranging these items to suit your needs can be the most time-consuming part of this project. To simplify that task, outline the dimensions of your plywood wall on the garage floor with masking tape. Then gather all the stuff you want to store and lay it out on your outline. Arrange and rearrange items to make the most of your wall space. Before you head to the hardware store or home center, make a list of the hardware you'll need.

WHAT IT TAKES		
TIME 4 hours	**COST** $100-$250	**SKILL LEVEL** Beginner
TOOLS Stud finder, drill/driver, circular saw, miter saw		

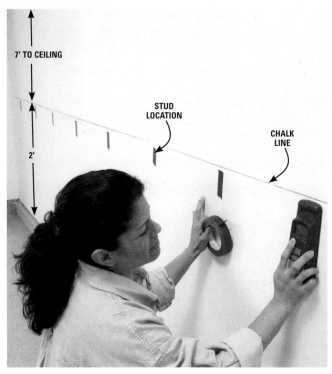

7' TO CEILING

2'

STUD LOCATION

CHALK LINE

1 Snap a level chalk line to mark the bottom edge of the plywood. Locate studs and mark them with masking tape.

2-1/4" SCREW

SUPPORT BLOCK

2 Screw temporary blocks to studs at the chalk line. Start a few screws in the plywood. Rest the plywood on the blocks and screw it to studs.

Storage supplies for every need

Wire closet shelves are sturdy and inexpensive, and they don't collect dust like solid shelving. They come in lengths up to 12 ft. and can be cut to any length using a hacksaw or bolt cutters. Standard depths are 12, 16 and 20 in. You will get more shelving for your money by cutting up long sections rather than buying shorter sections. Brackets and support clips (Photo 4) are usually sold separately.

Wire or plastic baskets are perfect for items that won't stay put on shelves (like balls and other toys) and for bags of charcoal or fertilizer that tend to tip and spill. Baskets are also convenient because they're mobile; hang them on hooks and lift them off to tote all your tools or toys to the garden or sandbox. You'll find baskets in a variety of shapes and sizes at home centers and discount stores. You can use just about any type of hook to hang the baskets. Heavy-duty mirror supports fit these types of baskets perfectly.

Hooks, hangers and brackets handle all the odd items that don't fit on shelves or in baskets. Basic hooks are often labeled for a specific purpose, but you can use them in other ways. Big "ladder brackets," for example, can hold several long-handled tools. "Ceiling hooks" for bikes also work on walls. Don't write off the wall area below the plywood—it's prime space for items that don't protrude far from the wall. We drove hooks into studs to hang an extension ladder.

MIRROR SUPPORT HOOK

MONEY, MATERIALS AND PLANNING

The total materials bill for the 6 x 16-ft. section of wall shown here was about $200. Everything you need is available at home centers. Shown is 3/4-in.-thick "BC" grade plywood, which has one side sanded smooth. You can save a few bucks by using 3/4-in. OSB "chip board" (oriented strand board) or MDF (medium-density fiberboard). But don't try to use particleboard; it doesn't hold screws well enough for this job. Aside from standard hand tools, all you need to complete this project is a drill to drive screws and a circular saw to cut plywood. You may also need a helper when handling plywood—full sheets are awkward and heavy.

This project doesn't require much planning; just decide how much of the wall you want to cover with plywood. You can cover an entire wall floor-to-ceiling or cover any section of a wall. In this garage, the lower 3 ft. of wall and upper 18 in. were left uncovered, since those high and low areas are best used for other types of storage. To make the most of the plywood, a course of full-width sheets was combined with a course of sheets cut in half. If your ceiling height is 9 ft. or less, a single 4-ft.-wide course of plywood may suit your needs.

COVER THE WALL WITH PLYWOOD

When you've determined the starting height of the plywood, measure up from the floor at one end of the wall and drive a nail. Then measure down to the nail from the ceiling and use that measurement to make a pencil mark at the other end of the wall. (Don't measure up from the floor, since garage floors often slope.) Hook your chalk line on the nail, stretch it to the pencil mark and snap a line **(Photo 1)**.

Cut the first sheet of plywood to length so it ends at the center of a stud. Place the end you cut in the corner.

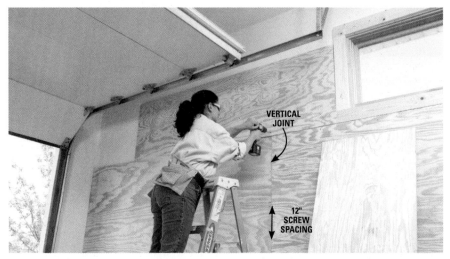

3 Set the upper course of plywood in place and screw it to studs. Stagger the vertical joints between the upper and lower courses.

4 Fasten the back edges of shelves with plastic clips. Set a level on the shelf and install the end brackets. Then add center brackets every 2 ft.

5 Acrylic photo frames make great label holders. Just slip in your labels and hot-glue the frames to the wire baskets. Frames are sold at office supply and discount stores.

That way the factory-cut edge will form a tight joint with the factory edge of the next sheet. Be sure to place the rough side of the plywood against the wall. Fasten the plywood with 10d finish nails or screws that are at least 2-1/4 in. long **(Photo 2)**. Shown here are trim screws, which have small heads that are easy to cover with a dab of spackling compound. Drive screws or nails every 12 in. into each stud. If you add a second course of plywood above the first as shown **(Photo 3)**, you'll have to cut the plywood to width. You can use a circular saw, but a table saw gives you faster, straighter cuts. Some home centers and lumberyards cut plywood for free or for a small charge.

With all the plywood in place, go ahead and mount the hardware, or take a few extra steps to dress up the wall first: You can add 3/4-in. cove molding along the lower edge of the plywood for a neater look and to cover up the chalk line and screw holes left by the support blocks.

You can also frame the window trim with doorstop molding to easily hide small gaps between the trim and the plywood. For a simple fix to this problem, caulk gaps between the sheets of plywood and fill screw holes. Finally, prime the plywood, lightly sand it with 100-grit sandpaper and paint it—the gaps will be gone.

More projects online

If you're looking for more garage storage projects, be sure to visit **familyhandyman. com** and search for "garage storage." Here are just a few of the projects you'll find: a hang-it-all storage wall, nifty rotating shelves and an above-your-head shelf system that holds a ton! So if you don't see anything that will work for you here, head to the Web!

Handy hooks

When you're out shopping, you might find elaborate hangers designed to hold specific toys and tools. These specialty hooks are nice, but you don't have to spend $10 or more just to hang a bike or garden tools. With a bit of ingenuity, you can hang just about anything on simple screw-in hooks that typically cost a dollar or two. You can place hooks anywhere on your plywood wall. If you don't put them on the plywood, be sure to locate them at studs.

Drill a hole at a 45-degree angle and turn in a screw hook to hang a bicycle by the front wheel.

Hang ladders on hooks below the plywood for easy access.

Circular saw jigs for table saw–quality cuts

You don't really need a full-size table saw or a portable table saw.

FACTORY EDGE

3"

3"

7"

A.

If you have a full-size table saw, you're all set for making plywood cuts. And if you have a portable table saw, you can use it for smaller ripping jobs, such as making shelving and drawer parts.

But if you don't have either of those, you can also do a fine job with a circular saw fitted with a cabinet-grade, smooth-cutting blade and a couple of simple, screw-together jigs made from cheap melamine closet shelving stock.

A. RIPPING JIG

Use an 8-ft. length of 16-in.-wide shelving to build the ripping jig. Draw a line 3 in. from the edge; cut along it with the circular saw. Screw this piece to the larger piece about 3 in. away from one edge with the factory edge facing the widest section of the shelving as shown. Then use that edge as a guide to cut off the melamine. Now it's just a matter of lining up that edge with marks on plywood stock and clamping it to make perfect cuts up to 8 ft. long on any piece of plywood.

B. CROSSCUTTING JIG

You can certainly use the ripping jig for crosscutting, too, but this crosscutting jig has the advantage of a stop on the bottom. Push the stop against the plywood, align it with the cutting mark and clamp for quick, accurate crosscuts. Make it from a 4-ft. length of 24-in.-wide melamine shelving (or plywood if wide shelving isn't available). Cut a 4-in.-wide strip for the stop from one end and another 4-in.-wide strip from one edge for the fence. Align the factory edge of the short piece with the factory edge at the other end of the shelving to make the stop. Then clamp and screw the two pieces together while checking the alignment with a carpenter's square.

Flip the jig over and measure from the long factory edge 6 in. to position and screw the long saw guide as shown. The key with both jigs is to use the straight factory edges when you are guiding the saw.

Garage floor coverings

Give your garage an entirely new look and feel with these eye-catching, easy-to-install, practical floor coverings.

Coverings come in two forms: interlocking tiles and rollout mats. The big advantage of coverings is how fast and easy they are to use. You can cover the floor of a three-car garage in a single morning. The only prep involved is a good thorough sweeping or vacuuming. Best of all, coverings hide cracks and craters and go right over damp concrete, so they can make a nasty floor look better than new.

A. INTERLOCKING FLEXIBLE TILES

These typically 12 x 12-in. or 18 x 18-in. flexible plastic tiles come in a bunch of cool patterns and colors that allow you to create custom designs in your garage. To install them, you cut the tiles with a utility knife and then tap or press the interlocking edges together with a rubber mallet or wallpaper roller. They're more slip-resistant than rollout flooring, and compared with rigid snap-together tiles, they offer better resistance to liquid seepage through the seams and are more comfortable underfoot. Like the rollout mats, flexible tiles are subject to staining, but unlike mats, damaged tiles can be quite easily replaced. The tiles do contract and expand in extreme temperature changes and with exposure to direct sunlight, so leave expansion room near walls and other obstacles.

B. RIGID SNAP-TOGETHER TILES

These are made of a stiffer plastic than flexible tiles. Because of that, they can handle heavier loads, which is important if you use floor jacks or kickstands. They also expand and contract less than the flexible tiles during extreme weather conditions. They come in many different colors and styles, including perforated versions that drain spills and snowmelt, making mold beneath the tiles and slippery spots on top less of an issue. They're easy to clean and are more chemical resistant than softer plastic tiles or mats. They do make a clacking noise when you walk on them. Like the other coverings, they're easy to install. All you do is line up the tiles, step on them, and then click the male and the female loops together.

A.

Interlocking flexible tiles are slip-resistant and soft underfoot.

B.

Snap-together tiles are easy to install and to clean.

Rollout mats are a breeze to install.

C. ROLLOUT MATS

Rollout flooring is a thick, rubbery mat that comes in a variety of lengths, widths, colors and patterns. You can use a single mat under a car or put several mats together to cover an entire garage. The mats are easy to clean and move. To install them, all you do is sweep the garage floor, unroll the flooring, butt the edges together or overlap them, and then trim the mats to fit with a utility knife. The mats are durable, but like most coverings, they can be permanently stained by hot tires and chemicals. These mats are also slippery in snowy or icy weather and are susceptible to being cut or gouged by motorcycle kickstands, hot metal shards and gravel. In extreme climates, the mats expand and contract (up to 2 percent). To ensure the mats are able to move during temperature fluctuations, don't tape them to the floor at the edges.

WHAT IT TAKES

TIME	COST	SKILL LEVEL
2 days	$250-$500	Intermediate

TOOLS
Table saw or circular saw, miter saw, drill/driver, basic hand tools

Bomb-proof woodworking bench

World-class workbench in a weekend.

If you're looking for a "real" woodworking bench but don't want to spend a year and a thousand bucks building one, here's a great design for you. It'll grow with you as your skills improve; it's flat and solid enough to help you do your best work; and it's sturdy enough that you can proudly pass it on to your grandchildren. One weekend and the simplest of tools are all you need to build it.

It does it all!

- **Hold long stock!**
  Clamp one end in the face vise; hold the other end with a pipe clamp under the bench top.
- **Pound away!**
  The 2-1/4-in.-thick solid maple top will never flinch.
- **Secure big stuff!**
  An easy-to-build bench jack supports large work.
- **Hold stock!**
  The centuries-old bench dog design secures work for machining.
- **Keep it flat!**
  A dead-flat top keeps your glue-ups flat and true.

1 **BUILD THE TORSION BOX LEGS. Assemble a 2x2 frame with screws. Be sure the joints are flush. Run a heavy bead of wood glue; screw or nail the plywood skin so edges are flush.**

3 top options

There are a few different ways you can build the top of your new workbench. Each are good options depending on how much you want to spend and what you want out of the bench. We used a ready-made, prefinished maple slab purchased online. The 2-1/4-in.-thick top is very flat and stable. You could also use a 1-3/4-in.-thick top.

You can also make a top from three sheets of 3/4-in. plywood. Cut them oversize, glue and screw two of them together, and then add the third. Use plenty of screws; they can be removed after the glue is dry. Noe that this top probably won't end up being perfectly flat.

Finally, it's possible to use a solid-core exterior door for this project. You can find them wherever recycled building materials are available or buy one at a home center. If you add 1/2-in. plywood as a wear surface, you'll have a 2-1/4-in.-thick top. It should be very flat and stable.

TIME-TESTED FEATURES

This bench includes the signature features of a traditional woodworking bench: a thick, flat top designed to take a pounding; a tail vise and a face vise, mounted one at each end, for securing stock; and an overhanging top that allows you to clamp stock to the edges.

We eliminated the traditional tool tray because it's a housekeeping hassle rather than an effective place to keep tools. Leaving it off gives you a larger work surface. And since most DIYers are short on workshop space, we went ahead and added a cabinet base for storage. The sliding doors are a cinch to make and mount, and they keep the contents free of sawdust.

The base is made from inexpensive 2x4s and plywood. The torsion box legs provide incredibly strong support and a place to mount trays and hooks to hold bench brushes, electrical cords and tools.

WHAT IT COSTS

You can spend as little as $250 if you mount only one vise and make the top yourself (see "3 top options" at left). If you go all out like we did, with two vises and a massive solid maple top, your cost will be closer to $800. The 2-1/4-in.-thick maple top we used comes prefinished. Check online for suppliers and prices, or order through a lumberyard. All you have to do is drill the dog holes, mount the vises and you're done. You can also find 1-3/4-in.-thick tops for $200, but if you go this route, you'll need to put spacer blocks under the vises so they fit properly.

You can buy unplaned maple for about half the cost of these tops, but you'll face many hours of surfacing, gluing and finishing—and getting the top dead-flat is tough, even for an expert.

TO BUILD A BENCH

Building this bench couldn't be any easier. The base is made with 2x4s, fir

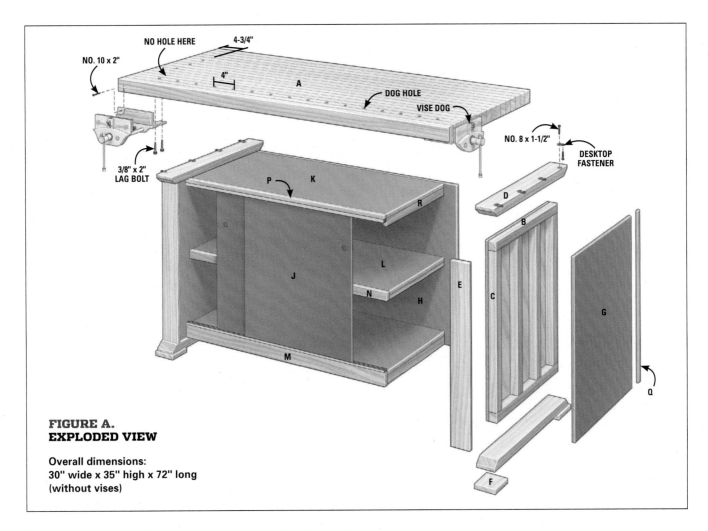

FIGURE A.
EXPLODED VIEW

Overall dimensions:
30" wide x 35" high x 72" long
(without vises)

Labels within figure: NO HOLE HERE · 4-3/4" · NO. 10 x 2" · 4" · A · DOG HOLE · VISE DOG · NO. 8 x 1-1/2" · DESKTOP FASTENER · 3/8" x 2" LAG BOLT · P · K · R · D · B · L · N · H · E · C · J · G · M · F · Q

plywood and a little maple trim. Start with torsion box legs. Torsion boxes are strong yet they don't add a ton of weight, and they're super easy to make **(Photo 1)**.

Cut the plywood shelves, the back, and the shelf cleats (K, L, H, R). Screw the base together to check the fit. Disassemble the bench and paint the pieces. It's a lot easier to paint all the plywood pieces before final assembly. After the paint's dry, attach the shelves to the legs. Cut the 2x4 supports (D). Add the feet to the bottom supports and attach them to the legs with screws. Turn the base upright and attach the back **(Photo 2)**. Add the top supports and the maple trim (M, N, P, Q). The trim piece Q is glued and nailed to the exposed edge of the back. Then secure the door tracks in the cabinet opening to complete the base **(Photo 3)**. Cut the doors to fit.

Materials List

ITEM	QTY.
2-1/4" x 30" x 72" maple top	1
Bd. ft. of maple	5
Sheet of 3/4" plywood	1
Sheets of 1/2" plywood	1-1/2
Sheet of 1/4" plywood	1/2
8' 2x4s	3
9" bench vises	2
Packs of desktop fasteners	2

Now turn your attention to the top. No matter what top you use (see "3 top options," p. 148), the following steps are the same.

Set the top on a pair of sawhorses and lay out the bench dog holes. Use a guide to drill the holes so they're square to the top **(Photo 4)**. We spaced the holes on 4-in. centers, 4-3/4 in. from the edges. Skip one hole in the front left corner, where it would interfere with the vise.

Flip the top over and mount the vises **(Photo 5)**. Line up the metal dog on the vise with the dog holes in the top.

Cutting List

KEY	PART	QTY.
A	2-1/4" x 30" x 72" (Maple top)	1
B	1-1/2" x 1-1/2" x 23-1/2" (2x2 torsion box rails)	4
C	1-1/2" x 1-1/2" x 26" (2x2 torsion box stiles)	8
D	1-1/2" x 3-1/2" x 28" (2x4 top/bottom support)	4
E	3/4" x 3" x 29" (Maple/pine front trim)	2
F	3/4" x 4" x 4" (Maple/pine feet)	4
G	1/2" x 23-1/2" x 29" (Plywood torsion box sides)	4
H	1/2" x 29" x 48" (Plywood back)	1
J	1/4" x 22" x 25-1/2" (Plywood doors)	2
K	3/4" x 20-1/4" x 43" (Plywood top/bottom shelf)	2
L	3/4" x 19-1/4" x 43" (Plywood middle shelf)	1
M	3/4" x 2-1/4" x 43" (Maple/pine bottom shelf trim)	1
N	3/4" x 1" x 43" (Maple/pine middle shelf trim)	1
P	3/4" x 3/4" x 43" (Maple/pine top shelf trim)	1
Q	1/4" x 3/4" x 29" (Maple/pine side trim)	2
R	3/4" x 1-1/2" x 19" (1x2 shelf cleats)	6

To protect wood that will be held in the vise, make wooden faces and attach them to the vise jaws. Use a soft wood, such as basswood or pine.

Mount figure-eight or other tabletop fasteners to the top supports. They may need to rest in a shallow hole in the support. These will allow the top to expand and contract without cracking. Get someone to help you set the top onto the base, then secure with screws through the fasteners. That's it. Your bench is ready for your first project!

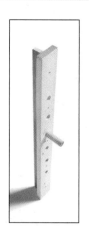

DIY accessories

Bench jack

The purpose of a bench jack is to support long, wide stock. To make a jack, screw together a couple of pieces of 3-in. x 36-in. pine or plywood to form a "T." Drill 3/4-in. holes in the face of the jack. Clamp the bench jack in the tail vise, and then insert a dowel at the desired height.

Bench dogs

Bench dogs work with the vise to hold stock on the bench surface They're easy to make. Drill a 1-in.-deep hole in 1-1/2-in. x 1-1/2-in. blocks of hardwood, then epoxy 3/4-in. dowel stock into the holes. To accommodate different stock thicknesses, cut the block to 1/4-in., 1/2-in., 3/4-in., 1-in. and 1-1/2-in. heights.

2 ATTACH THE BACK. Screw the back to the shelves and legs. It's best to paint the plywood surfaces before final assembly.

3 MOUNT THE DOOR TRACKS. Apply a bead of construction adhesive and clamp the door tracks in place. Cut the bottom track about 1/2 in. shorter than the opening. Center the track to leave gaps at each end so the door motion sweeps out accumulated sawdust.

DRILL GUIDE

4 DRILL THE BENCH DOG HOLES. Fit a drill with a 3/4-in. drill bit and drill the dog holes. A drill guide made from a couple of plywood scraps attached at 90 degrees ensures you make perpendicular holes.

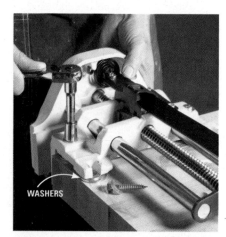

WASHERS

5 BOLT THE VISE TO THE TOP. Mount each vise so the metal jaws are slightly below the surface of the wood top. This may require some shimming. We used some metal fender washers to fine-tune the vise position.

Yard tool slant rack

This may take the record for the world's simplest storage project!

Stashing stuff in the unused spaces between studs is a smart move; adding slant boxes to expand the space is smarter yet. These boxes give your tools more headroom and give you easier access to long- and short-handled tools.

For the tall unit, use the bottom wall plate for the bottom of your box. Attach the plywood to create a 1-in. gap at the bottom for removing dirt or dropped items. For the shorter slant boxes, install your own blocking to create the bottom; leave a gap at the bottom of the plywood for those, too. We show 48-in. and 16-in. versions; you can make yours any depth or length you want.

Note: If your garage has a short ceiling (or your tools have extra-long handles), create a cutout in the top of the plywood face, as shown in **Figure A**, to allow more entrance and exit leeway for your tools.

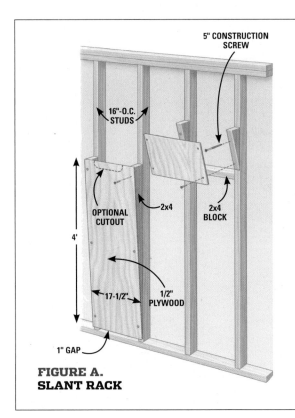

FIGURE A.
SLANT RACK

Labels in figure: 5" CONSTRUCTION SCREW; 16"-O.C. STUDS; OPTIONAL CUTOUT; 2x4; 2x4 BLOCK; 4'; 17-1/2"; 1/2" PLYWOOD; 1" GAP

Rip a 2x4 diagonally to create the sides. Screw each wedge to the face of a stud. Install a plywood face, and you're ready to store stuff.

WHAT IT TAKES		
TIME	**COST**	**SKILL LEVEL**
1 hour	Less than $50	Beginner

TOOLS
Circular saw, drill

Compact compressor station

Save floor space and get organized with this sturdy compressor stand.

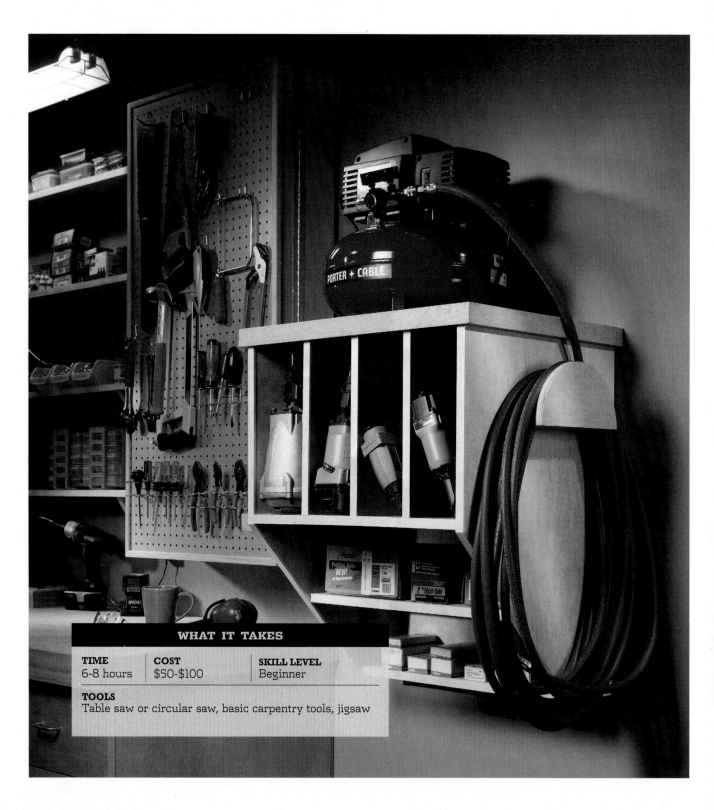

WHAT IT TAKES

TIME	COST	SKILL LEVEL
6-8 hours	$50-$100	Beginner

TOOLS
Table saw or circular saw, basic carpentry tools, jigsaw

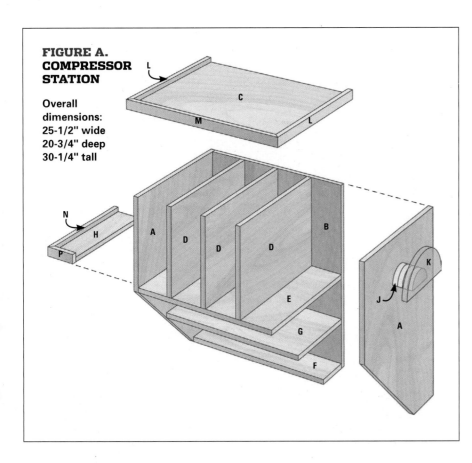

FIGURE A. COMPRESSOR STATION

Overall
dimensions:
25-1/2" wide
20-3/4" deep
30-1/4" tall

FIGURE B.
PLYWOOD CUTTING DIAGRAM

6"

14-3/4"

Materials List

ITEM	QTY.
4' x 8' x 3/4" plywood	1
1x2 x 8'	1
1/4" x 3/4" strips of wood (optional)	16
1-5/8" screws	1 lb.
2" finish nails	1/2 lb.
Wood glue	

Cutting List

KEY	PART	QTY.
A	3/4" x 20" x 28-3/4" (Plywood)	2
B	3/4" x 22-1/2" x 28-3/4" (Plywood)	1
C	3/4" x 20" x 24" (Plywood)	1
D	3/4" x 14" x 19-1/4" (Plywood)	3
E	3/4" x 19-1/4" x 22-1/2" (Plywood)	1
F	3/4" x 5-1/4" x 22-1/2" (Plywood)	1
G	3/4" x 12-1/4" x 22-1/2" (Plywood)	1
H	3/4" x 4" x 16" (Plywood)	1
J	3/4" x 6-1/2" diameter (Half circles of plywood)	4
K	3/4" x 10-1/4" diameter (Half circle of plywood)	1
L	3/4" x 1-1/2" x 21" (Miter to fit)	2
M	3/4" x 1-1/2" x 26" (Miter to fit)	1
N	3/4" x 1-1/2" x 17" (Miter to fit)	1
P	3/4" x 1-1/2" x 5" (Miter to fit)	1

You can get your nail guns, fasteners, hose and more off your workbench and out of your way by building this nifty, wall-mounted compressor station. This easy project requires just one sheet of 3/4-in. plywood, about 8 ft. of 1x2 lumber and only standard carpentry tools, plus a circular saw and a jigsaw. We used a table saw for most of the plywood cuts and a miter saw for the trim, but a circular saw and straightedge will give good results, too. We spent more for birch plywood and birch 1x2 for this station, but you can cut the cost in half by using less expensive wood.

Start by cutting out the plywood pieces according to **Figure B**. Use a table saw or a circular saw fitted with a sharp carbide-tooth blade to minimize splintering. If you're using a circular saw, clamp a straightedge or a saw guide to the plywood for straight, accurate cuts. **Photo 1** shows how to make the diagonal cuts for the sides.

Build the hose holder by marking four half circles with a gallon paint can and one half circle with a 5-gallon bucket on a plywood strip. Cut out the parts with a jigsaw (**Photo 2**). Glue and clamp the four small half circles together. After the glue dries, use a belt sander to smooth the edges, then glue the half round block to the larger half circle.

Once the parts are cut, assembly is straightforward. Mark the centerline of the shelves (E, F and G) on the sides and the centerline of the dividers (D) on the top (C) and upper shelf (E). Drill holes and countersinks for screws on the centerline of all shelves and dividers. Space screws about 1-1/2 in. from plywood ends and about 8 in. apart.

Start by driving 1-5/8-in. screws through the sides into the back and attaching the shelf and hose holder with screws. Then screw the top to the sides and back and add the dividers (**Photo 3**). We made the first space 6 in. wide and the three remaining spaces 4-3/4 in. wide to fit our nail guns. Adjust these dimensions to fit your own tools. Screw the wide shelf (E) to the dividers and then screw through the sides into the three shelves (E, F and G).

Finish station by adding a 1x2 edge to the top and to the accessory shelf (**Photo 4**). Align the 1x2s with the plywood so they protrude 3/4 in. above the top and shelf to create a lip. Glue and nail the 1x2s to the plywood. For a more finished appearance, we covered the raw plywood edges with 1/4-in. strips of wood, but screen molding would work fine.

We brushed two coats of clear polyurethane on the station before hanging it on the wall. When you mount the station, be sure to locate wall studs and attach the station firmly to them with four 1/4-in. x 3-1/2-in. lag screws and washers.

To reduce irksome issues like noise and compressor movement, just cut a rubber mat or piece of carpet to fit under the compressor.

1 Cut the angled sides using a straightedge to guide your saw. Cut the rectangular pieces with a table saw or a circular saw and straightedge.

2 Saw out the hose holder parts with a jigsaw. Trace around one half of a paint can and one half of a 5-gallon bucket to mark the pieces. Glue and screw the half circles together to make the hose holder.

TEMPORARY SPACER

3 Position the dividers with temporary spacers. This eliminates the need for measuring and marking and makes alignment easier. Use the same spacers when you install the shelf below the dividers.

ACCESSORY SHELF

4 Wrap the top of the station with a sturdy lip to prevent the compressor from "walking" off. Use both glue and nails for a strong connection.

Saw blade roost

Here's a double-duty holder for storing and cleaning table saw and circular saw blades.

This roost features a slotted dowel to keep stored blades spaced apart so the teeth stay sharp.

Using a handsaw, cut notches spaced at 3/8-in. intervals halfway through a 5/8-in. dowel. Glue the dowel in a hole drilled in a 16 x 12-in. piece of 3/4-in. plywood. Frame the sides and lower edge of the plywood with 2-in. strips of plywood and add a lower facing piece to create a basin at the bottom. When a blade needs cleaning, remove the other blades and line the rack with aluminum foil. Then mount the gunked-up blade on the dowel, spray one side with oven cleaner and flip it over to spray the other side. Any drips go in the basin, and the sides minimize overspray. Let the cleaner work for an hour or so, then use a moistened kitchen scrub pad to scour the dissolved gunk and burned sawdust off the blade. Lastly, throw away the foil and store your blades.

WHAT IT TAKES		
TIME	**COST**	**SKILL LEVEL**
1 hour	Under $20	Beginner
TOOLS		
Circular saw, drill		

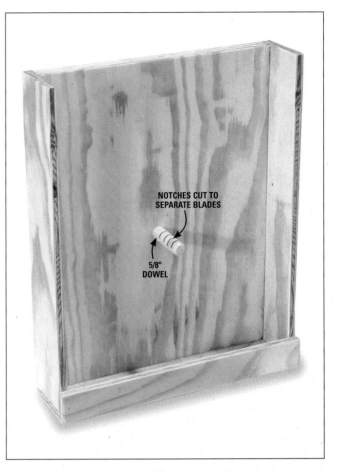

NOTCHES CUT TO SEPARATE BLADES

5/8" DOWEL

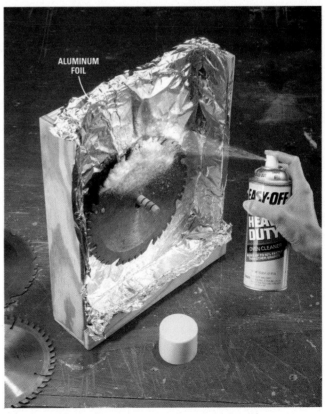

ALUMINUM FOIL

EASY-OFF HEAVY DUTY OVEN CLEANER

This roost makes it easier than ever to keep your blades from getting gunky, and cleanup is a breeze.

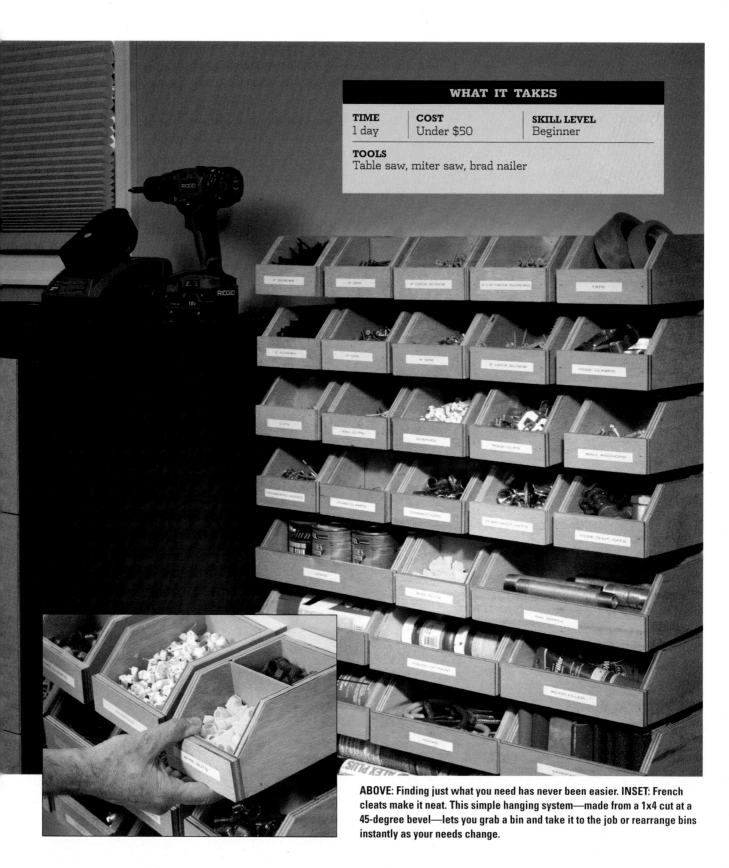

WHAT IT TAKES

TIME	COST	SKILL LEVEL
1 day	Under $50	Beginner

TOOLS
Table saw, miter saw, brad nailer

ABOVE: Finding just what you need has never been easier. **INSET:** French cleats make it neat. This simple hanging system—made from a 1x4 cut at a 45-degree bevel—lets you grab a bin and take it to the job or rearrange bins instantly as your needs change.

Hardware organizer

Portable and possibly free, it's a fantastic way to manage inventory!

DIY isn't just about building and fixing things. It is also about maintaining a supply of the stuff you need and knowing right where to find it. This simple bin system is the perfect project to get you organized. It is modeled on the systems used in cabinet shops, plumbers' vans and mechanics' garages.

The materials cost for the bins shown here will depend on the type of plywood you choose. A store-bought light-duty system would cost just a few bucks more, but these homemade bins offer two big advantages: They're far tougher than plastic bins and you can customize them to suit your stuff. Plus, they make the perfect scrap-wood project because all the parts are small. We built these bins from leftovers and didn't spend a dime.

MASS-PRODUCE PARTS

Begin by measuring the items you want to store. We found that the basic bin **(see Figure A)** was just right for most stuff: nuts, bolts, construction screws, and plumbing and electrical parts. For larger items, we made a few bins wider but didn't change the bin sides (A). That approach is the most efficient because the sides are the most complex parts and changing them requires fuss.

Once you've determined the sizes you want, fire up your table saw and rip plywood into strips. If you are following our plan, you'll need strips 1-3/4, 3-1/2 and 6 in. wide. Then cut the strips to length, making parts for one box only. Test-assemble the box to check the fit of the parts.

Note: "Half-inch" plywood is just slightly less than a 1/2 in. thick, so the bin bottom (B) needs to be slightly longer than 6 in. Start at 6-1/8 in., then trim as needed. When you've confirmed all the parts are the right size, mass-produce them by chopping the strips to length **(Photo 1)**.

If you want dividers (E) in any of the bins, your next step is to cut the divider slots. Set your table saw blade to a height of 3/16 in. Screw a long fence

1 CUT THE PARTS. Rip strips of plywood to width on a table saw, then cut them to length with a miter saw. Clamp a scrap of plywood to the saw's fence to act as a stop block. That lets you cut identical lengths from several strips with one chop.

CAUTIONARY INSTRUCTIONS
You have to remove the guard for this step. Be extra careful!

2 CUT DIVIDER SLOTS. Mount a fence on your saw's miter gauge and position a stop block on the fence. Run the bin side across the blade. Then rotate the side 180 degrees and make a second pass to widen the slot.

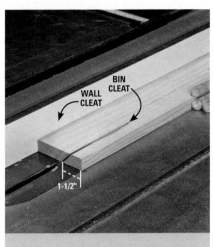

CAUTIONARY INSTRUCTIONS
Our guard was removed for photo clarity. Use yours!

3 CUT THE CLEATS. Tilt the blade to 45 degrees and set the fence so that the bin cleat is 1-1/2 in. wide. Getting the fence positioned may take some trial and error, so cut a test scrap first.

4 ASSEMBLE THE BINS. Join the parts with glue and brads. The glue will provide plenty of strength, so drive only as many brads as needed to hold the parts together while the glue sets.

Materials List

ITEM	QTY.
4' x 8' x 1/2" plywood	1
2' x 4' x 1/8" hardboard	1
1x4 x 8' pine	3
1" brads, 2-1/2" screws, wood glue and Danish oil	

Cutting List

KEY	PART	QTY.
A	3-1/2" x 6-1/2" (sides)	2
B	4" x 6" (bottom)	1
C	3-1/2" x 4" (back)	1
D	1-3/4" x 5" (front)	1
E	3" x 4-5/16" (divider)	1
F	3/4" x 1-1/2" x 5" (cleat)	1

Dividers are hardboard. Cleats are pine.
All other parts are plywood.

to your miter gauge and run the fence across the blade to cut a notch on the fence. Position a stop block 3-1/4 in. from the center of the notch. Place a side (A) against the block, run it across the blade, rotate it and cut it again **(Photo 2)**. Check the fit of a divider in the slot and reposition the block slightly to adjust the width of the slot. It may take two or three tries before you get the width right.

When you're done cutting slots, it's time to clip off one corner of each side. Set your miter saw 45 degrees to the right. Clamp on a stop block and "gang-cut" sides just as you did when cutting parts to length (similar to **Photo 1**). Remember this: Slotted sides require left/right pairs. For every side that you cut with the slot facing up, cut another with the slot down.

Next, cut the cleats **(Photo 3)**. The 45-degree bevel cuts will leave sharp, splintery edges, so crank the table saw blade back to zero degrees and shave 1/8 in. off each cleat before cutting them to length.

ASSEMBLE THEM AND HANG THEM UP

Assembly is fast and easy with glue and an 18-gauge brad nailer. First, tack the back (C) to the bottom (B), then add the sides (A), the front (D) and finally the cleat (F). After assembly, we wiped on two coats of penetrating oil finish to keep the wood from absorbing greasy fingerprints and oils from hardware.

When mounting the wall cleats, start at the bottom. Make sure the bottom cleat is level and straight. Then cut spacers at least 1-3/4 in. tall and use them to position the remaining wall cleats **(Photo 5)**.

Larger cleats will create more space between rows of bins, making it easier to reach in and grab stuff. Bins filled with hardware put a heavy load on the cleats, so be sure to go ahead and drive a screw into every wall stud. And just like that, you've built yourself a perfect organizer for all your DIY hardware.

5 **MOUNT THE WALL CLEATS. Mark the stud locations with tape and screw on the lowest cleat. Then work your way up the wall, using spacers to position each cleat.**

SPACER

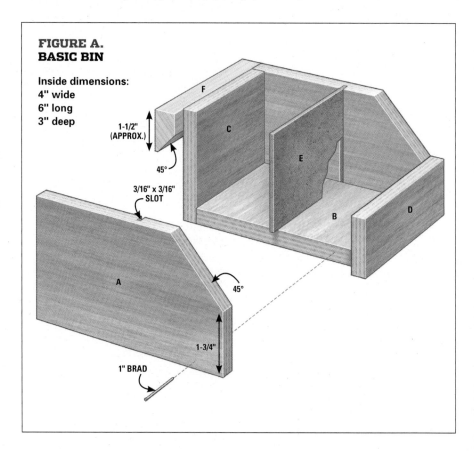

FIGURE A.
BASIC BIN

Inside dimensions:
4" wide
6" long
3" deep

1-1/2" (APPROX.)

45°

3/16" x 3/16" SLOT

45°

1-3/4"

1" BRAD

F
C
E
B
D
A

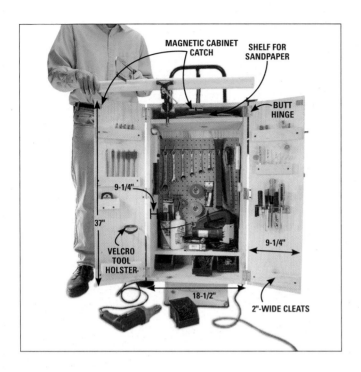

MAGNETIC CABINET CATCH

SHELF FOR SANDPAPER

BUTT HINGE

9-1/4"

37"

VELCRO TOOL HOLSTER

9-1/4"

18-1/2"

2"-WIDE CLEATS

BARREL BOLT LATCH

BASE

Mobile tool chest

Take all your tools in one trip.

To make the chest, first screw the cabinet together with 1-5/8-in. drywall screws after drilling pilot holes. Clamp on the plywood back, check for square, then screw it to the sides, top and floor with 1-5/8-in. drywall screws. Attach the doors with 2-1/2-in. butt hinges. Pine boards tend to warp, so to keep the doors flat, screw several 2-in.-wide cleats across the inside.

To raise the cabinet, screw four scrap boards into a frame and attach this base to the dolly's base with lag screws. Next drill holes in the base, then rest the cabinet on the base and attach it with 1-5/8-in. drywall screws through the floor into the base. To attach the upper part of the cabinet to the dolly, drive two 5/16-in.-diameter bolts through a board positioned behind the dolly's frame and into two 5/16-in. tee nuts set in the cabinet back. If this won't work for your dolly or design, use metal strapping or drill bolt holes through the dolly.

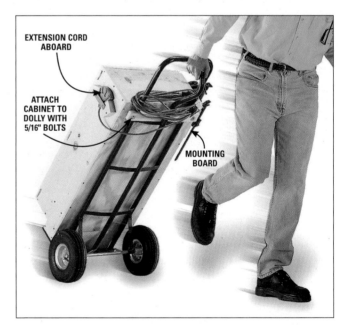

EXTENSION CORD ABOARD

ATTACH CABINET TO DOLLY WITH 5/16" BOLTS

MOUNTING BOARD

Materials List

ITEM	QTY.
37" long 1x10 pine boards (actually 3/4" x 9-1/4") for the doors and sides	4
18-1/2" long 1x10 pine boards for the cabinet top and floor	2
18-1/2" x 36" piece of 1/2" thick plywood for the back	1
Scrap boards for a base	
Assorted fasteners	

WHAT IT TAKES		
TIME 4 hours	**COST** Under $50	**SKILL LEVEL** Beginner
TOOLS Circular saw or table saw, drill/driver		

This design has stood the test of time, and for good reason: It's practical, efficient and will last for years.

A classic workbench

Here's a timeless design that's simple and strong.

If this workbench looks familiar, it's probably because you have seen one a lot like it in your parents' or grandfather's shop. Variations of this design have been around for decades. The bench is strong, practical and super easy to build. You can run to the lumberyard in the morning to grab a few boards and by noon you'll have a perfectly functional, eye-catching workbench.

WHAT IT TAKES		
TIME 4-5 hours	**COST** $100-$250	**SKILL LEVEL** Beginner
TOOLS Small square, tape measure, circular saw, drill/driver		

PRO TIP

Perfect fit

If your car is too small for the long boards, you can ask to have the boards cut to length. Remember to take the Cutting List with you to the store.

This workbench isn't fancy—it's built from standard construction lumber—but you can easily customize it with drawers or other features now or later.

If you can cut a board, you can build this bench. And you don't need any fancy tools either. In addition to a small square and a tape measure, you will need a circular saw to cut the parts and a drill to drive the screws.

GETTING STARTED

Find the materials at a lumberyard or home center (see Materials List, p. 163). Choose lumber that is straight, is flat and doesn't have too many gouges, slivers or cracks. We used Torx-head screws with self-drilling tips, but you can substitute any construction screw. If you're not using screws with self-drilling tips, drill pilot holes to avoid splitting the wood.

Cut the parts according to the Cutting List, p. 163. We used a miter saw, but a circular saw will work fine. Mark the 2x4s with a Speed square or combination square. Then carefully cut the boards to length. If you plan to stain or paint the bench, now is the time to sand the parts. And to really simplify your job, you could also stain or paint the parts before you assemble the bench.

START BY BUILDING THE TOP AND SHELF FRAMES

We used an old door propped up on sawhorses as a work surface, but the floor will work, too. Lay the 2x4s for the front and back of the top and for the shelf on the work surface. Mark the

1 BUILD THE FRAMES. Use 3-in. screws to assemble the frames that support the top and the shelf. To avoid splitting the 2x4s, either drill pilot holes or use self-drilling screws. Build both frames and set the top frame aside.

2 ATTACH THE SHELF BOARDS. Attach the outside boards first. Then position the two remaining boards to create equal spaces between them, and screw them to the frame. Before driving screws, drill pilot holes with a countersink bit.

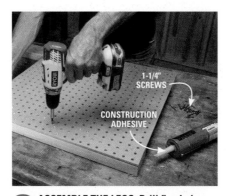

3 ASSEMBLE THE LEGS. Drill five holes with the countersink bit about 2 in. from the edge of the pegboard. Spread a bead of construction adhesive on the legs and attach the pegboard with 1-1/4-in. screws. If glue oozes through the holes, wait for it to dry. Then shave it off with a sharp chisel.

4 SCREW THE LEGS TO THE TOP FRAME. Apply construction adhesive where the legs contact the top frame. Then proceed to attach the legs with screws.

5 ADD THE SHELF. Rest the bench on one end. Slide the shelf between the legs and line it up with the bottom of the pegboard. Screw through the shelf into the legs.

SHELF

BOTTOM OF PEGBOARD

6 MOUNT THE TOP BOARDS. Align the first 2x6 flush to the back and measure for the 2-in. overhang on the side. Attach the 2x6s with trim screws. The front 2x6 will overhang the frame about 2 in.

TRIM SCREW

2" OVERHANG

7 INSTALL THE BACKBOARD. Attach the 1x4 shelf to the 1x10 backboard. Then add a 2x4 block at each end. Rest the assembly on the workbench and drive screws through the back to hold it in place.

centers. Remember, if you're not using self-drilling screws, drill pilot holes for the screws. **Photo 1** shows how to assemble the frames. Set the top frame aside and screw the shelf boards to the shelf frame **(Photo 2)**.

BUILD AND ATTACH THE LEG ASSEMBLIES

Photo 3 shows how to build the leg assemblies. You'll notice the leg assemblies are 1/8 in. narrower than the inside dimension of the top. That's so you can install the legs without binding, which would cause the pegboard to bow. Also, if the only pegboard you can find is thinner than the 1/4-in. pegboard specified, add the difference to the front and back of the shelf frame (C). For example, if you buy 1/8-in. pegboard, add 1/4 in. to parts C.

The pegboard is useful for hanging tools, but its real function is to stabilize the workbench as a brace. We added the construction adhesive to make sure the assemblies stayed strong and rigid. Be aware, though, that some of the adhesive will end up being visible through the holes.

The pegboard holes are a little too big to use as screw holes, so use a No. 6 countersink bit to drill pilot holes for the screws. Secure five evenly spaced 1-1/4-in. screws into each leg.

The next step is to attach the legs to the top frame. Apply construction adhesive to the top 3 in. of the legs. Then attach the leg assemblies with 3-in. screws **(Photo 4)**.

ADD THE SHELF AND THE TOP

Stand the workbench on one end so it's simple to slide the shelf into place and line it up with the pegboard **(Photo 5)**. Drive 3-in. screws through the shelf frame into the legs to support the shelf.

The top of this bench is 2x6s, placed tight together. The boards overhang the frame 2 in. on the sides and front. The overhang makes it easier to use clamps on the edges of the workbench. **Photo 6** shows how to get started. We attached the 2x6s with trim screws, but you could substitute 16d casing nails.

ATTACH THE BACK BRACE AND THE BACKBOARD

The 1x10 back brace keeps things from falling off the back of the shelf, but it also stiffens the bench to prevent side-to-side rocking. Apply construction adhesive before attaching the brace. The backboard is a 1x10 with a 1x4 shelf attached. On the side of the 1x10 you want facing out, draw a line the length of the board

Torx-head screws

A star-shaped Torx bit fits tightly into the star-shaped recess in the head of the screw, providing a firm grip that rarely slips out or strips the screw head. It's easier to drive these screws because you don't have to press down as hard to maintain good bit contact. Plus, most Torx-head screws are premium-quality fasteners available with other features, such as self-drilling points, self-setting heads and corrosion-resistant coatings.

Torx-head screws require star-shaped bits that are labeled with a "T" followed by a number. Some screw packages include a driver bit, but if yours doesn't, check the package to see what size is required.

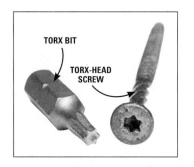

TORX BIT

TORX-HEAD SCREW

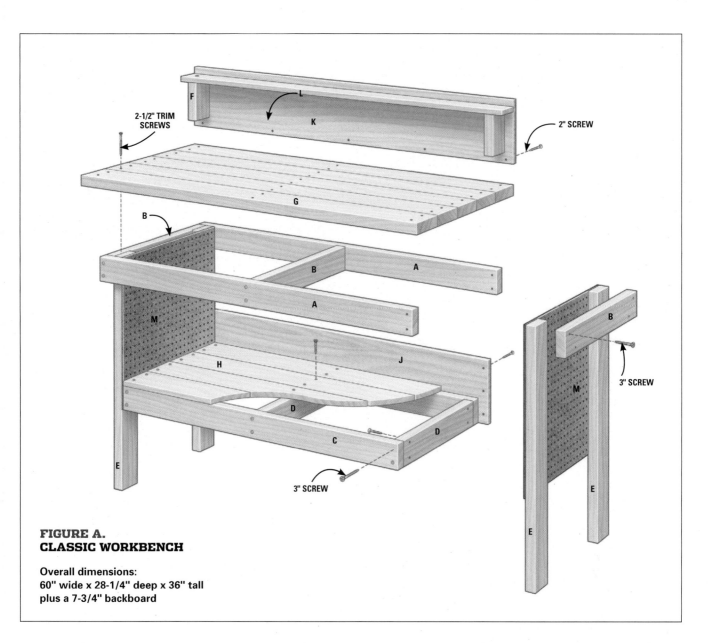

2-1/2" TRIM SCREWS

2" SCREW

3" SCREW

3" SCREW

**FIGURE A.
CLASSIC WORKBENCH**

**Overall dimensions:
60" wide x 28-1/4" deep x 36" tall
plus a 7-3/4" backboard**

1-3/4 in. down from the top. Here, you'll align the bottom of the 1x4.

Draw a second line 1-3/8 in. from the top. Drill pilot holes with the countersink bit every 8 in. along this line. Now ask a helper to hold the 1x4 on the line while you drive 2-in. screws into the shelf through the pilot holes. After the shelf and 2x4 block at each end are attached, screw the backboard to the workbench **(Photo 7)**.

You can modify your bench in quite a few ways. We mounted a woodworking vise on the front of the workbench and drilled holes in the 1x4 shelf to hold some screwdrivers.

Cutting List

KEY	PART	QTY.
A	1-1/2" x 3-1/2" x 56" (top frame front and back)	2
B	1-1/2" x 3-1/2" x 22-1/2" (top frame crosspieces)	3
C	1-1/2" x 3-1/2" x 49-1/2" (shelf frame front and back)	2
D	1-1/2" x 3-1/2" x 19-1/2" (shelf crosspieces)	3
E	1-1/2" x 3-1/2" x 34-1/2" (legs)	4
F	1-1/2" x 3-1/2" x 6" (back shelf supports)	2
G	1-1/2" x 5-1/2" x 60" (top boards)	5
H	3/4" x 5-1/2" x 49-1/2" (shelf boards)	4
J	3/4" x 9-1/4" x 53" (back brace)	1
K	3/4" x 9-1/4" x 60" (backboard)	1
L	3/4" x 3-1/2" x 60" (backboard shelf)	1
M	22-3/8" x 22-3/8" x 1/4" (pegboard leg braces)	2

Materials List

ITEM	QTY.
2x4 x 8' pine	6
2x6 x 10' pine	2
2x6 x 8' pine	1
1x10 x 10' pine	1
1x6 x 10' pine	2
1x4 x 6' pine	1
2' x 4' x 1/4" pegboard	1
3" self-drilling screws	42
2" self-drilling screws	50
1-1/4" self-drilling screws	20
2-1/2" trim screws	30
Tube of construction adhesive	1

WHAT IT TAKES

TIME	COST	SKILL LEVEL
2-4 hours	Under $50	Beginner

TOOLS
Circular saw, miter saw, drill/driver

Build a rolling shop cart

Whether your garage shop is big or small, it's sure handy to have a cart for moving stacks of parts from one machine to another.

Constructing this cart is simple—all the parts are just glued and screwed or nailed together. You'll need one full sheet of 3/4-in. plywood and a box of 1-1/4-in. screws.

You can use a cart to support table saw work if you build the cart the same height as your saw, so buy the casters for your cart before cutting any parts to size. (We recommend using casters that are at least 2-1/2 in. in diameter.) Then measure the total height of one caster and alter the lengths of the cart's legs as needed.

We've laid out the parts so you can crosscut your plywood into three 32-in. pieces before having to cut anything to exact size. It's OK if these crosscuts are rough; a jigsaw or circular saw would work fine. After this, it's best to use a table saw for ripping the parts and a miter saw or table saw for cutting them to length.

After breaking down the plywood into manageable sizes, cut all the leg pieces (A and B). Glue them together, using nails or screws to hold them together while the glue dries. Make sure their ends are even.

Cut the parts for the upper and lower boxes (C, D, E and F), and glue and screw them together. Next, cut the shelf and bottom (G) to fit the boxes, and glue and screw these pieces into place. (Adding a bottom to the upper box makes it easier to clamp things to the top of the cart. Without a bottom, you'd only have a narrow 3/4-in. edge to clamp to.) Make sure the shelf and bottom don't overhang each box or the legs won't fit correctly. To avoid any overhang, you could cut the shelf and bottom 1/16 in. smaller all around.

Fasten the legs to the boxes, using three screws at each corner. Finally, cut the caster supports (H) and the top (J) to size, and add them to the cart. Fasten the casters using 3/4-in. No. 14 sheet metal screws.

FIGURE A. ROLLING SHOP CART

Overall dimensions: 20" wide x 32" long x 34-1/4" tall
All materials are 3/4" thick.

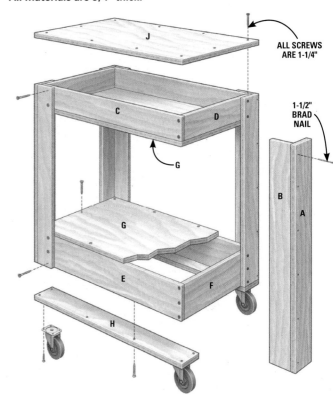

ALL SCREWS ARE 1-1/4"

1-1/2" BRAD NAIL

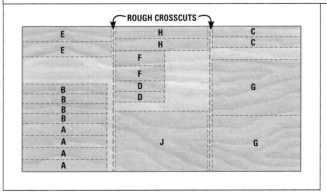

ROUGH CROSSCUTS

Cutting List

KEY	PART	QTY.
A	3/4" x 4" x 29" (Wide leg pieces)	4
B	3/4" x 3-1/4" x 29" (Narrow leg pieces)	4
C	3/4" x 3-1/2" x 30-1/2" (Upper box, long sides)	2
D	3/4" x 3-1/2" x 17" (Upper box, short sides)	2
E	3/4" x 5" x 30-1/2" (Lower box, long sides)	2
F	3/4" x 5" x 17" (Lower box, short sides)	2
G	3/4" x 18-1/2" x 30-1/2" (Shelf and bottom)	2
H	3/4" x 4" x 32" (Caster supports)	2
J	3/4" x 20" x 32" (Top)	1

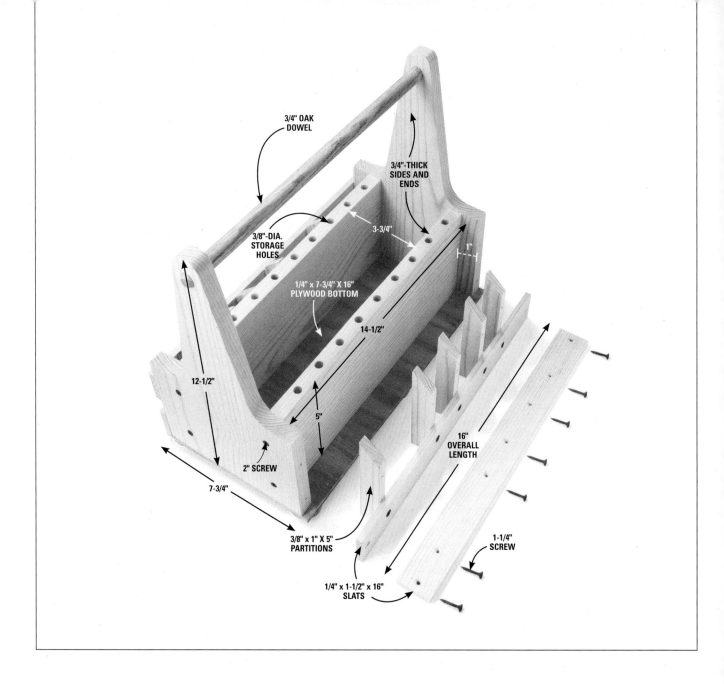

3/4" OAK DOWEL

3/4"-THICK SIDES AND ENDS

3/8"-DIA. STORAGE HOLES

3-3/4"

1"

1/4" x 7-3/4" X 16" PLYWOOD BOTTOM

14-1/2"

12-1/2"

5"

2" SCREW

7-3/4"

16" OVERALL LENGTH

3/8" x 1" X 5" PARTITIONS

1-1/4" SCREW

1/4" x 1-1/2" x 16" SLATS

Tool tote

Use it for gardening gear, craft materials or cleaning supplies, too.

To build this wonderfully useful tool tote, you can use our dimensions or customize it to suit the person on your gift list. We cut our slats and partitions from 2x4 scraps with a table saw. Then we glued the partitions in place before adding the slats.

■ Drill the 3/8-in. storage holes in the top edges of the sides before assembly.

■ Drill holes in the tops of the ends for a 3/4-in. dowel handle, and tap it in the holes before assembling the ends and sides. Screw together the sides and ends with the ends protruding 1 in. beyond the sides.

■ Cut and screw on the 1/4-in. plywood bottom.

■ Cut partitions and screw them to the slats to create custom-width pockets for tools.

■ Saw 1/4-in. x 1-1/2-in. x 16-in. pine strips for the side slats and screw them to the protruding ends.

WHAT IT TAKES		
TIME 2-4 hours	**COST** Under $50	**SKILL LEVEL** Beginner
TOOLS Table saw, miter saw, drill/driver		

The foldable shelf adds stability, and it's a great place to store tools and fasteners off the ground while doing a project.

Folding sawhorse with built-in shelf

These horses are plenty of fun to build.

Some horses have a shelf and some fold up—this design combines both features. To make a pair, you'll need a 4 x 4-ft. sheet of 3/4-in. plywood, one 8-ft. 2x6, one 8-ft. 2x4, two 12-ft. 2x4s and eight hinges.

Legs: After cutting the top 2x6 to length, cut both sides of each leg at a 15-degree angle. Make sure the angles are parallel. Fasten hinges to the ends of two of the legs, then attach those legs by fastening the hinges to the top piece. Attach the other two legs with 3-in. screws.

Shelf: Cut the 2x4 that supports one side of the shelf. Mark a line 8 in. up from the bottom of the leg, line up the bottom of the 2x4 with that line and attach it with two 3-in. screws on each side. Cut the shelf to size and notch the two corners using a jigsaw. Fasten the hinges to the shelf, then use two 11-1/8-in. blocks of wood to temporarily hold the shelf in place while you fasten the hinged side of the shelf to the legs. Cut a 23-3/4-in. x 1-1/2-in. strip of plywood to overlap the 2x4 shelf brace. Attach it with wood glue and 1-1/4-in. screws. You may have to trim it a bit before fastening.

Cut two blocks of wood to temporarily hold the shelf in place while you fasten the hinged side of the shelf to the legs.

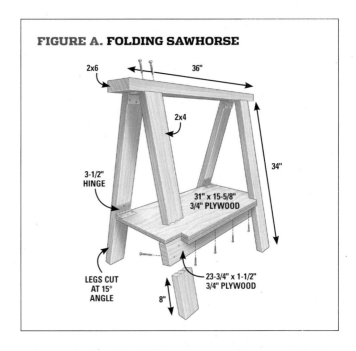

FIGURE A. FOLDING SAWHORSE

- 2x6
- 36"
- 2x4
- 34"
- 3-1/2" HINGE
- 31" x 15-5/8" 3/4" PLYWOOD
- LEGS CUT AT 15° ANGLE
- 8"
- 23-3/4" x 1-1/2" 3/4" PLYWOOD

WHAT IT TAKES		
TIME	**COST**	**SKILL LEVEL**
2 hours	Under $50	Beginner

TOOLS
Circular saw, miter saw, drill/driver

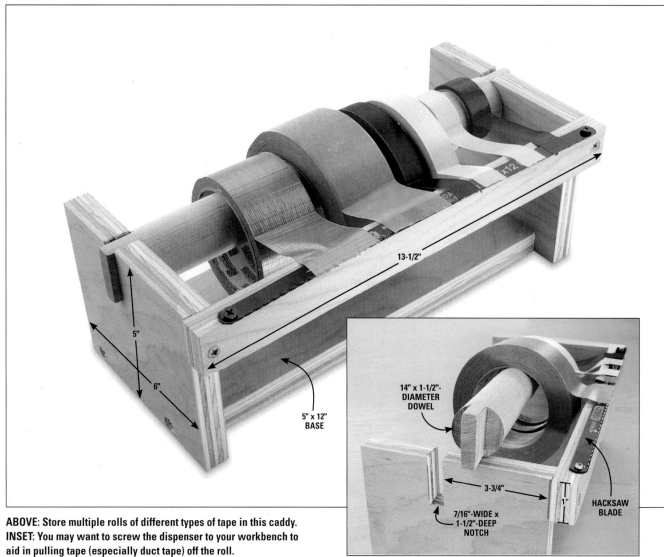

**ABOVE: Store multiple rolls of different types of tape in this caddy.
INSET: You may want to screw the dispenser to your workbench to aid in pulling tape (especially duct tape) off the roll.**

Tape caddy

Keep your tape rolls in one place with this plywood dispenser.

It always seems like the tape's nowhere in sight right when you need it most. Thankfully, this easy-to-build tape caddy solves the missing-tape problem with ease. When you run out of tape, just lift the dowel out of the notches, reload and slide it back in the notches. You'll need:

- Two 5-in. x 6-in. side pieces of 3/4-in. plywood
- One 5-in. x 12-in. plywood base
- One 1-in. x 13-1/2-in. hacksaw blade support
- One 14-in. x 1-1/2-in.-diameter dowel rod
- An 18-tooth, 12-in. hacksaw blade
- Notch the sides to the dimensions shown and screw the sides to the base, along with the hacksaw blade support.
- Saw the dowel ends to fit in the notched sides and screw

the hacksaw blade on the support, positioning it so the saw teeth extend a little beyond the edge of the plywood. That's all you have to do.

- Well, your last step is to load it up with tape—you'll never have to go hunting for stray rolls again.

WHAT IT TAKES		
TIME 1-2 hours	**COST** Under $50	**SKILL LEVEL** Beginner
TOOLS Table saw, drill/driver		

Chisel pockets

Build it from scrap boards.

Here's a neat tabletop chisel storage idea that's a snap to build. It angles the handles toward you for easy reach.

Start with a 4-in.-wide board. Using your table saw, cut stopped slots to match the width and depth of each chisel (plus some wiggle room). Screw or glue on another board to create the pockets, then run the lower edge of the doubled board through a table saw with the blade set at 15 degrees. Now cut three triangular legs with 75-degree bottom corners and glue them to the pocket board.

If you like, drill a few holes through the boards for pegboard hooks so the holder is easy to store on the wall.

Shop-made parts boxes

Have you priced those plastic parts bins? Too expensive! Instead, make your own out of scrap. The trick is to keep them modular. Make the front, back and bottom from 3/4- or 1/2-in. material, and the sides from 1/4-in. plywood. Nailed and glued together, they're plenty tough. The ones shown here are 12 in. front to back (to fit in old kitchen upper cabinets), 3 in. tall, and either 3-1/2 in. or 7 in. wide. Save up some scrap and you can make a couple dozen in an hour or so.

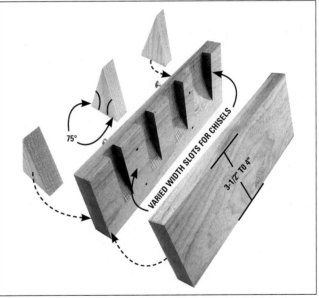

75°

VARIED WIDTH SLOTS FOR CHISELS

3-1/2" TO 4"

ABOVE: Use a dado blade to cut grooves to fit your chisels, then glue on the face board. Cut small triangular "feet" as shown and glue them to the back, so your rack stands up for easy use.

WHAT IT TAKES		
TIME 1 hour	**COST** Under $20	**SKILL LEVEL** Beginner
TOOLS Table saw, miter saw, dado set, drill/driver		

Make your garage floor last

Sealing your concrete garage floor is the best way to prevent damage from road salt and freezing temperatures. With so many concrete sealing/waterproofing products on the market, choosing the right product can be confusing.

To get the scoop on choosing the right sealer, we contacted Dave Barnes, president of SaverSystems Inc., a manufacturer of concrete sealing/waterproofing products. Here's what we learned about concrete sealing technology.

FOUR TYPES OF SEALERS

Film-forming acrylic, epoxy and polyurethane products seal the concrete pores and impart a sheen or "wet-look" gloss to the entire garage floor for a really sharp style. These coatings are easy to clean, but they require more rigorous surface preparation. They're also slippery, especially when wet.

Silane/siloxane formulas penetrate the concrete and react with minerals to form a "hydrophobic" surface that repels water, road salt and other de-icing chemicals. The product won't darken the concrete or look shiny, so your garage floor will still look like dull concrete.

WE CHOSE SILANE/SILOXANE

This garage is in Minnesota, so preventing damage from freezing water and road salt was critical. We didn't care about gloss, but we wanted to avoid two steps that are required for many film-forming sealers: acid etching and roughening the surface. We chose MasonrySaver All-Purpose Heavy Duty Water Repellent, a water-based silane/siloxane. It took us 5 gallons to seal the floor of this three-car garage.

IT'S ALL ABOUT SURFACE PREP

Start by cleaning the floor with a concrete cleaner and power washer **(Photo 1)**. If you have oil stains, treat them before you power wash. Apply the sealer with a paint pad to get an even application and avoid puddles **(Photo 2)**. After it dries, fill floor cracks with a polyurethane crack filler **(Photo 3)**.

POWER WASHER

CAUTIONARY INSTRUCTIONS
To avoid electrical shock or carbon monoxide poisoning, locate your power washer in an open area outside the garage.

1 **APPLY CLEANER, SCRUB AND POWER WASH.** Mask the walls with poly. Use the power washer to apply concrete cleaner. Scrub with a push broom. Then rinse with high pressure and a 40-degree nozzle. Squeegee and let dry.

PAINT PAD

2 **APPLY AND SPREAD.** Dip the paint pad into the sealer and spread it evenly across the floor to avoid puddling. Let the product soak in and dry.

POLYURETHANE CAULK

3 **FORCE FILLER INTO THE CRACKS.** Cut a small opening in the tube tip. Then hold the caulk gun perpendicular to the floor, pressing the tip into the crack. Squeeze the trigger and force the crack filler deep into the crack.

Great Goofs®

Laughs and lessons from our readers

IT'S A MONSTER, ALL RIGHT

My latest gearhead project was the most challenging: converting my stock Ford pickup to a manly mini monster truck. I had tricked it out with a lift package, giant struts, enormous tires—the whole bit! When it was done, I couldn't wait to take it out to show my friends.

But as I was getting ready to drive it out of the garage, I came to the ridiculously late realization that my truck was too high to get through the door! With my tail between my legs, I had to take off the wheels, rest the truck on dollies and have a tow truck pull it out like a beached whale. Nothing manly about that.

JEFF ROSS

DIY OIL CHANGE DIDN'T PAN OUT

I'd been feeling like a sucker for paying quick-change oil joints 25 bucks or more when I was so capable of changing the oil myself. It was time I got my hands dirty. Ten minutes to save $15? No problemo!

I rounded up everything I needed and went to work. I pulled the plug and watched the black gold start to flow. While the oil drained, I headed to the kitchen for a cup of joe. When I came back out, my garage floor looked like the Exxon Valdez oil spill. I didn't know it, but my old oil pan had a crack in the bottom. Have you ever tried cleaning 5 qts. of dirty oil off a concrete floor? Well, it takes longer than 10 minutes!

LOU BELANGER

GARAGE DOOR GAFFE

We were about to put our house on the market and wanted to spruce up the garage to boost the home's resale value. We were painting the garage walls and everything was going fine until we decided to take a break. Before climbing down the ladder, I set my can of paint on top of the open garage door.

Out of habit, I hit the garage door opener right as I entered the house, which caused the paint can to fall on the driveway. Paint splattered all over the car, the garage door, the driveway and everything else within the "splash zone." We spent two hours scrubbing and washing off all the paint. It was quite a while before I attempted painting again.

GARY SCHEIDEMANTLE

MAGIC CABINET MYSTERY SOLVED

The metal cabinet where I store my cans of spray paint used to drive me crazy. Every time I opened the door, a can would fall out and land on my foot. I'd pick up the can and put it back on the shelf. This happened at least a dozen times.

For the life of me, I couldn't figure out why a can would fall out every time I opened the cabinet. Finally, I saw it: A magnet was stuck to the inside of the door and had been pulling out the cans.

MARK YAX

CHAPTER **FIVE**

FLOORS

SUBFLOOR

POLYURETHANE CONSTRUCTION ADHESIVE

JOIST

1 Locate the floor squeak and inject polyurethane caulk into the gaps between the joists and plywood subfloor. Ventilate the area while using this caulk.

Squeaky floor fix using caulk

Don't ignore your squeaky floor. Instead, use this cheap and simple fix to silence the noise.

Squeaky floors are an irritant homeowners endure for a long time before repairing. A whole doodad industry is devoted to solving this problem. Here's one fix: When the floor framing in your house is accessible and there's a slight gap between the floor joists and the subfloor, try using polyurethane caulk to silence the squeak **(Photo 1)**.

Inject caulk into the gap and work it deep with a plastic spoon so the caulk flows toward the nail shanks that are causing the squeaks **(Photo 2)**.

PLASTIC SPOON

2 Push the bead of polyurethane caulk deeper into the flooring gap with a plastic spoon instead of your finger. This caulk is extremely sticky. Wear gloves when handling it and expect that any tools you use to work the caulk will have to be cleaned with paint thinner or, in the case of the spoon, just thrown away.

WHAT IT TAKES		
TIME 10 minutes	**COST** $5-$10 per tube	**SKILL LEVEL** Beginner

TOOLS
Polyurethane caulk, plastic spoon, gloves, paint thinner

A.

Concrete stain gives concrete the mottled look of natural stone.

B.

Concrete sealers come in clear and tinted versions.

Stain or seal a concrete floor

Here's your guide to making your garage floor shine like new.

A. CONCRETE STAIN

A stain isn't really a coating; it is a translucent decorative coloring that soaks into the concrete and creates a pigmented, marbled appearance resembling natural stone. It typically requires two coats and is applied with a roller or a sprayer and then immediately worked into the concrete with a nylon scrubbing brush.

The stain itself doesn't protect the concrete, so after it dries, rinse the surface and then apply one or two coats of urethane sealer to protect against moisture, chemicals and stains (see "urethane sealer"). Depending on the traffic your floor gets, you may need to wax the sealer annually and touch up the stain and reseal the floor every two years. You can find the right concrete stain for your floor at various home centers and at online retailers.

B. CONCRETE SEALERS

Sealers are like floor paint, but tougher. After paints, they're the least expensive coating, and they're very easy to apply with basic tools like a brush or roller. They dry to a clear satin or semigloss finish, depending on the product, and you can also get them tinted. There are water-based and solvent-based versions.

Acrylic/latex sealer

Like floor paint, acrylic/latex sealer is vulnerable to chemicals and it isn't as tough as an epoxy, so you'll find it'll benefit from an annual protective waxing or even a reapplication every few years. Acrylic/latex sealer will stick better to a concrete floor than urethane sealer, which is why it's sometimes used as a primer for oil-based floor paint or epoxy.

Urethane sealer

Urethane sealer is significantly tougher than acrylic/latex sealer, but it's important to know that it doesn't bond well with bare concrete. It provides a clear, high-gloss finish that resists chemicals better than epoxy alone and is less likely to yellow in sunlight, which is why it's used as a seal coat over epoxy and concrete stain. However, urethane sealer is more expensive than acrylic sealer, and solvent-based versions require the use of a respirator during application. Be sure to take all necessary safety precautions.

WHAT IT TAKES

TIME	COST	SKILL LEVEL
2 days	$5-$15 per sq. ft.	Beginner

TOOLS
Circular saw, jigsaw, flooring installation kit, pull saw, basic hand tools

Install a floating wood floor

No glue, no nails and best of all, you can do it in just one weekend.

Here's a wood floor that's so easy to install you can complete an average-size room in just one weekend. The joints easily snap together. Simple carpentry skills and a few basic tools are all you need to cut the floorboards and notch them around corners.

In this article, we'll show you how to prepare your room and lay the snap-together flooring. The flooring we're using is similar to snap-together laminate floors except that it has a surface layer of real wood. The 5/16-in.-thick flooring has specially shaped tongues and grooves that interlock to form a strong, tight joint without glue or nails. Once assembled, the entire floor "floats" in one large sheet. You leave a small expansion space all around the edges so the floor can expand and contract with humidity changes.

Wood veneer floors cost $5 to $15 per sq. ft., depending on species, thickness of the top wood layer, underlayment and trim. Most home centers sell a few types of snap-together floors, but you'll find a better selection and expert advice at your local flooring retailer or even online.

Before you go shopping, draw a sketch of your room with dimensions. Make note of transitions to other types of flooring and other features like stair landings and exterior doors. Ask your salesperson for help choosing the right

LEFT: You'll want to spend quality family time on this super simple (and comfortable) floor. ABOVE: The floor joints snap together with ease, which makes this project a walk in the park.

transition moldings for these areas. You'll need a few special tools in addition to basic hand tools like a tape measure, square and utility knife. We purchased an installation kit from the manufacturer that included plastic shims, a tapping block and a last-board puller, but if you're handy, you could fabricate these tools. You'll also need a circular saw and a jigsaw to cut the flooring, and a miter box to cut the shoe molding. A table saw and a power miter saw would make your job easier but aren't necessary.

MAKE SURE YOUR FLOOR IS DRY

Don't lay this type of floor over damp concrete or in damp crawl spaces. Check all concrete for excess moisture. As a starting point, use the plastic mat test shown in **Photo 1**. Even though some manufacturers allow it, professional installers we spoke to advised against installing floating floors in kitchens, full or three-quarter baths, or even entryways, all areas where they might be subjected to standing water.

PREPARE YOUR ROOM FOR NEW FLOORING

You have to make sure the existing floor is smooth and flat before you install a floating floor on top. Clear the old floor, and then smooth it by scraping off lumps and sweeping it. Carefully check the floor with an 8-ft. straightedge, marking high spots and depressions. Sand or grind down ridges and fill low spots **(Photo 2)**. Most manufacturers recommend no more than an 1/8-in. variation in flatness

---

PRO TIP

Essential tool

A pull saw works great to undercut doorjambs and casing **(Photo 3)**. It's difficult to get close enough to the floor with a standard handsaw.

1 Test for excess moisture in concrete floors by sealing the edges of a 3-ft. square of plastic sheeting to the floor with duct tape. Wait 24 hours before you peel back the plastic to check for moisture. Water droplets on the plastic or darkened concrete indicate a possible problem with excess moisture. Ask your flooring supplier for advice before installing.

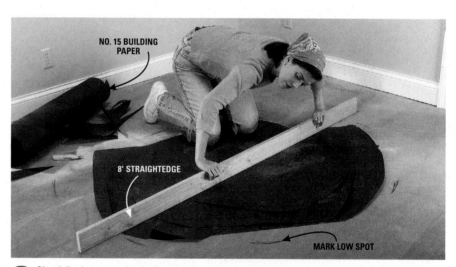

2 Check for low spots in the floor with an 8-ft. straightedge and mark their perimeter with a pencil. Fill depressions less than 1/4 in.-deep with layers of building paper. Fill deeper depressions with a hardening-type floor filler available from flooring stores.

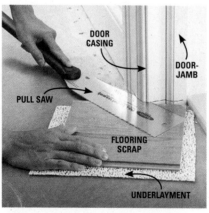

3 Undercut doorjambs and casings to make space for the flooring to slip underneath. Guide the saw with a scrap of flooring stacked on a piece of underlayment.

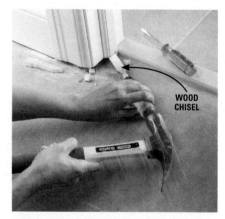

4 Break and pry out the cutoff chunks of jamb and casing with a screwdriver. Use a sharp chisel or utility knife to complete the cut in areas the saw couldn't reach.

5 Unroll the underlayment and lap it up the baseboards or walls 2 in. Temporarily secure the edges with masking tape. Butt the sheets together and seal the seams with the tape recommended by the manufacturer. Cut the first row of boards narrower if necessary to ensure that the last row of flooring will be at least 2 in. wide. Start the installation by locking in the ends of the first row of flooring. Measure and cut the last piece to fit, allowing a 3/8-in. expansion space.

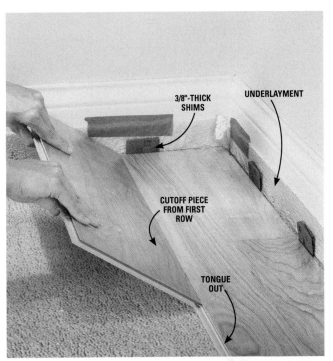

6 Start the second row with the leftover cutoff piece from the first row, making sure the end joints are offset at least 12 in. from the end joints in the first row. With the board held at about a 45-degree angle, engage the tongue in the groove. Push in while you rotate the starter piece down toward the floor. The click indicates the pieces have locked together. The joint between boards should draw tight.

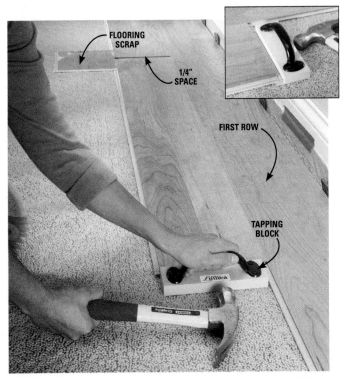

7 Leave a 1/4-in. space between the next full piece of flooring and the previous piece. Snap this piece into the first row. Snap a scrap of flooring across the ends being joined to hold them in alignment while you tap them together. Place the tapping block against the end of the floor piece and tap it with a hammer to close the gap.

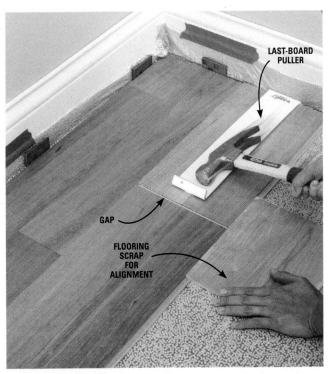

8 Close a gap at the end of the row by hooking the last-board puller tool over the end of the plank and tapping it with a hammer to pull the end joints together.

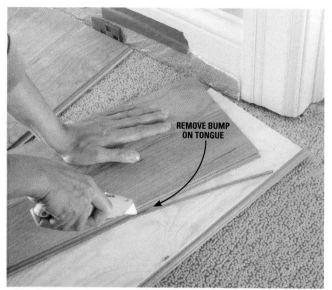

9 Plan ahead when you get near a doorjamb. Usually you have to slide the next piece of flooring under the jamb rather than tilting and snapping it into place. To accomplish this, you must slice off the locking section of the tongue from the preceding row with a sharp utility knife before installing it.

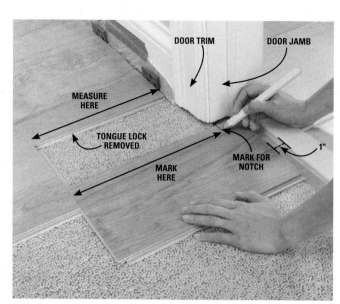

10 Cut the plank to be notched to length, allowing a 1-in. space for the future transition piece. Align the end with the end of the last plank laid and mark 3/8 in. inside the jamb to make sure the flooring extends under the door trim.

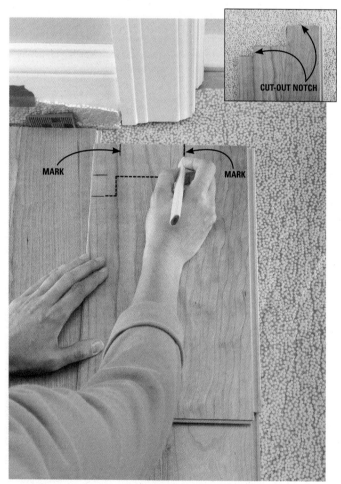

11 Align the flooring lengthwise and mark for the notches in the other direction, allowing for the floor to slide under the doorjamb about 3/8 in. Connect the marks with a square and cut out the notch with a jigsaw.

12 Apply a thin bead of the manufacturer's recommended glue along the edge where the portion of the tongue was removed. Slide the notched piece of flooring into place and tighten the glued edge by pounding on the special tapping block.

over an 8-ft. length. Allowing the floor to expand and contract freely is critical. Leave at least a 3/8-in. expansion space along the edges. You can hide the gap under the baseboards or leave those baseboards in place and cover the gap with shoe molding or quarter round as we did. Cover the expansion space at any openings or transitions to other types of flooring with special transition moldings **(Photo 13)**. Buy these from the dealer.

Finally, saw off the bottoms of door jambs and trim to allow for the flooring to slide underneath **(Photo 3)**. Leaving an expansion gap at any exterior doors presents a unique challenge. In older houses, you could carefully remove the threshold and notch it to allow the flooring to slide underneath. For most newer exterior doors, you can butt a square-nosed transition piece against the threshold.

Floating floors must be installed over a thin cushioning pad, which is called underlayment **(Photo 5)**. Underlayment is usually sold in rolls. It's a good idea to ask your flooring dealer to suggest the best one for your situation. Some types combine a vapor barrier and padding. Install this type over concrete or other floors where moisture might be a problem. Take extra care when installing underlayment that includes a vapor barrier. Lap the edges up the wall and carefully seal all the seams as recommended by the manufacturer. Keep a roll of tape handy to patch rips and tears as you install the floor.

After the first few rows, installing the floor is a snap; you may have to cut your first row of flooring narrower to make sure the last row is at least 2 in. wide. To figure this, measure across the room and divide by the width of the exposed face on the flooring. The number remaining is the width of the last row. If the remainder is less than 2, cut the first row narrower to make this last row wider. Then continue the installation as shown in **Photos 6 – 8**.

The same tilt-and-snap installation technique cannot be used where the flooring fits under door jambs. Instead, you have to slide the flooring together. **Photos 9 – 12** show how. If the specific opening requires a transition molding, cut the flooring short to leave space for it **(Photo 13)**.

Complete the floor by cutting the last row to the correct width to fit against the wall. Make sure to leave the required expansion space. Finally, reinstall the baseboards if you removed them, or install new quarter-round or shoe molding to cover the expansion space **(Photo 14)**. That's it — enjoy your brand-new floor.

CONSTRUCTION ADHESIVE

SQUARE NOSE TRANSITION

TEMPORARY WEIGHTS

BAND OF ADHESIVE

13 Cut a transition molding, in this case a square nose transition, to fit between the doorstops or jambs. Spread a bead of construction adhesive only on the area of the floor that will be in contact with the transition piece. Set the transition in place and weight it down overnight.

NAIL SET

4d FINISH NAILS

14 Complete the flooring project by trimming off the protruding underlayment with a utility knife and installing shoe molding. Predrill 1/16-in. holes through the shoe molding. Then nail the shoe molding to the baseboard with 4d finish nails. Set and fill the nails. Do not nail the shoe molding down into the flooring.

PRO TIP

Fix it first!

If you have wood floors, fix squeaks and tighten loose boards by screwing them to the joists with deck screws before you go ahead with installing your new flooring.

WHAT IT TAKES		
TIME	**COST**	**SKILL LEVEL**
1 day	Under $50	Beginner
TOOLS		
Drill, flat bar		

Stop stair squeaks

If you're tired of the whole house hearing when you sneak downstairs for a midnight snack, this is the project for you.

Squeaky stairs are easy to fix from underneath—provided they're exposed. A simple fix is to tap shims into voids between the treads and the stringers, and add some glue. Then screw the stringer to each stud. But most stairs are finished on the underside with drywall or plaster. Squeaks

in these stairs need to be fixed from the top. That's why the perfect time to fix them is when you're replacing the carpeting—then you can remove the treads and get at the squeaky culprits. (If you're not replacing the carpet but have a squeak that's driving you nuts, see the box on p. 185 for how to fix tread squeaks right through the carpeting.) Here are four easy steps to permanently fix the treads that squeak and keep the rest from ever starting.

After you've removed the carpet, use a flat bar to pry off the treads, working from the top down (**Photo 1**). Since you'll be reusing the treads, remove the nails and any leftover carpet pad or staples. Screw the outside stringers to each stud with 4-1/2-in. screws (**Photo 2**). Starting with the bottom tread, apply a bead of subfloor adhesive (two brands are PL 400 and Liquid Nails) along the top of the riser, the stringers and the back of the tread. Press the tread back into place. Next, drive three 2-1/2-in. screws through the top of the same tread into each stringer (**Photo 3**). Then, drive a 2-in. screw through the riser into the back of the tread between the stringers (**Photo 4**). Repeat these steps with each tread, working your way up to the top of the stairs.

Note: Your stairs will be out of commission for a couple of hours, so let everyone in the house know. Make sure you cordon off the top to keep someone from tumbling down the steps while you're working!

1 Pry off each tread with a flat bar. Remove the nails, and clean off any carpet pad or staples.

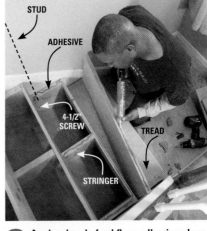
2 Apply a bead of subfloor adhesive along the top of the riser, the stringers and the tread's back. Press the tread back into place.

3 Drive three 2-1/2-in. screws through the top of the tread into each stringer.

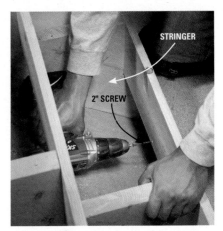
4 Drive a 2-in. screw through the riser into the back of the tread.

Fix squeaks through carpet

If you have carpeted stairs and a squeak, try the Squeeeeek No More Kit (123itsdone.com). The kit is designed to send a snap-off screw through the carpet without damaging fibers. Find the squeak by bouncing up and down on each step, then drive the specially scored screw through the middle of the depth control jig, down through the carpeted tread, and into the stringer or riser nearest the squeak. The jig stops the scored screw right below the tread's surface. Use the screw gripper located on one side of the jig to rock the screw back and forth until the excess length snaps off.

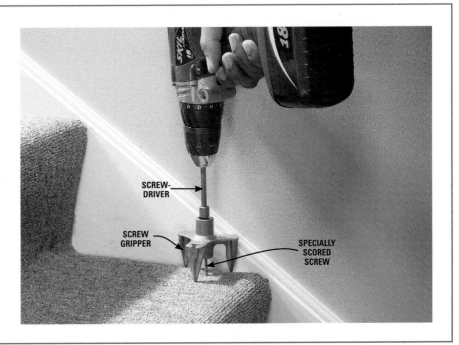

1 Remove metal buttons on furniture legs. If a button is sunk deep into the wood and you can't pry it out, drill a 1/4-in. hole and lever it out with a small screwdriver.

2 Stick self-adhesive pads to the legs or drive in nail-type feet. On hardwood legs, drill a pilot hole slightly smaller than the nail shank.

Damage prevention

Floor-friendly feet for furniture.

Most manufacturers put small metal buttons on furniture legs. Metal feet slide easily across factory and warehouse floors, but they can damage any type of hard flooring in your house (even ceramic tile). On carpet, a spilled drink can even lead to rust stains. So whenever you get a new piece of furniture, run to your local home center or hardware store to find a variety of furniture feet for less than $5.

WHAT IT TAKES		
TIME 10 minutes	**COST** $5-$10	**SKILL LEVEL** Beginner
TOOLS Drill, flat blade screwdriver, hammer		

Pads

Felt or cloth pads are gentle on floors, but they don't slide as easily as plastic feet.

Glides

Plastic glides slide across hard flooring, but don't use plastic or rubber on wood flooring—chemicals in plastics stain finishes.

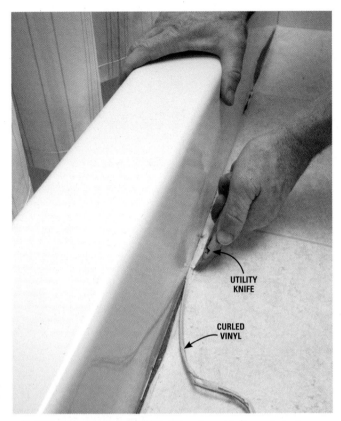

1 **CUT OUT THE CURLED VINYL.** Slice alongside the curled edge of vinyl flooring with a utility knife. Then peel off the thin strip of vinyl and clean out any dirt or old caulk.

UTILITY KNIFE

CURLED VINYL

Curling vinyl cure

Solving this issue is easier than you think.

When water gets under the sheet vinyl along the edge of a shower or tub and the vinyl starts to curl, no amount of caulk can hide the problem. But there's an easy fix: Buy a solid-surface threshold strip at a home center or tile shop. Strips are available in various lengths and thicknesses; the one shown is a 1/2 in. thick. The material cuts like wood, so you can use a handsaw or miter saw to cut a piece to the right length. **Photos 1 – 3** show how to complete the repair.

WHAT IT TAKES		
TIME 30 minutes	**COST** $50-$100	**SKILL LEVEL** Beginner

TOOLS
Basic hand tools, clamps, caulking gun

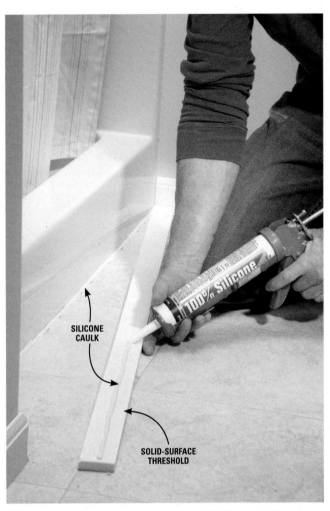

SILICONE CAULK

SOLID-SURFACE THRESHOLD

2 **ATTACH A THRESHOLD.** Spread a bead of silicone caulk on the back of the threshold and along the base of the shower.

3 **CLAMP THE THRESHOLD.** Press the threshold against the shower base. If there are gaps, use clamps to hold the threshold tight until the caulk sets.

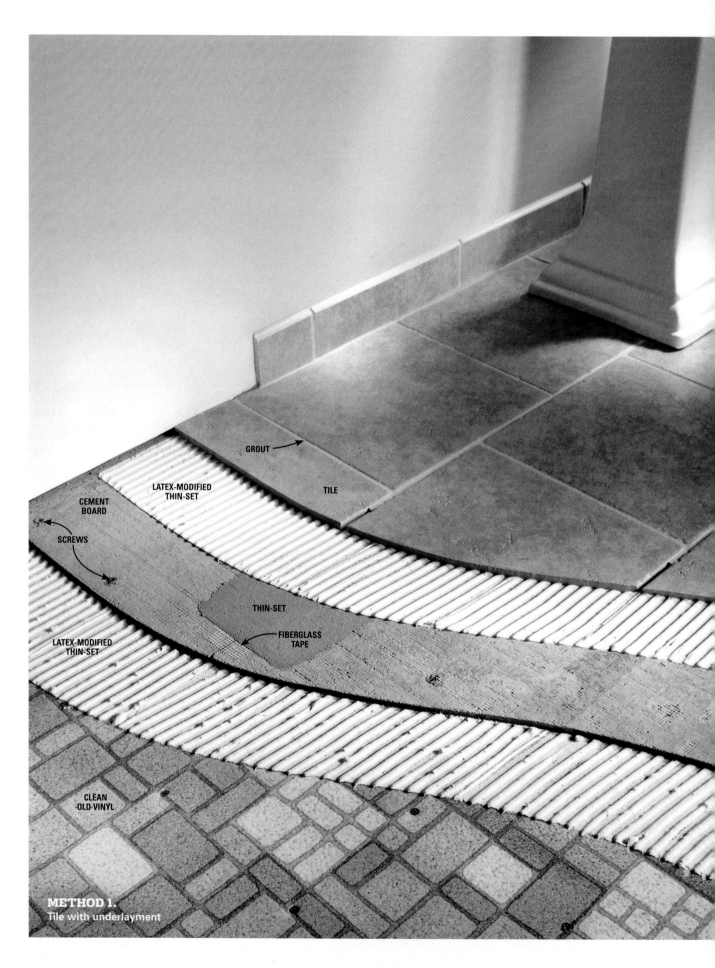

GROUT

TILE

LATEX-MODIFIED THIN-SET

CEMENT BOARD

SCREWS

THIN-SET

FIBERGLASS TAPE

LATEX-MODIFIED THIN-SET

CLEAN OLD VINYL

METHOD 1.
Tile with underlayment

Tile over a vinyl floor

If you have a drab vinyl floor in your bathroom or kitchen, chances are you can tile right over it.

Ceramic tile requires a stiff base to keep it and the grout from cracking. First, check the thickness of your floor. You can usually figure the thickness by pulling up a floor register or removing a door threshold. If the ceiling is open below the floor, you can often tell from where plumbing penetrates the floor. As a last resort, remove the toilet to examine the area around the ring; in kitchens, pull out the dishwasher or oven. If your floor framing is spaced 16 in. apart, the combination of subfloor plus underlayment (a second layer of plywood directly under the vinyl) should add up to at least 1-1/8 in. If the framing is 24 in. apart, the subfloor and underlayment should add up to 1-1/2 in.

If your floor has a vinyl covering with any "give," it probably isn't stiff enough to install tile right over the top. Use tiling **Method 1**, and add either 1/4- or 1/2-in. cement board to build it up. Keep in mind that in doing so, you'll be raising the floor level 1/2 to 3/4 in. (cement board plus 1/4-in. tile), which means that you'll have to trim the door, raise the vanity or appliances, extend the toilet ring and make a new transition to the hallway.

If your floor is already stiff enough, you can lay the tile directly over the vinyl using **Method 2**. With this method you only build your floor up 1/4 in. However, if you choose this method, you should be aware of the possibility that the flooring might contain asbestos. Asbestos is a known carcinogen that was used in many products including vinyl tile, asphalt tile, sheet flooring and adhesives made until 1980. If your floor was laid after 1980, it won't contain asbestos unless the installer used older materials. You can clean and sand it to improve tile adhesion or even tear it out.

However, if you have an older home and don't know when the floor was laid, do not sand it or disturb it. Simply strip off the grime and old wax with an ammonia-based cleaner. When it's dry, apply a little tile adhesive and let it dry to test for good adhesion. If thin-set mortar with an acrylic additive doesn't stick well, try a mastic-type adhesive. Both of them are available at home centers and tile stores.

Tighten loose flooring by screwing down the entire surface with galvanized wood screws spaced every 6 in. Add more screws in obviously loose areas. For complete instructions and more, visit familyhandyman.com and search for the term "tile floor."

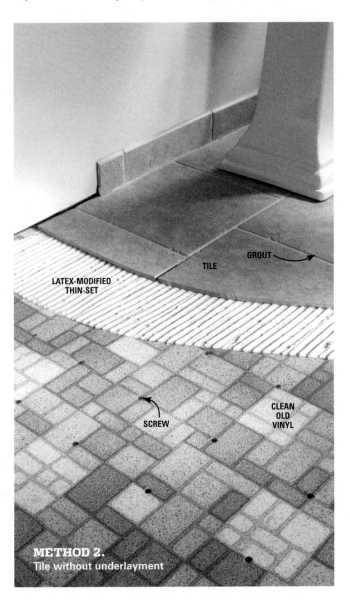

LATEX-MODIFIED THIN-SET

GROUT

TILE

SCREW

CLEAN OLD VINYL

METHOD 2.
Tile without underlayment

WHAT IT TAKES		
TIME	**COST**	**SKILL LEVEL**
3 days	Over $500	Intermediate

TOOLS
Drill, tile cutter, notched trowel, margin trowel, 5- gallon buckets, mixing paddles, rubber grout float, sponges

Pull wrinkles out of your carpet

Make your carpet look younger (and avoid calling a pro) with a few rental tools and these easy-to-follow steps.

Wall-to-wall carpets sometimes develop loose, wrinkled areas, usually due to installation issues. If you ignore the wrinkles, they'll wear and become permanent eyesores, even if you stretch them later. You don't have to hire a carpet layer— fix it yourself with rental tools and our instructions. Rent a power stretcher and knee kicker at an equipment rental store. Buy a carpet knife (not a utility knife) at any home center.

You'll be stretching from the center of the carpet and pulling it at an angle into a corner, so move any furniture that'll be in the path of the stretch. First, loosen the carpet in the corner **(Photo 1)**. Next, set up the power stretcher at an angle across the room. Set the tooth depth on the power stretcher based on the carpet pile depth **(Photo 2)**.

Operate stretcher with the lever, capturing excess carpet in the tack strip as it stretches. Use the knee kicker on each side of the locked stretcher to help lock the carpet into the tacks.

Once the wrinkles are out and the carpet is secure in the tack strip, cut off the excess **(Photo 4)**.

WHAT IT TAKES		
TIME 1 day	**COST** Under $50	**SKILL LEVEL** Beginner
TOOLS Power stretcher, knee kicker, carpet knife		

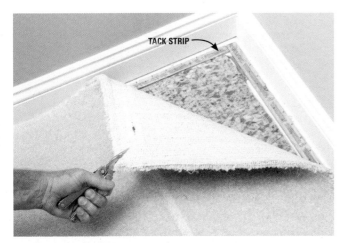

1 **PULL THE CARPET FREE.** Grab the carpet right next to the baseboard and pull it straight up. Then loosen the rest of the carpet along the wall.

2 **DIAL IN THE CORRECT TOOTH DEPTH.** Adjust the tooth depth by loosening or tightening the screws on the spacer bar. Set the bar so the teeth grab just the carpet pile, not the jute backing or pad (the pad is stapled to the floor and shouldn't be stretched).

3 **SINK AND STRETCH.** Set the teeth into carpet near the wall and push down on the stretcher handle. Lock stretched carpet into place by jamming it behind the tack strip with a putty or linoleum knife.

4 **TRIM OFF EXCESS CARPET.** Fold the excess carpet so the backing is facing up. Then cut it off with a carpet knife.

Smooth talk about wrinkles

Professional carpet installer Steve Hoover explains how carpet gets wrinkled. "Carpet has to acclimate to interior conditions before it's installed. That's especially important if the carpet has been in a cold truck or exposed to high humidity. If it's installed while it's still cold or humid, you are going to have wrinkling problems later on," he says.

Improper stretching during installation is another cause. "Some installers lay the pad and carpet and then secure the carpet with just the knee kicker. Since it was never really stretched, it's going to wrinkle after it's seen some traffic. If the carpet wasn't stretched during installation, it's going to wrinkle later," he adds.

Steve's advice? Make sure the installers of your carpet allow enough time for the carpet to acclimate, and insist that they actually stretch it with a power stretcher during the installation.

Great Goofs®

Laughs and lessons from our readers

SAFE, BUT SORRY

I decided to buy a floor safe to protect my wife's jewelry. The locksmith wanted $200 to install it in my concrete floor—which was more than the safe cost! To do the job myself, I rented the biggest jackhammer known to humankind and bought some concrete mix for the patchwork. I fired up the jackhammer and it broke through the basement slab just fine. Then it hammered through the main water line, sending water shooting up like a geyser.

The project took some extra time and an emergency visit from my plumber, but you know what? That $200 locksmith would have caused the same disaster!

PATRICK FINDLEY

A SNAG IN THE SHAG

A few years ago, I was installing bypass closet doors in a customer's newly finished basement, which had beautiful, expensive new carpet. Everything was going fine until it was time to screw the door guides to the concrete floor. I got out my hammer drill to drill the pilot holes for the concrete screws.

In a split second, the drill bit grabbed a carpet fiber and ripped a perfectly straight snag right down the middle of the $30-a-yard woven carpet. I had to recruit my friend, a carpet expert, to fix the problem—he said it happens to carpenters all the time. I just wish I had cut a little slit in the carpeting before drilling. Then I wouldn't have lost money on that job.

PETE BOUMAN

NAILED IT PERFECTLY!

To prepare for putting in my wood floor, I removed all the base trim. I labeled the trim to make sure the pieces would go back in the same order. I installed the floor in a single day and, in all modesty, it looked terrific. Then I got out my compressor and trusty nail gun to reinstall the base trim.

I had just nailed the last piece of base when my wife walked in and asked me why the pocket door wouldn't pull out of the pocket. I was baffled. After using every muscle in my body to try to pull the stuck door closed, I realized the problem: While reinstalling the base, I had shot nails through the trim, drywall and pocket door framing, and right into the door itself. Oh, well. Who needs to close a bathroom door anyway?

WILL HANSON

TWO INCHES OFF THE TOP

With the motto "measure twice, cut once" in mind, I borrowed my husband's tape measure and twice measured the closet floor where I was planning to install carpet. I wrote down the dimensions, grabbed my piece of carpet and headed to the garage.

I used a yardstick to measure the carpet in the garage. Soon my masterpiece was ready, and I hurried to install it. When I laid it out, I was shocked to find that it was 2 in. short on two sides. My measurements were right, which left me puzzled. Then my husband solved the mystery. Weeks ago, he'd cut 2 in. off the end of the yardstick to use as a shim. I never noticed.

DARLENE LOCKERT

CHAPTER SIX

WALLS & CEILINGS

The prospect of painting a ceiling can feel daunting, but there's no need to fret—just follow Bill Nunn's tips.

How to paint a ceiling

Ceilings present unique challenges, which is why we called in an expert to give his advice.

Painting a ceiling can be difficult. For starters, a ceiling is usually much larger than any single room wall and is often illuminated with raking light that accentuates even the smallest flaw in the paint. Add to that the challenge of working overhead and things can get messy in a hurry. That's why we called in Bill Nunn, one of our favorite painting consultants, to help out with his best ceiling painting tips; keep them in mind next time you have a room-painting project.

A. USE A STAIN-BLOCKING PRIMER TO COVER FLAWS

Roof leaks, overflowing sinks, tobacco smoke and big spills can all leave ugly ceiling stains or dingy areas that are impossible to conceal with plain old paint. But cover the stain with a coat of stain-blocking primer and your troubles are over. Bill's favorite is white pigmented shellac. You can buy spray cans of pigmented shellac, but Bill prefers brushing it on. Just don't forget to pick up some ammonia or denatured alcohol to clean your brush. If you're painting over a ceiling that's yellow from smoke, roll a coat of shellac over the ceiling before painting with latex.

B. SAND BEFORE YOU PAINT

Over time, and as the layers of paint build up, bumps and crud can get stuck to the ceiling. On untextured ceilings, Bill starts out with a quick once-over, sanding with 100-grit drywall sanding paper. This helps ensure a perfectly smooth paint job and increases paint bonding. The easiest way to do this is with a sanding pole. When you're done sanding, wipe the ceiling with a damp sponge to remove the dust.

C. CUT IN BEFORE YOU ROLL

Cutting in before you roll allows you to cover most of the brush marks with the roller. Bill likes to carefully brush paint along the edge of the ceiling a section at a time. He'll cut in about 10 linear ft. and then roll that section.

D. ROLL BOTH DIRECTIONS

There are several tricks to getting a smooth, consistent coat of paint on the ceiling. First, work in sections about 5 or 6 ft. square. Move quickly from one section to the next to make sure the paint along the edge doesn't dry before you roll the adjoining section. This is the key to avoiding lap marks.

Bill says you'll get the best coverage by immediately rerolling as you go, each section at a right angle to your first roller direction.

E. BUY SPECIAL CEILING PAINT

While there are exceptions, you'll usually experience the best results with paint that's formulated for ceiling application. For a ceiling, you want paint that doesn't spatter, has a long open time and is flat instead of glossy. Most ceiling paints are formulated with these qualities. And of course you can have ceiling paint tinted if you want a color other than "ceiling white."

F. LAP YOUR CUT-IN ONTO THE WALLS

If you're also planning to paint the walls, lap the paint onto the walls a little. Then when you paint, you can err on the side of leaving a little ceiling color showing when you cut in and it won't be noticeable. Some painters skip this cutting-in step and save time by mashing the roller into the corner instead. Bill objects to this method because it is sloppy, builds up excess paint in the corner, and can leave runs or a thick paint line on the wall.

G. DON'T BE AFRAID OF COLOR

You may not want to paint your ceiling yellow, but don't be afraid to deviate from plain old white. Bill says painting the ceiling a color can make a small room seem bigger or a room with a high ceiling seem more intimate. Plus, it's just more interesting. Ask at any full-service paint store for help in choosing complementary wall and ceiling colors, or search online for examples of rooms you like.

H. YOU DON'T NEED AN EXPENSIVE POLE

Bill is sort of old-school when it comes to equipment, actually preferring low-tech solutions. You can buy all kinds

PRO TIP

Clear the room

Bill prefers to move everything out of the room and to cover the floors with drop cloths before going to paint a ceiling. But if this isn't possible, he groups furniture in the center and covers it with painter's plastic. Sometimes it may be necessary to make two or more small groups so you can reach over them with the roller.

D.

E.

F.

of fancy extendable paint poles, but Bill prefers a simple wooden broom handle. And his reasons are simple: They're cheap and light, and they do the job.

I. USE A THICK, PREMIUM ROLLER COVER

Here's a tip that applies to most paint jobs but is even more important for ceilings. You want to get as much paint on the ceiling as you can in the shortest amount of time possible while minimizing spatters. To do this, you need the best roller cover you can buy. Bill prefers a 1/2-in.-nap lambswool cover. If you've never tried a lambswool roller cover, you owe it to yourself to experience the difference. If you're worried about the cost, keep in mind that lambswool covers are easy to clean and last a long time if you take good care of them. One costs about $8.

J. ROLL GENTLY ON TEXTURED CEILINGS

Painting textured ceilings is a bit of a crapshoot. If the texture has been painted over, it's probably safe to paint again. If the texture has never been painted, there's a risk the water in the paint could loosen the texture, causing it to fall off in sheets. If you have a closet or other inconspicuous area, do a test by rolling on some paint to see what happens. If the texture loosens, painting over the larger ceiling is risky. Thankfully, Bill has a few handy tips for painting over texture.

If possible, spray on the paint—it's less likely to loosen the texture than rolling—but spraying paint in an occupied house is usually impractical. Bill says the best tip for rolling on paint in this instance is to avoid overworking the paint. Just roll it on and leave it. Don't go back and forth, since this is likely to pull the texture from the ceiling. If the ceiling needs another coat, wait for the first to dry. Then roll another coat perpendicular to the first one, using the same careful technique.

G.

H.

I. LAMBSWOOL ROLLER   INEXPENSIVE ROLLER

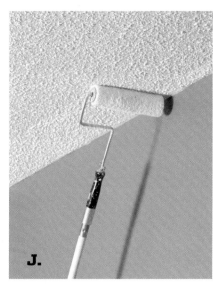

J.

Hang pictures straight and level

The first challenge in hanging a picture is deciding exactly where you want it. It's not so hard with just one picture. You can ask a helper to hold it up while you stand back and judge the position.

Most experts recommend hanging a picture with its center about 60 in. from the floor or its bottom edge 6 to 8 in. above a piece of furniture. Use these heights as a starting point. Then adjust the position of the picture to your liking, and mark the top center with the corner of a sticky note.

A group of pictures is trickier. First, cut out paper patterns and arrange them on the wall with low-adhesive masking tape. The temporary red line from a laser level is helpful for aligning a series of photos level with one another **(Photo 1)**. A standard carpenter's level will also work. When you arrive at a good grouping, mark the top center of each pattern with the corner of a sticky note **(Photo 1)**. You'll use the bottom corners as a reference point for locating the picture hangers.

Now you're ready to position the picture hangers **(Photos 2 – 4)**. Use two hangers for each picture for extra support and to help keep the picture from tipping. Choose picture hangers that are rated to support the weight of your art. We recommend professional hangers like the one shown in the inset on p. 201. They work fine in drywall. These are available at home centers or from most picture-framing shops. OOK is one popular brand. Plaster may not support pictures as well as drywall does. To hang heavier art on plaster walls, use picture hangers with double or triple nails.

Photos 2 and 3 show how to measure the space between the hangers and the distance from the top of the picture frame. The distance between hangers isn't critical. Just space your fingers several inches from the outside edges of the picture frame. Transfer these measurements to the wall **(Photo 4)**. An inexpensive level with inches marked along an edge is a great picture-hanging tool **(Photo 4)**. Otherwise, just stick masking tape to the edge of a level and transfer measurements to the tape. Then line up the bottom of the hooks with the marks and drive the picture-hanger nails through the angled guides on the hooks **(Photo 5)**.

PRO TIP

Do this first!

Before you hang the picture, stick a pair of clear rubber bumpers on the back lower corners of the frame to protect the wall and help keep the picture level. You'll find these with the picture hanging supplies or in the cabinet hardware department (they're called "door bumpers").

WHAT IT TAKES

TIME	COST	SKILL LEVEL
30 minutes	Under $50	Beginner

TOOLS
Level, tape measure, nails, basic hand tools

1 Project a level line and tape exact-size paper patterns on the wall. Mark the top center of each pattern with a sticky note corner.

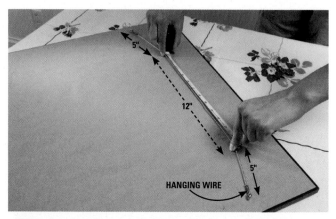

2 Stretch the hanger wire with two fingers spaced an equal distance from the edges of the frame. Keep the wire parallel to the top of the frame. Measure the distance between your fingertips.

3 Leave one finger in place and measure from the wire to the top. Use this dimension and the dimension from Photo 2 to position the picture hangers.

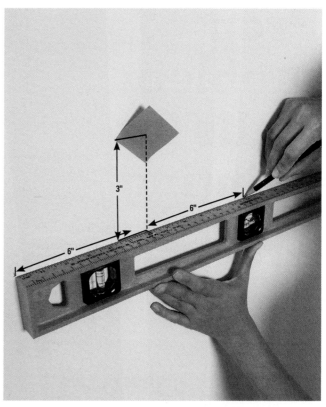

4 Find the hanger positions by measuring down from the sticky note and to each side from the center. Keep the hangers level.

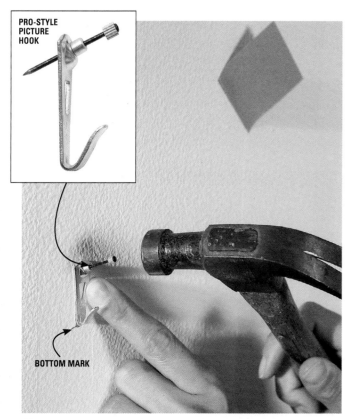

PRO-STYLE PICTURE HOOK

BOTTOM MARK

5 Align the bottom edge of a picture hook with the mark and drive a nail through the hook's guide.

6 Slip the wire over both hooks. Slide the picture sideways across the wires until it is level. Use the same process to hang the remaining pictures.

Prep problem walls for painting

If you hired a pro for this, you'd pay hundreds of dollars. Save your wallet and do it yourself!

Here you'll learn how to fix common wall problems before you paint. Everything you need is available at home centers. For small fixes, pick up spackling compound. For any larger repairs, use all-purpose joint compound. You may also need mesh tape.

A. HIGHLIGHT HIDDEN FLAWS

Minor wall flaws are often hard to spot—until the afternoon sun hits them and makes them embarrassingly obvious. Find and mark any imperfections in the walls. Start by turning off all the lights in the room and closing the curtains. Then hold a trouble light next to the wall and move it across the surface (a process called "raking").

Wherever the light highlights a problem, even a small one, stick a piece of tape next to it so you can easily find it when you come through with spackling or joint compound.

B. FILL HOLES THREE TIMES

Fill small holes and indents (less than 1/8 in.) with spackling compound. For larger holes, use joint compound instead.

Apply either compound with a putty knife, spreading it thin on the wall. You'll apply two more coats, so don't worry if the hole isn't filled perfectly the first time. Let each coat of compound dry according to the directions.

Do not believe spackling labels that say you don't have to sand—you do. You'll have to sand between coats if there's any excess compound. After the final coat, use fine-grit paper.

C. FIX HOLES FAST WITH AN ALUMINUM PATCH

The old method of repairing large holes was to cut out a square in the drywall, attach wood backing and then screw on a new patch of drywall. Aluminum patches are a faster, easier solution. Cut the patch so it covers the hole by at least 1 in. on each side, then place it over the hole. One side is sticky to adhere to the wall. Cover the patch with joint compound. Let it dry overnight, then recoat.

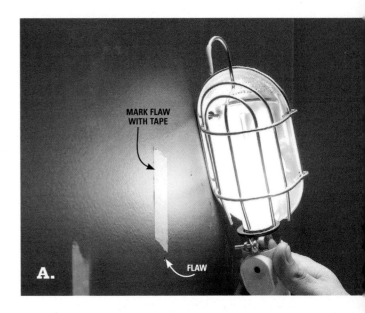

A. MARK FLAW WITH TAPE / FLAW

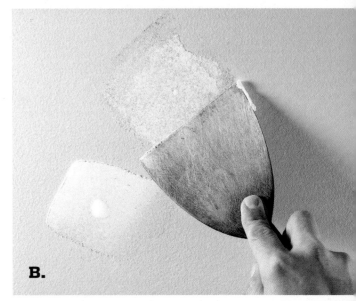

B.

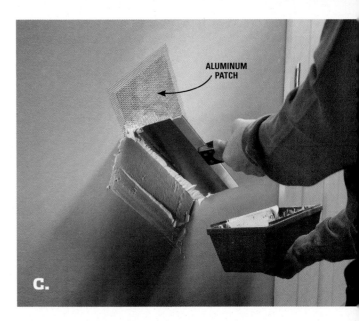

C. ALUMINUM PATCH

D.

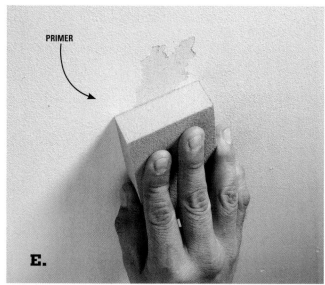

PRIMER

E.

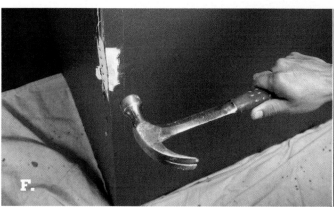

F.

DRY COMPOUND

TAPE

D. CUT AROUND GLUE SPOTS

Mirrors and paneling are sometimes installed with adhesive backing to help hold them in place. When you take them down, the glue sticks to the drywall. Don't try to pull it off—you'll tear the drywall face, making rips across the wall. Instead, cut around the glue with a utility knife, cutting through the drywall face.

Scrape off the glue with a putty knife. You'll still tear the paper, but the tears will be confined to the outline you cut in the drywall. Use sandpaper on small areas of glue that won't scrape off. Fill gouges that you made in the wall with joint compound.

E. SEAL TORN PAPER

The back of a chair, a flying video game controller or a playful kid with a toy truck can tear the drywall paper face. A coat of paint or joint compound over torn paper will create a fuzzy texture. For a smooth finish, seal the torn paper. Start by cutting away any loose paper. Then seal the exposed drywall with a stain-blocking primer. Wait for the primer to dry, then sand the exposed drywall edges to remove paper nubs. Cover the gouge with a thin layer of joint compound, feathering it out along the wall.

F. TAPE AND FILL DAMAGED CORNERS

Metal corner bead dents easily, causing cracks in the wall. Fortunately, the fix is relatively simple, too. Use a hammer to knock the bead right back into shape with several light taps instead of hard blows. Use a level to make sure the bead doesn't stick out past the finished walls or you won't get a clean corner. Round any sharp edges on the bead with a file.

When you hit the bead with the hammer, you probably sent cracks up and down the corner, especially if the bead wasn't taped. Place mesh tape over the cracks, then on one side only apply joint compound over the tape and corner bead. Work on one side at a time—the first side needs to be hard so you can square the other side. Once the first side is dry, apply joint compound to the second side. Then recoat the corner, let it dry and sand it smooth.

G. FIX NAIL POPS FOREVER

Seasonal expansion and contraction of studs can push nails out of drywall. You can't just resink the nail and apply joint

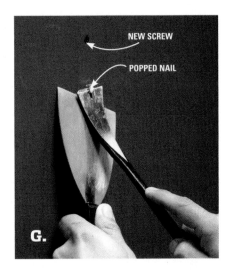

G.

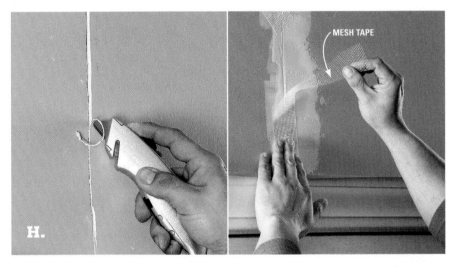

H.

I.

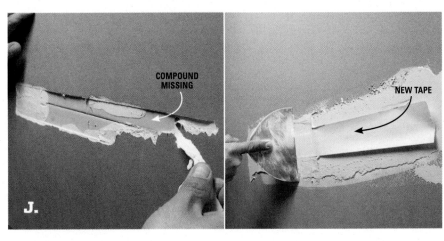

J.

compound over the top—the nail will pop back out. To permanently fix the problem, drive a drywall screw about 2 in. above or below the popped nail. Use a 1-1/4-in. screw. A longer screw isn't better; it's more likely to pop out than a shorter one.

Pull out the nail, holding a wide putty knife under your pry bar to ensure the wall is protected. Tap the empty nail hole with the putty knife handle to knock protruding drywall fragments into the wall. Finally, cover the screw head and fill the nail hole with three coats of joint compound.

H. CUT OUT WALL CRACKS

When homes settle, drywall cracks sometimes shoot out above or below windows and above doors. You can't just cover or fill the cracks with joint compound—they'll come back. Instead, fix the cracks with joint compound and mesh tape. Protect the window or door trim with masking tape before starting.

To fill the crack, use a utility knife to cut a V-shaped groove along its entire length. Fill the groove with joint compound, let it dry, then sand it flush with the wall. Place the mesh tape over the crack. Apply joint compound over the tape and feather it out 2 to 4 in. on each side of the tape. Let the compound dry, then apply a second and third coat, feathering it out 8 to 10 in. from the tape with a 10-in. taping blade.

I. BLOCK STAINS WITH SPECIAL PRIMER

Don't expect regular primer or paint to cover marker or crayon marks; they will bleed through. The same goes for water stains. First try to wash off the marker or crayon with a Mr. Clean Magic Eraser dipped in warm water. If that doesn't work, cover the marks with stain-blocking primer. Apply the primer with a roller so the texture matches the rest of the wall. Buy a cheap roller and then throw it away when you're done.

J. REPLACE LIFTING TAPE

Tape will lift off the wall if there isn't enough joint compound underneath to adhere it to the drywall. You'll have to cut away the loose tape and replace it. Start by cutting through the paint and compound to remove each piece of tape. Go beyond the cracked area. Peel away the tape until you see the underlying drywall. Fill the hole with compound and wait for it to harden. Embed mesh or paper tape in joint compound over the hole. Extend the tape a few inches past the hole on each side. Once dry, apply a second coat. Feather it to blend the patch with the wall.

Space-saving wall niche

If you need more storage in your bathroom, this is the project for you.

Bathrooms are notoriously cramped, so this cabinet fits inside a wall, where it won't take up space. The width is narrower than the 14-1/2-in. stud space, so the cabinet will fit even if the studs are a little off center or bowed.

The following pages show you how to build and install the cabinet. You can complete the project in one weekend: Build and stain (or paint) it on Saturday, then stick it in the wall on Sunday.

TOOLS AND MATERIALS

Everything you need for this project is available at home centers. It's made out of oak, and you'd pay several times as much to buy a cabinet like this in a store.

To complete the project, you'll need a miter saw, a circular saw or table saw, and a drywall saw. A brad nailer will make nailing fast and easy, but it's not absolutely necessary (you can hand-nail instead). You'll also need a router with a 1/4-in. round-over bit and a 1/4-in. Roman ogee bit to rout the shelves and sill nose.

WHERE TO PUT THE CABINET

This cabinet was installed next to the shower, but it'd also fit nicely behind the bathroom door if there's no other available space. In most cases, it won't work over a toilet because there's a vent pipe in the wall. Also avoid exterior walls because they're filled with insulation. When choosing a location, check both sides of the wall for obstructions. A light switch or showerhead on the other side of the wall means the wall contains electrical cable or plumbing pipes.

You could also choose a different room. The cabinet can store—or display—anything you like in the hallway,

The cabinet fits between studs inside the wall, so it'll work in even the tiniest bathroom. Unlike a wall-hung shelf, the cabinet lets you gain storage space without sacrificing elbow room.

WHAT IT TAKES		
TIME 2 days	**COST** $50-$100	**SKILL LEVEL** Intermediate

TOOLS
Miter saw, circular or table saw, drywall saw, brad nailer (optional), router with 1/4-in. round-over bit and 1/4-in. Roman ogee bit

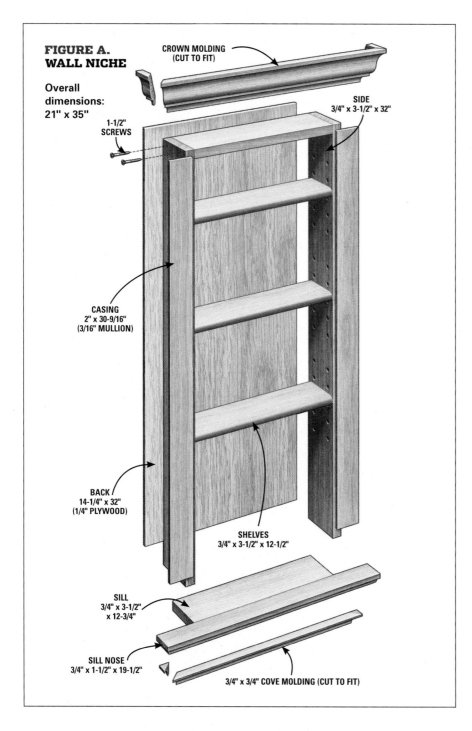

FIGURE A.
WALL NICHE

Overall
dimensions:
21" x 35"

CROWN MOLDING
(CUT TO FIT)

1-1/2"
SCREWS

SIDE
3/4" x 3-1/2" x 32"

CASING
2" x 30-9/16"
(3/16" MULLION)

BACK
14-1/4" x 32"
(1/4" PLYWOOD)

SHELVES
3/4" x 3-1/2" x 12-1/2"

SILL
3/4" x 3-1/2"
x 12-3/4"

SILL NOSE
3/4" x 1-1/2" x 19-1/2"

3/4" x 3/4" COVE MOLDING (CUT TO FIT)

Materials List

ITEM	QTY.
1x4 x 96" oak	2
1x2 x 24" oak	1
1/4" x 24" x 48" oak plywood	1
3/16" x 2" x 72" mullion	1
11/16" x 3-1/4" x 36" crown molding	1
3/4" x 3/4" x 36" cove molding	1
Shelf brackets	12

a bedroom or the family room. The
location is up to you—anywhere you
need extra storage space, this cabinet
will come in handy.

CUT, ROUT AND DRILL THE PIECES

Get started by cutting all the pieces to
size **(refer to Figure A)**. Then run a
router with a Roman ogee bit along the
bottom front and both bottom sides of
the sill nose. Use a round-over bit to
rout the top and the bottom front of
the shelves.

Apply wood glue along the front
edge of the sill, center the sill nose

over it, then clamp the pieces together
until the glue dries. Use a damp cloth
to wipe away any glue that oozes out.
If the sill and sill nose surfaces aren't
flush, be sure to sand the pieces flat
with 80-grit sandpaper.

Lay out the sides for the shelf
bracket holes, following **Figure A**.
Drill the holes 3/4 in. from the edges
and spaced 1 in. apart. Use a 1/4-in.
drill bit (or whatever bit size is required
for your brackets). You need to drill
the holes only 3/8 in. deep (wrap tape
3/8 in. from the end of the drill bit
to mark the depth), although it's OK
to drill all the way through the sides
since the other side will end up being
hidden inside the wall.

After drilling the holes, sand off the
pencil lines remaining on the sides with
120-grit sandpaper.

ASSEMBLE THE CABINET

Use wood glue and 1-1/4-in. brad
nails to assemble the cabinet frame
(Photo 1), following **Figure A**. Then
drill two 1/8-in. pilot holes in each
corner and drive in 1-1/2-in. screws
to hold the corners together.

Run a thin bead of glue along the
back of the entire frame, then set the
back panel over it. Use the back panel
to square the frame, then tack panel
into place with 5/8-in. brad nails.

Lay the cabinet on its back and
fasten the casing **(Photo 2)**. Three
5/8-in. nails will hold the casing
until the glue dries.

Precision cuts are required for the
molding corners to fit tightly. Measure
along the bottom edge of the molding
when you make the cuts (the top
measurements will vary depending
on the type of molding).

To get accurate cuts, build a simple
jig to hold the molding in place.
Screw or nail wood scraps together
at a 90-degree angle. Set the crown
molding upside down in the jig so the
flat part on the back (the part that sits
against the cabinet after installation) is

flush against the vertical part of the jig. Fasten a stop block to the horizontal part of the jig along the top of the molding. Screw or hot-glue the jig to the fence on your miter saw so it won't move.

Set the crown molding upside down in the jig and cut it **(Photo 3)**. If the molding moves in the jig even a tiny bit during the cut, recut the molding or the corners will not fit tightly together. To cut the molding returns (sides), use the jig to make the angle cuts, then cut the 90-degree angles.

Nailing the mitered corners together won't work—the molding will crack or move as you nail it. Instead, simply glue the corners **(Photo 4)**. Cut the cove molding for the bottom of the cabinet in the miter saw (without using the jig), then glue the cove molding pieces together.

Glue and tack the assembled crown and cove moldings to the cabinet with 5/8-in. brad nails.

APPLY A FINISH AND STICK THE CABINET IN THE WALL

Sand the entire cabinet with 120-grit sandpaper and wipe away the dust with a clean cloth. Then brush on a finish. This cabinet has golden oak stain and two coats of polyurethane.

Get the wall ready. Using a drywall saw, cut a small inspection hole in the wall where the cabinet will go. Shine a light in the opening and use a small mirror to look for obstructions in the wall. If you find electrical cable or plumbing pipe, patch the hole and move over a stud space.

Make an outline on the wall between two studs, 1/4 in. larger than the back of the cabinet (so it'll fit easily), and cut out the drywall with a drywall saw. Be careful not to cut into the drywall on the other side of the wall.

Finally, put the cabinet into the wall, level it, then nail through the stiles into the studs with 2-1/2-in. finish nails. Enjoy your increased storage space!

SHELF BRACKET HOLES
ROMAN OGEE ROUT
SILL NOSE
SILL

1 Tack the cabinet box together quickly with a brad nailer. Then add screws for rock-solid corners. Glue the sill nose to the sill before assembling the cabinet.

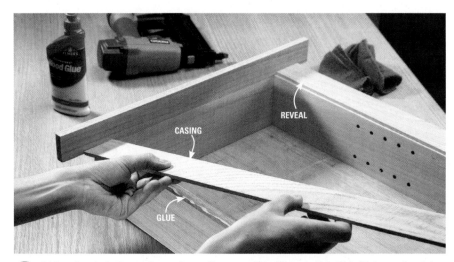

REVEAL
CASING
GLUE

2 Add casing to the box using as few nails as possible. Three nails will hold the casing tight while the glue dries.

STOP BLOCK
JIG

3 Cut the crown molding using a simple homemade jig. The jig holds the crown upside down as you make the cuts.

4 Glue the crown corners together without using nails or clamps. Just hold each return tightly in place for about 60 seconds. Set the completed crown aside for 20 minutes, then attach it to the cabinet.

WHAT IT TAKES

TIME	COST	SKILL LEVEL
1 day	$50-$100	Beginner

TOOLS
Hammer, handsaw, level, screw driver and drill (If you have a miter saw and an 18-gauge brad nailer, great!)

Custom picture ledges

Make them in any length in any color for any wall.

Picture ledges are the perfect marriage of beauty and function. They elegantly display your picture collections, large or small, and are ultra easy to use. You don't even have to mess with positioning hooks. Your photos and artwork will never go crooked, and best of all, you can redecorate instantly by just swapping things around.

There's no need to patch holes after you move a picture.

These shelves are super simple to build, too. It's mostly a matter of gluing and nailing together two boards and a length of molding—no fancy cuts, tools or skills required. This is a great woodworking project for beginners.

PLAN YOUR SHELVES

Even though you'll likely be swapping out and rearranging pictures down the road, it's still a good idea to lay out the initial arrangement of pictures on the floor. That way you can sketch a plan for the length of your ledges and the spacing between them. The other advantage is that you'll be able to assemble a materials list to take to the home center.

You can build your ledges any length that you wish. It takes two 1x3s for every ledge: one for the apron (back) and one for the shelf (**Photo 1**). A 1-1/4 x 1/4-in. molding nailed to the front (**Photo 2**) acts as a lip to hold frames in place.

These ledges are made from clear pine because they will be painted. If you prefer a natural wood look, oak is available at the home center along with the 1/4-in. matching molding. You can choose any wood you want if you're capable of making your own molding.

Remember to get wood glue along with the nails. Finish washers are a

1 **GLUE AND NAIL THE PARTS.** Glue and nail the 1x3 apron onto the 1x3 shelf with 2-in. brads.

2 **ADD THE LIP.** Use the benchtop to make the shelf and molding flush while you glue and nail them together with 1-in. brads.

3 **TRIM THE ENDS.** Cut to final length after the ledge has been assembled. Sand the freshly cut ends before painting.

Easy as 1, 2, 3!

You need only three parts, so these ledges are fast and easy to build. Even a beginner can do them—no experience needed.

- You need basic tools. If you don't have a brad nailer or miter saw, you can assemble the ledges using a hammer and nails, then cut each with a handsaw.
- Each ledge is made from just three parts. All you have to do is glue and tack them together.

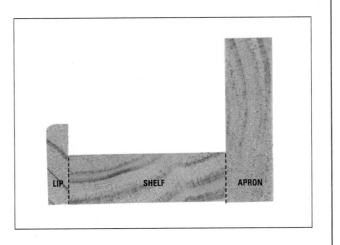

4 DRAW A GUIDELINE. Scribe a line on the back of the apron 3/4 in. down from the top.

3/4"

5 DRILL PILOT HOLES. Mark for a screw hole 2 to 3 in. from each end. Then space holes evenly every 8 to 12 in. between them. Drill 1/8-in. holes.

6 SAND AND PAINT. Fill the brad holes with filler, sand them flush, and prime and paint the ledges. (Or use a combination primer/paint product.)

LEDGE LOCATION

MARK ON TAPE

7 MARK LEDGE LOCATIONS ON MASKING TAPE. Stick a vertical strip of masking tape to the wall to position one end of the ledges. Mark the top of each ledge on the tape, and use those marks to draw level lines on the wall for each ledge.

simple, elegant way to dress up screw heads. The heads will largely be hidden behind the pictures, but you can paint them to help them blend in better if you wish. You'll need 2-1/2-in. screws, about one for every 8 in. of shelf, plus a package of screw-in anchors that accept conventional threaded wood screws. (E-Z Ancor is one brand.) You can use other drywall anchors if you wish.

ASSEMBLY TAKES MINUTES

You'll glue the pieces together and then nail them with an 18-gauge brad nailer **(Photo 1)**. Fasten the apron to the shelf with 2-in. brads, and secure the 1/4-in. molding to the front with 1-in. brads. If you don't have a brad nailer, you can certainly do it the old–fashioned way with finish nails and a hammer. It's smart to assemble all three parts first and then cut the ends so they are flush. If you don't have a miter saw, make the cuts with a handsaw.

FINISH AFTER ASSEMBLY

Whether you paint the ledges or stain and varnish for a natural wood finish, do it after the shelves are built but before they get put on the wall. If you choose to paint, start with a coat of primer. The best topcoat is acrylic latex enamel. It's easy to apply, tougher than ordinary latex paint to resist scratches and wear, and easier to dust.

HANG THE LEDGES

Use screws with finish washers along with drywall anchors to hang the ledges—no glue. That way, if you want to remove them later for repainting, you won't have to patch the walls. The screws will be mostly hidden by pictures, but if you want, you can paint them after installation. Some screws will fall over studs. You'll find the studs when you drill pilot holes with a Phillips screwdriver. You can skip the anchors and drive those screws directly into the studs.

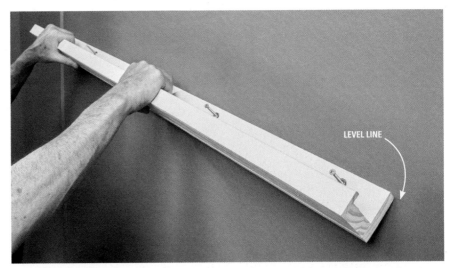

8 MARK THE ANCHOR HOLES. Start screws so the tips project through the back of the apron about 1/4 in. Hold the top of the apron even with the level line and push the screw tips into the drywall to mark the wall for anchors. (Have a buddy help with longer ledges.)

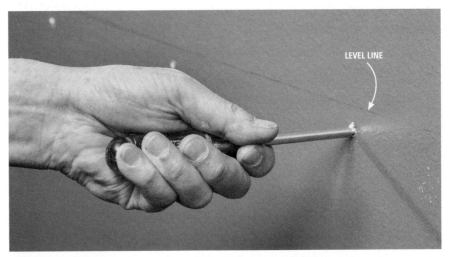

9 DRILL ANCHOR HOLES. Twist and drive a Phillips screwdriver through the marks. Draw a circle around any holes that have studs behind them.

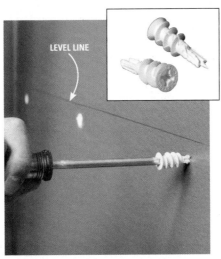

10 SINK THE DRYWALL ANCHORS. Screw a drywall anchor into each hole, except the ones over studs.

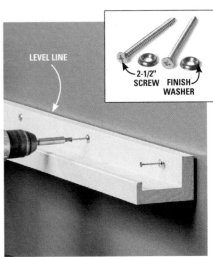

11 SCREW THE LEDGES TO THE WALL. Screw each shelf to the anchors or into the studs.

Repainting chipped, flaking or dirty moldings can turn a dull room into your favorite place in the house.

Trim painting tips

For a crisp, professional-looking job, you have to go beyond just brushing on a coat of paint.

From prep work to the final coat, here are tips for making your painted woodwork look like new.

A. CAREFUL SANDING IS THE KEY TO A PERFECT JOB

If your woodwork is smooth, just give it a once-over with 120-grit sandpaper. But if your trim is in rough shape like the trim shown here, start with 80-grit sandpaper. Switch to 100-grit for smoothing and blending in the areas with layered paint. Finally, go over all the wood with 120-grit. Buy sandpaper labeled "no-load." No-load sandpaper won't clog as easily and is better for sanding painted surfaces.

B. FILL HOLES AND DENTS

To repair large dents or gouges on edges that are vulnerable to abuse, use hardening-type two-part wood filler (Minwax High Performance Wood Filler is one brand). Fill any smaller dents and holes with spackling compound. Since spackling compound shrinks as it dries, you'll have to apply a second (and possibly a third) coat after the previous coat dries.

Shine a strong light across the woodwork to highlight depressions and to ensure that you don't miss any spots as you're applying the filler. Let the filler dry and sand it smooth.

C. CAULK FOR A SEAMLESS LOOK

Here's a step that many beginners don't know about but pros swear by. Caulk every crack or gap, no matter how small. Use latex caulk or a paintable latex/silicone blend. The key is to cut the caulk tube tip very carefully to create a tiny, 1/16-in.-diameter hole. Fill all the small cracks first. Then, if you have wider cracks to fill, recut the caulk tube tip to make a larger hole. Move the caulk gun swiftly along the cracks to avoid an excess buildup of caulk. If necessary, smooth the caulk with your fingertip. Keep a damp rag in your pocket to clean caulk from your finger and to keep the tip of the caulk tube clean. If caulk piles up in the corners, remove the excess with a flexible putty knife.

D. SPOT-PRIME TO AVOID BLOTCHES

Brush a stain-blocking primer over the areas that you've patched or filled, and over areas where you've sanded down to bare wood. If you have a lot of patches and bare spots, it'll be faster and easier to just prime the entire surface. Also seal discolored areas or marks left by crayons, pens or markers to prevent them from bleeding through the finish coat of paint.

E. ADD AN EXTENDER TO LATEX PAINT

Most pros prefer to use oil-based paint on trim for two reasons: Oil-based paint doesn't dry as fast as water-based paint, leaving more time to brush, and oil-based paint levels out better than most water-based paints, leaving a

A.

NO-LOAD SANDPAPER

B.

SPACKLING COMPOUND

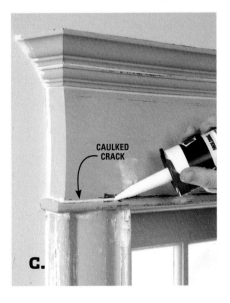

C.

CAULKED CRACK

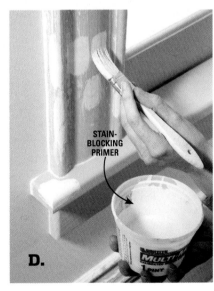

D.

STAIN-BLOCKING PRIMER

smoother surface with few visible brush marks. But because water-based paint is more environmentally friendly, less stinky and easier to clean up, it is a better choice for DIYers.

You can make water-based paint perform more like oil paint by adding latex paint conditioner. Floetrol is one brand. Conditioners, also called extenders, make paint flow better and slow down the drying time, allowing you more time to spread the paint without leaving brush marks. Check with the manufacturer of the paint you're using to see if it recommends a particular brand of conditioner.

LATEX PAINT CONDITIONER

E.

F. PAINT FROM A SEPARATE PAIL

Pour paint about 1-1/2 in. deep into a separate pail. A metal painter's pail (shown here), a specialty pail called a Handy Paint Pail or even an empty 5-quart ice cream pail would work great. Placing a small amount of paint in a pail allows you to easily load the bristles of the brush by dipping them about 1 in. into the paint.

Slap the brush gently against each side of the pail to remove excess paint. This method of brush loading is best for laying on paint because it keeps the bristles fully loaded with paint. To use the brush for cutting-in, follow up by wiping each side of the brush gently on the rim to remove a little bit more of the paint.

F.

G. CUT IN EDGES BEFORE YOU FILL THE CENTER

Cutting-in is a skill that takes practice to master, but it's worth the effort. To cut in, first load the brush. Then wipe most of the excess paint off by gently scraping the bristles on the edge of the can. Start by pulling the brush along the edge, but keep the bristles about 1/4 in. away from the wall or ceiling to deposit some paint on the wood. Now return with another brushstroke, this time a little closer. Sneaking up to the

G.

LAYING-OFF STROKE

H.

line like this is easier than trying to get it perfect on the first try. At the end of the stroke, arc the brush away from the cut-in line. Cut in a few feet and then fill the middle using the lay-on, lay-off technique we show in the next section.

H. LAY ON, LAY OFF

The biggest mistake beginners make is to work the paint too long after it's applied. Remember, the paint starts to dry as soon as you put it on, and you have to smooth it out before it dries or you'll end up with brushstrokes or worse. So here's the tip: Load your brush, then quickly unload on the surface with a few back-and-forth brushstrokes. This is called "laying on" the paint. Repeat this until you have covered a few feet of trim with paint.

Now, without reloading the brush, drag the tips of the bristles over the wet paint in one long stroke to "lay off" the paint. Start in the unpainted area and drag into the previously painted trim. Sweep your brush up off the surface at the end of each stroke. Areas wider than your brush will require several parallel laying-off strokes to finish. When you're done laying off a section, move on and repeat the process, always working quickly to avoid brushing over partially dried paint. Try to complete any shorter pieces of the trim with a continuous laying-off brushstroke.

What not to do...

DON'T

BRUSH MARK

DON'T START A BRUSHSTROKE ON ALREADY-SMOOTHED PAINT. Setting the paintbrush on an area that has already been smoothed out with laying-off strokes will leave an unsightly mark. Try to start laying-off strokes at the end of a trim piece or board, or in an unpainted area. Brush toward the finished area. Then sweep the brush up and off, like an airplane taking off from a runway, to avoid leaving a mark.

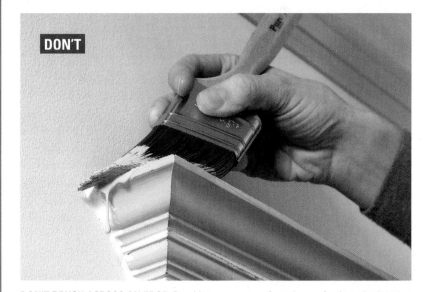

DON'T

DON'T BRUSH ACROSS AN EDGE. Brushing across an edge wipes paint from the bristles and creates a heavy buildup of paint that will run or drip. Avoid this by brushing toward edges whenever possible. If you must start a brushstroke at an edge, align the bristles carefully as if you are cutting-in, instead of wiping them against the edge. If you accidentally get a buildup of paint that could cause a run, spread it out right away with a dry paintbrush or wipe it off with a damp rag or your finger.

STIFF
METAL ARM

GRIPPING TEETH

Learn the right way to roll with these simple steps.

Paint a room in a day

Let's be clear—this isn't a fancy method. But it'll get the job done quickly, easily and correctly.

Most people have used paint rollers before, with varying degrees of success. Maybe you just plunged right in and started rolling, developing your own technique as you went. Or maybe you read the instructions telling you to apply the paint in some pattern, usually a "W," before rolling it out. Here you'll learn a slightly different approach: how to simply and quickly spread a smooth, even coat of latex paint on the wall. It's not fancy, but it gets the job done in record time and eliminates common problems like light areas, roller marks and built-up ridges. This technique definitely guarantees pro-quality results.

However, even the best technique won't work with poor-quality equipment. Don't waste your money on those all-in-one throwaway roller setups when you can buy a pro setup that will last a lifetime for less than $30. Start with a good roller frame. Buy one that is sturdy and designed to keep the roller cover from slipping off while you paint.

To extend your reach and give you better control, screw a 48-in. wood handle onto the end of the roller. You could also use a threaded broom handle.

You will need a container for the paint. While most homeowners use paint trays, you'll rarely see a pro using one. That's because a 5-gallon bucket with a special bucket screen hung over the edge works a lot better.

Here are a few of the advantages of a bucket and screen over a roller pan:

WHAT IT TAKES		
TIME 1 day	**COST** $50-$100	**SKILL LEVEL** Beginner
TOOLS Roller frame, 48-in wood handle, 5-gallon bucket, bucket screen, drop clothes, putty knife		

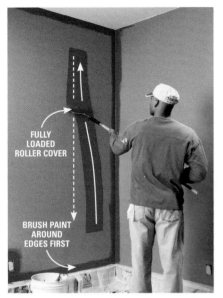

1 Lay the paint on the wall with sweeping strokes. Start a foot from the bottom and 6 in. from the corner and roll upward at a slight angle using light pressure. Stop a few inches from the ceiling. Now roll up and down, back toward the corner to quickly spread the paint. You can leave paint buildup and roller marks at this step. Don't worry about a perfect job yet.

2 Reload the roller and repeat the process in the adjacent space, working back toward the painted area.

3 Roll back over the area you've covered to smooth and blend the paint. Don't reload the roller with paint. Use very light pressure. Roll up and down, from floor to ceiling, and move over about three-quarters of a roller width each time so you're always overlapping the previous stroke. When you reach the corner, roll as close as you can to the adjacent wall without touching it.

- It's easy to move the bucket without dealing with spills.
- The bucket holds more paint. You won't have to frequently refill a pan.
- You're less likely to trip over or step in a bucket of paint.
- It is quicker and easier to load the roller cover with paint from a bucket.
- It's easy to cover a bucket with a damp cloth to prevent the paint from drying out while you take a lunch break.
- Use an old drywall compound bucket or buy a clean new bucket for about $5. Add a $4 bucket screen and you're ready to go.

TAKE A WOOL-BLEND ROLLER COVER FOR A SPIN

The most important part of your paint-rolling setup is the roller cover, also known as a sleeve. It's tempting to buy the cheapest cover available and throw it away when you're done. But you won't mind the few extra minutes of cleanup time once you experience the

difference a good roller cover makes. Cheap roller covers don't hold enough paint to do a good job. It'll take you four times as long to paint a room. And you'll likely end up with an inconsistent layer of paint, lap marks and built-up ridges of paint.

Instead, buy a 1/2-in. nap, wool-blend roller cover and give it a try ($10). (A good one has a combination of polyester for ease of use and wool for maximum paint capacity.) With proper care, this may be the last roller cover you'll ever buy.

Wool covers have a few drawbacks, though. They tend to shed fibers when they're first used. To minimize shedding, wrap the new roller cover with masking tape and peel it off to remove loose fibers. Repeat this a few times. Wool covers also tend to become matted down if you apply too much pressure while painting. Rolling demands a light touch. No matter what roller cover you're using, always let the paint do the work. Keep the roller cover loaded with paint and use

PRO TIP

Let's roll!

Load the roller cover by dipping it into the paint about 1/2 in. and then rolling it against the screen. Filling a dry roller cover with paint will require five or six repetitions. After that, two or three dips are all you need. Leave the roller almost dripping with paint.

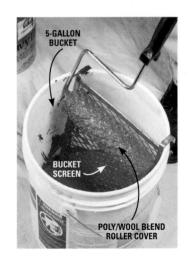

5-GALLON BUCKET

BUCKET SCREEN

POLY/WOOL BLEND ROLLER COVER

only enough pressure to release and spread the paint. Pushing on the roller to squeeze out the last drop will only cause problems.

TIPS FOR A PERFECT PAINT JOB

■ Get as close as you can. Since rollers can't get tight to edges, the first painting step is to brush along the ceiling and moldings and inside corners. This cutting-in process leaves brush marks that won't match the roller texture on the rest of the wall. For the best-looking job, you'll want to cover as many brush marks as possible with the roller. Do this

Paint neatly along textured ceilings

It's almost impossible to paint right next to rough-textured ceilings (cutting in) without getting paint on the ceiling. Taping off the ceiling doesn't work either. The solution? Knock off the texture at the edge with a putty knife. Hold the knife at a 45-degree angle to the wall and run the blade along the edge of the ceiling. The blade scrapes away the texture and leaves a small groove in the ceiling. Clean out the groove with a duster or a dry paintbrush. Now when you cut in along the top of the wall, the paintbrush bristles will slide into the groove, giving you a crisp paint line without getting paint on the ceiling.

GROOVE

4 Smooth the paint along the ceiling using a long horizontal stroke without reloading the roller with paint.

5 Lay paint on wall areas above and below windows and doors with a long horizontal stroke. Then smooth it off with short vertical strokes so the texture will match the rest of the wall.

Avoid fat edges and roller marks

Ridges of paint left by the edge of the roller, or "fat edges," are a common problem. And if left to dry, they can be difficult to get rid of without heavy sanding or patching. Here are a few ways to avoid the problem:

- Don't submerge the roller in the paint to load it. Paint can seep inside the cover and leak out while you're rolling. Try to dip only the nap. Then spin it against the screen and dip again until it's loaded with paint.
- Don't press too hard when smoothing out the paint.
- Never start against an edge, like a corner or molding, with a full roller of paint. You'll leave a heavy buildup of paint that can't be spread out. Starting about 6 in. from the edge, unload the paint from the roller. Then work back toward the edge.
- Unload excess paint from the open end of the roller before you roll back over the wall to smooth it out. Do this by tilting the roller and applying a little extra pressure to the open side of the roller while rolling it up and down in the area you've just painted.

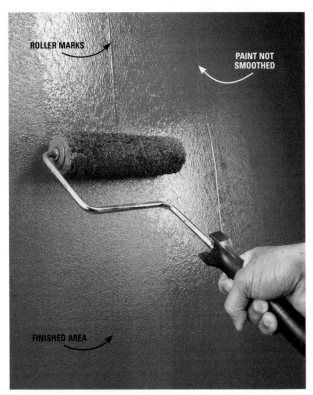

ROLLER MARKS

PAINT NOT SMOOTHED

FINISHED AREA

Smooth walls by rolling back over the wet paint without reloading the roller. Roll lightly without pressing.

by carefully rolling up close to inside corners, moldings and the ceiling. Face the open end of the roller toward the edge and remember not to use a roller that's fully loaded with paint. With practice, you'll be able to get within an inch of the ceiling rolling vertically and avoid crawling up on a ladder to paint horizontally, as shown in **Photo 4**.

- Keep a wet edge. Keeping a wet edge is crucial to all top-quality finish jobs, whether you're enameling a door, finishing furniture or rolling paint on a wall. The idea is to plan the sequence of work and work fast enough so that you're always lapping newly applied paint onto paint that's still wet. If you stop for a break in the middle of a wall, for example, and then start painting after this section has dried, you'll likely see a lap mark where the two areas join. The rolling technique shown here avoids this problem by allowing you

to quickly cover a large area with paint and then return to smooth it.

- Lay it on, smooth it off. The biggest mistake most beginning painters make, whether they're brushing or rolling, is taking too long to apply the paint. **Photo 1** shows how to lay on the paint. Then quickly spread it out and repeat the laying-on process again **(Photo 2)**. This will work only with a good-quality roller cover that holds a lot of paint. Until you are comfortable with the technique and get a feel for how quickly the paint is drying, cover only about 3 or 4 ft. of wall before smoothing off the whole area **(Photo 3)**. If you find the paint is drying slowly, you can cover an entire wall before smoothing it off.
- Pick out the lumps before they dry. It's inevitable that you'll end up with an occasional lump in your paint. Keep the roller cover away from the floor where it might pick up bits of debris that are later spread against the

wall. Drying bits of paint from the edge of the bucket or bucket screen can also cause this problem. Cover the bucket with a damp cloth when you're not using it. If partially dried paint is sloughing off the screen, take it out and clean it. Keep a wet rag in your pocket and pick lumps off the wall as you go. Strain used paint through a mesh paint strainer to remove lumps. Five-gallon size strainers are available at paint stores.

- Scrape off any excess paint from the roller before you wash it. Use your putty knife or, better yet, a special roller-scraping tool with a semicircular cutout in the blade. Then rinse the roller cover until the water runs clear. A roller and paint brush spinning tool, available at most hardware and paint stores, simplifies the cleaning task. Just slip the roller cover onto the spinner and then repeatedly wet and spin out the roller until it's clean.

Great Goofs®

Laughs and lessons from our readers

NOT A FAN OF BIG FANS

When the ceiling fan in our kitchen started making a loud noise, we decided to replace it. We bought a new one with larger blades for more air circulation. My husband and I worked on the installation together (that's usually a challenge in itself!). We turned the fan on, then stood back and admired how quiet it was.

A couple of days later, I was working in the kitchen with the fan on and opened an upper cupboard door. I felt and heard a loud collision, which scared the daylights out of me. You guessed it—the longer fan blades whacked the edge of the door. Now we keep a small rubber band on the handle of that cupboard to remind us not to open it when the fan is on.

PAM MARTIN

SCREW LOOSE

To free up floor space in my kid's bedroom, I built a bed box to hold the mattress. Then I hung one side of the box from the ceiling joists with chains and screwed the other side to the wall studs.

To convince my skeptical family that the box was safely hung, I set down my tools, hopped up on it and started jumping around. As my family stood back and watched, the box pulled loose from the wall, dropping straight down and dumping me out onto the floor. The ceiling chains were secure enough, but the drywall screws in the wall pulled right out. I patched the wall and reinstalled the box with longer screws, but my family never lets me forget how I got thrown out of the bed.

GARY HAVENS

SHORT-CIRCUIT SHORTCUT

When Mike, a carpenter buddy of mine, encounters a hump in a wall caused by a bowed stud, he cuts through the drywall and into the stud with a long reciprocating saw blade. The cut relieves the stress and the stud straightens itself. Brilliant! I had that problem in my downstairs bedroom.

I stuck the saw blade into the drywall and started cutting. All of a sudden, the room went black. The bad stud was the one with an electrical cable stapled to the side to feed the light; I had cut through the cable and blown the circuit breaker. There was a lot of electrical work, drywall patching and painting ahead of me.

MILO AMUNDSEN

THE NOSE KNEW

Recently, I bought speakers to hang from the ceiling of our family room. I tapped on the ceiling to locate the joists and then drilled small holes to make sure I'd found solid backing. Confident, I screwed the brackets to the ceiling and mounted the speakers. A few days later, we smelled something awful. We suspected our 2-year-old, who was in the midst of potty training. He denied any wrongdoing, so I followed my nose and found a stain on the speaker bracket. The "solid backing" I'd screwed the bracket into was the toilet drainpipe instead of the ceiling joist! Every time we flushed we got a small leak. I tore out the ceiling and replaced the drainpipe while offering my son a sincere and heartfelt apology.

JOEY SHEAT

CHAPTER **SEVEN**

FURNITURE & SHELVING

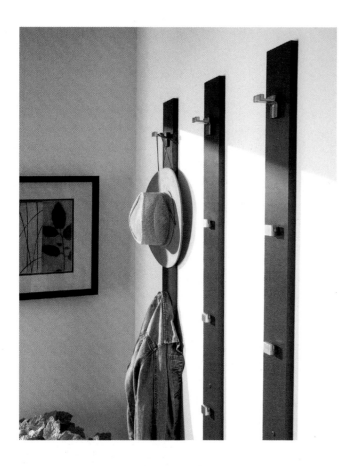

Coat & hat rack

Putting together this attractive entryway feature is as easy as painting a couple of boards and then screwing them to the wall.

Organize your entryway or mudroom with this handsome, simple coat and hat rack. Just cut the boards to fit your space, paint them, outfit them with different kinds of hooks to suit your needs and then screw them to the wall. Shown are 6-ft.-long 1x4s, but use whatever length works for you and the space available. Shown is poplar, which is the best choice if you want a painted finish. If you're after a natural wood look, choose any species you want.

Finish the boards first and then attach your hooks. Shown here are drawer pulls down the middle and a robe hook near the top to hold backpacks and larger items. You'll find hooks in a tremendous range of styles, colors and prices at hardware stores and online retailers.

Attach the boards to studs or to the drywall with screw-in drywall anchors. Drive three screws in each board: one at the top, one in the middle and one at the bottom.

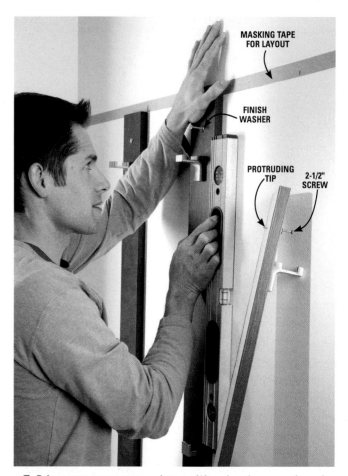

MASKING TAPE FOR LAYOUT

FINISH WASHER

PROTRUDING TIP

2-1/2" SCREW

1 Drive your screws partway into each board so the screw tips poke out the back. Place the boards where you want them, and press the screws hard to mark the spots for your drywall anchors.

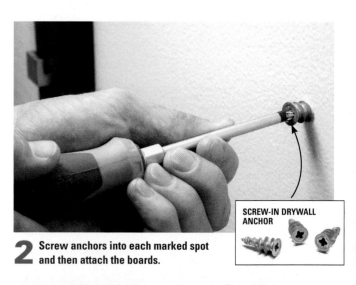

SCREW-IN DRYWALL ANCHOR

2 Screw anchors into each marked spot and then attach the boards.

WHAT IT TAKES		
TIME 2 hrs.	**COST** Under $50	**SKILL LEVEL** Beginner

TOOLS
Screwdriver

Light-duty table

Sewing, painting, school projects—this table lets you do it all (and it doesn't take long to build).

If you ever need a light-duty work surface anywhere in the house, this one's for you. Get to the home center and buy a hollow-core door, four toilet flanges, a 10-ft. length of 3-in. PVC pipe, 16 No. 10 x 1-1/4-in.-long screws, and a tube of construction adhesive. Inside of a half hour, you'll have the flanges glued and screwed to the door and you'll be ready to slip in the 30-in.-long PVC legs.

WHAT IT TAKES		
TIME 30 minutes	**COST** Under $50	**SKILL LEVEL** Beginner
TOOLS Drill/driver, caulk gun		

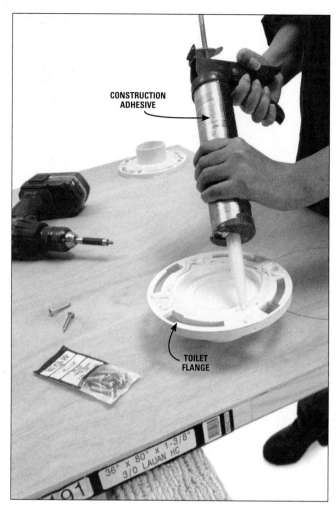

CONSTRUCTION ADHESIVE

TOILET FLANGE

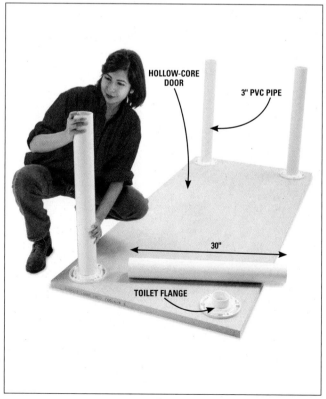

HOLLOW-CORE DOOR

3" PVC PIPE

30"

TOILET FLANGE

ABOVE: These shelves are more than just functional; they're a wonderful feature for a living or family room. LEFT: You can even stick them in your basement to hold files.

Multi-purpose shelves

Don't settle for a shelving unit from a huge store. Make this one yourself, and customize it to hold everything you need.

WHAT IT TAKES		
TIME 4 hrs	**COST** $50 - $100	**SKILL LEVEL** Beginner
TOOLS Tablesaw, miter saw, drill/driver		

Customizing your shelves

You can modify these super sturdy storage shelves and create a stylish storage center like the one pictured here and at the top of p. 226. Simply add one shelf by changing the 22-1/2-in. measurements to 14 in. and the 4-in. measurement to 6 in. Then apply the finish of your choice.

Store-bought shelving units are either hard to assemble, flimsy or awfully expensive. These shelves are a better solution. They are strong, easy to build and budget-friendly. The sturdy shelf unit shown on the bottom of p. 226 is sized to hold standard records and storage boxes. If you want deeper storage, build the shelves 24 in. deep and buy 24-in.-deep boxes. If you prefer plastic storage bins, measure the size of the containers and modify the shelf and upright spacing to fit.

Refer to the dimensions in **Figure A** to mark the location of the horizontal 2x2s on the backs of four 2x4s. Also mark the positions of the 2x4 uprights on the 2x2s. Then simply line up the marks and screw the 2x2s to the 2x4s with pairs of 2-1/2-in. wood screws. Be sure to keep the 2x2s and 2x4s at right angles. Rip a 4 x 8-ft. sheet of 1/2-in. MDF, plywood or OSB into 16-in.-wide strips and screw the strips to the 2x2s to connect the two frames and form the shelving unit.

FIGURE A. MULITPURPOSE SHELVES

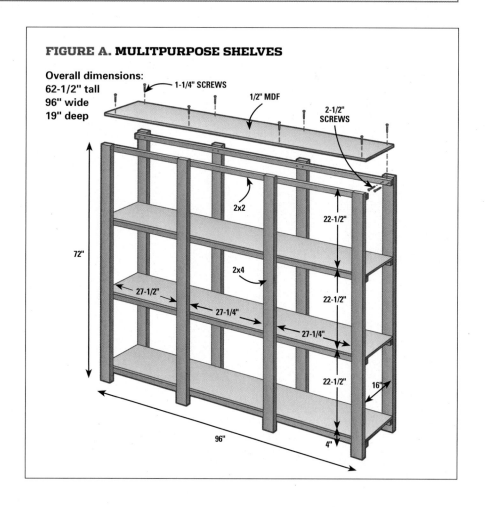

Overall dimensions:
62-1/2" tall
96" wide
19" deep

1-1/4" SCREWS
1/2" MDF
2-1/2" SCREWS
2x2
2x4
72"
27-1/2"
27-1/4"
27-1/4"
22-1/2"
22-1/2"
22-1/2"
16"
4"
96"

Stone-top table

Tough enough for outdoors. Attractive enough for indoors.

WHAT IT TAKES

TIME	COST	SKILL LEVEL
2 hrs.	Under $50	Beginner

TOOLS
Miter saw, drill/driver

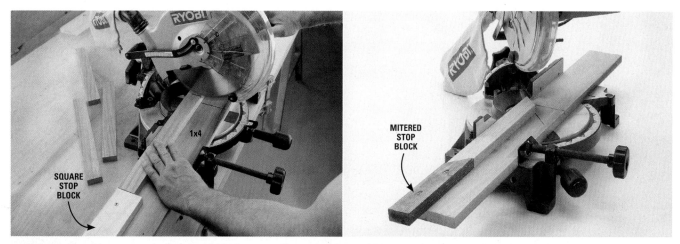

1 Make a jig with square and mitered stop blocks screwed to a straight 1x4. Slide the 1x4 to the right length for each piece and clamp it down. When you cut the miters, set the saw for 45-1/2 degrees. That way, the outside corners of the top—the only parts that show—will be tight even if the top isn't perfectly square. Sand all the oak pieces before beginning assembly.

The inspiration for this small end table came while browsing through a local tile store. The table top shown here is 16-in.-square copper slate—a perfect match for the oak base—but a variety of other stone tiles in the same price range are available.

To make this table, you'll need a power miter saw, a drill and your hand tools. The stone top doesn't need any cutting—just soften the sharp edges with 120-grit sandpaper. The table's base is made from standard dimension oak, available at home centers. And once you put together the cutting and assembly jigs shown in the photos, the table base almost builds itself.

Materials List

ITEM	QTY.
Wood	
2x2 x 3' oak	2
1x2 x 14' oak	1
Stone Tile	
16" x 16" x 1/2"	1
Hardware	
1-1/2" galvanized finishing nails	1 lb.
No. 8 x 1-5/8" galvanized screws	8
Nylon chair glides	4
Exterior wood glue	
Exterior construction adhesive	

Cutting List

KEY	PART	QTY.
A	2x2 x 16-3/4" (leg)	4
B	1x2 x 13-3/4" (shelf supports)	2
C	1x2 x 10-3/4" (shelf slats)	5
D	1x2 x 13-3/4" (miltered top support)	4

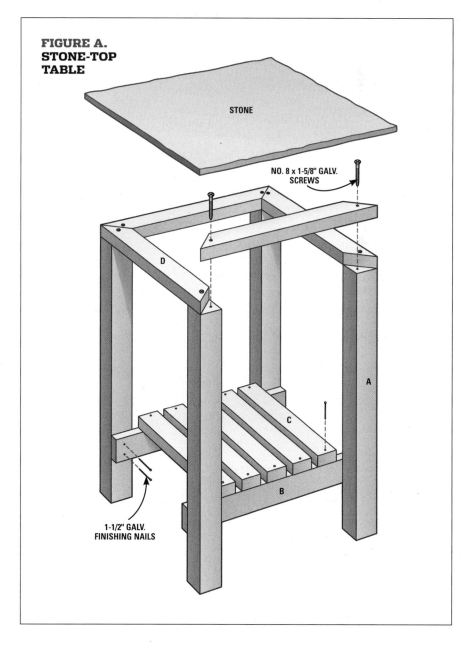

FIGURE A. STONE-TOP TABLE

STONE

NO. 8 x 1-5/8" GALV. SCREWS

D

A

C

B

1-1/2" GALV. FINISHING NAILS

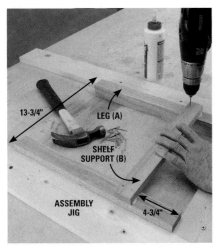

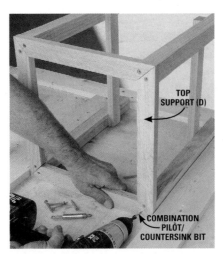

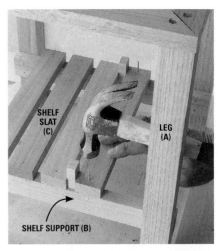

2 Set up a square assembly jig with 1x4s attached to your workbench. Use two shelf supports as spacers to ensure that the jig is the correct width. Set two table legs (A) in the jig and attach a shelf support (B) with glue and nails. Predrill with a 5/64-in. drill bit, or use one of the nails with the head clipped off as the drill bit.

3 Screw down the mitered top supports (D) with the table still in the jig, using glue and 1-5/8-in. galvanized screws. Predrill and countersink with a combination bit at a slight angle, toward the center of the leg.

4 Predrill and nail the shelf slats with the legs tight and square against the sides of the assembly jig. Attach the center slat first, centering it on the shelf support. Wipe off excess glue and set the remaining slats, using two 1/2-in. spacers. Set the nails, fill the holes, then sand.

5 Glue the stone top to the base. First, center the table and trace the top onto the tile. Lay a bead of construction adhesive within the outline, keeping glue away from the outer edge to avoid oozing. Press the table into the glue. Place a weight on the table for 24 hours until the glue sets. Leave excess glue until it's dry, and then peel it away. Finish the wood with exterior oil or varnish, and add a nylon chair glide on the bottom of each leg.

Magnetic office supplies holder

Say goodbye to the junk drawer.

If you have an hour to spare, use it to organize all those paper clips, rubber bands and pushpins. All it takes is a magnetic knife/tool holder strip, small jars with lids and a few fender washers. (The strips are available at bath stores, hardware stores, home centers and online retailers.) You don't even need the fender washers if you buy jars with steel lids that will stick to the magnet on their own.

Clamp the magnetic strips to the underside of a shelf or cabinet. Drill pilot holes and screw the strip into place **(Photo 1)**. If the jars have steel lids, fill them with office supplies and stick them up on the magnetic strip. If the jar lids are aluminum or plastic, use cyanoacrylate glue (Super Glue is one brand) to attach a fender washer to the top of each lid **(Photo 2)**. After they dry, fill the jars and stick them up on the magnet.

1 Clamp the magnetic strip in place, drill pilot holes and drive in the screws that came with the strip.

FENDER WASHER

2 Glue fender washers to plastic or aluminum jar lids so they'll stick to the strip. Skip this step if your jars have steel lids.

WHAT IT TAKES		
TIME	**COST**	**SKILL LEVEL**
1 hour	Under $50	Beginner
TOOLS		
Drill, cyanoacrylate glue		

PRO TIP

Protect your electronics
It's important to keep computer components at least 6 in. away from magnets.

WHAT IT TAKES		
TIME 4-6 hrs.	**COST** $50 - $100	**SKILL LEVEL** Intermediate
TOOLS Tablesaw, miter saw, drill/driver, doweling jig, basic hand tools		

This nifty stand is a perfect place to keep your magazines organized, and off your countertops and floors.

Magazine stand

Keep your reading material looking lovely with this charming hardwood stand.

The magazine stand shown is made from Merbau, a tropical hardwood. You can substitute any hardwood. Aluminum tube was used to join the frame, and aluminum flat bars were used to hang the magazines. Be sure to get your wood before starting, and use 5/16-in. dowels to join the frame, with 3/8-in. dowels for a tight fit with the tubes.

FIGURE A. MAGAZINE STAND

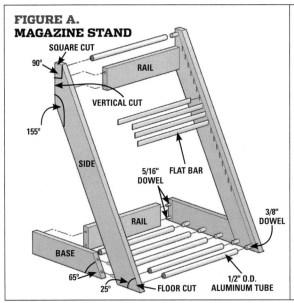

SQUARE CUT
90°
RAIL
VERTICAL CUT
155°
SIDE
5/16" DOWEL
FLAT BAR
RAIL
3/8" DOWEL
BASE
65°
25°
FLOOR CUT
1/2" O.D. ALUMINUM TUBE

FIGURE B. SIDE DETAIL

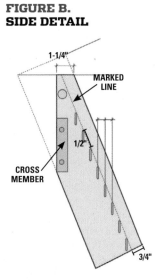

1-1/4"
MARKED LINE
1/2"
CROSS MEMBER
3/4"

FIGURE C. BASE DETAIL

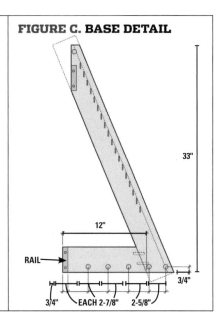

33"
12"
RAIL
3/4"
3/4"   EACH 2-7/8"   2-5/8"

Cutting List

KEY	PART	QTY.
Hardwood		
A	39-1/4" x 3-1/2" x 3/4" (side)	2
B	12" x 3-1/2" x 3/4" (base)	2
C	12-1/4" x 3-1/2" x 3/4" (rail)	2
Aluminum		
D	12-3/4" x 3/4" x 1/8" (flat bars)	18
E	12-1/4" x 1/2" (tube)	6

1 CUT SIDE AND BASE ENDS. Mark a 65-degree angle on the ends of the bases. On the sides, mark 25 degrees as the floor cut and 155 degrees as the vertical wall cut at the top (see Figure A for reference), then cut with a sliding compound miter saw. Square-cut the top of the sides 1-1/4 in. wide.

2 MARK THE SLOT SETBACK. Set a marking gauge to 3/4 in. to scribe a setback line down the long inside front edges of the sides. Use this line as a guide for the beginning of each slot that will house an aluminum flat bar.

3/4"
SETBACK LINE
MARKING GAUGE

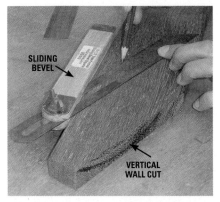

3 MARK THE SLOT POSITIONS. Set a sliding bevel to match the 155-degree cut at the top. Beginning 1-1/2 in. from the top, mark 3/4-in.-long lines from the setback line. Measure down 1/2 in. to make the next mark, marking 18 slots in each side.

SLIDING BEVEL
VERTICAL WALL CUT

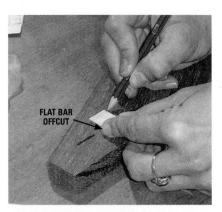

4 MARK SLOTS IN THE SIDES. Cut a small piece of aluminum flat bar offcut as a template to mark the slot shapes on the sides, centering it on the vertical lines, against the setback line, to trace the shape (see Figure B for reference).

FLAT BAR OFFCUT

5 ROUT THE SLOTS. Clamp the sides to a workbench and clamp a guide board set at the same angle as the slots as a jig to guide the router. Use a 1/8-in. bit to make 1/8-in.-wide x 1/2-in.-deep slots. TIP: Reverse the jig to make cuts on the opposite side piece.

6 CUT THE ALUMINUM. Use a miter saw to cut each aluminum tube and flat bar, lightly sanding the ends of each piece to remove the burrs.

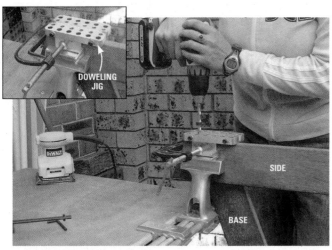

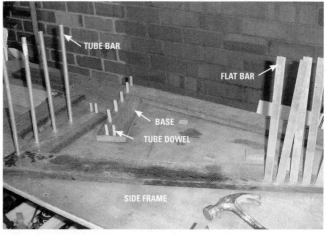

7 DRILL DOWEL HOLES. Use a drill with a 5/16-in. bit and a doweling jig to make dowel holes in the front end of the base and back edge of the side. Drill holes in rails, bases and sides, drilling five holes for tube dowels on the base, 3/4 in. from the edge (see Figure C).

8 ASSEMBLE ONE SIDE FRAME. Secure the base to the side using glue and dowels. Secure the rails to the side frame using glue and dowels, then glue in the tube dowels, tapping the tubes over the dowels and inserting flat bars into the slots.

PRO TIP

Finishing

Lightly sand and round over edges with 180-grit sandpaper. Wipe clean. Finish with carnauba wax or a clear polyurethane to bring out the natural wood color and grain.

9 ASSEMBLE THE SIDES. Assemble the remaining side and base, inserting the tube dowel with glue added to the dowel holes. Position this side frame over the assembled frame and slot together, clamping until dry.

Knock-apart table

This table is perfect for gatherings and for the great outdoors; it's easy to set up and take down.

This table is made from one full sheet of 5/8-in. plywood for the interlocking base stand and one sheet of 3/4-in. plywood for the work surface and shelves. You'll also need four 10-ft. lengths of 1x3 pine for the edge banding and cleats.

Cut two 30-in.-high by 48-in.-long pieces from the 5/8-in. plywood for the base pieces. Then cut a slightly oversize 5/8-in.-wide slot in the bottom half of one base and in the top half of the other. Make both slots about 15-1/2 in. long. Assemble the base and position the top so the corners are aligned with the legs. Screw loose-fitting 12-in.-long 1x3s along each side of each leg to hold everything stable.

The table is much more stable if you use the 3/4-in. waste from the top to make triangular braces (which also act as shelves) with 20-in.-long sides. Using 1-1/4-in. drywall screws, attach 1x2s to the base about 12 in. up from the floor and screw the shelves down.

WHAT IT TAKES		
TIME 1/2 day	**COST** $50 - $100	**SKILL LEVEL** Beginner-Intermediate
TOOLS Tablesaw or circular saw, drill/driver		

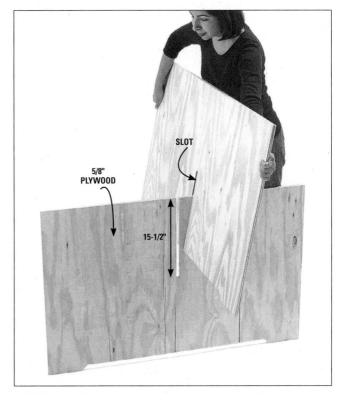

1 Using a tablesaw or circular saw, cut the legs to size, then cut a slot to the mid-point centered on each leg.

2 Cut the top to size and apply the edge banding. Set the top on the base and attach the stabilizer boards to it's underside on both sides of each leg.

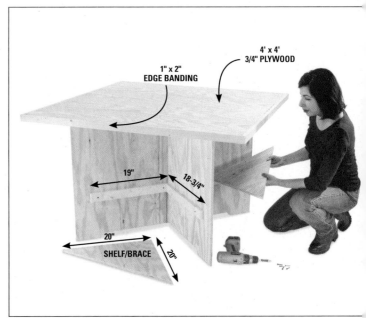

3 Screw shelf supports to the legs. Cut and install the triangular shelves using screws.

Whether you're a veteran woodworker or a newbie in the world of DIY, everyone can appreciate a well-made bookcase.

Super simple bookcase

This bookcase is a true classic that looks amazing in any room and will last for decades to come.

There are few pieces of furniture as timeless as the bookcase. Like the literature sitting on them, these shelves will stand proud from year to year and even decade to decade, if they are made right. You can build this bookcase in your garage with nothing more than a table saw, a drill and a pocket hole jig. If you don't own a pocket hole jig, you owe it to yourself to buy one. Pocket screws aren't as strong as most other types of joinery, but they are plenty strong for this bookcase, and you can't beat their speed and simplicity. You'll agree, especially when you hear that $40 can buy a complete pocket hole system. For tips on using pocket screws, go to familyhandyman.com and search for "pocket screws." You'll also need at least four pipe clamps for this project, which will cost about $60 altogether.

WOOD SELECTION MATTERS

At the home center, take your time picking through the oak boards. You want straight and flat boards, of course, but also look closely at grain pattern. Novice woodworkers usually skip this tedious process, but they shouldn't. It has a big impact on the final look of the project.

For the legs, examine the end grain and choose boards with grain running diagonally across the ends **(see Photo 4)**. This "rift sawn" wood has straight grain on both the face and the edge of the board. ("Plain sawn" boards typically have wilder grain on the face.) Straight grain will give the legs a look that suits the Stickley style. Also, glue joints disappear in straight grain wood, so the legs—which are made from sandwiched

WHAT IT TAKES		
TIME 2-3 days	**COST** $100-$250	**SKILL LEVEL** Beginner

TOOLS
Tablesaw, miter saw, drill/driver, pocket hole jig, clamps, jig saw, orbital sander

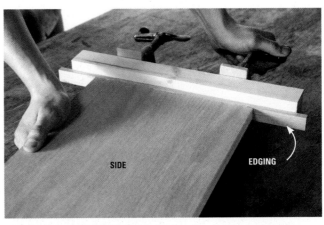

1 ADD EDGING TO THE SIDES. Cut the plywood box parts to size, then glue strips of wood to the bottom edges of the box sides. This edging keeps the plywood veneer from chipping. Trim off the excess edging with a handsaw and sand it flush with the plywood. Take care not to sand through the thin veneer.

SIDE *EDGING*

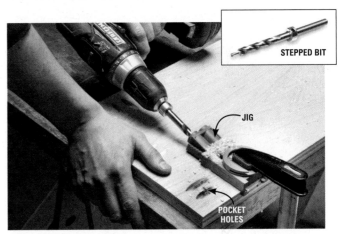

STEPPED BIT *JIG* *POCKET HOLES*

2 DRILL POCKET HOLES. Pocket hole jigs are super easy to use: Place the jig where you want the holes, clamp and drill. The stepped bit bores a pocket hole and a pilot hole at the same time. The holes on the ends are for attaching the top to the sides. The holes along the front and back are used to attach the box to the face frame.

3 ASSEMBLE THE BOX. Drive in the pocket screws with a drill. To avoid stripping the screws in plywood and softwoods, switch to a screwdriver for the final tightening. Long clamps make assembly easier, but they aren't absolutely necessary.

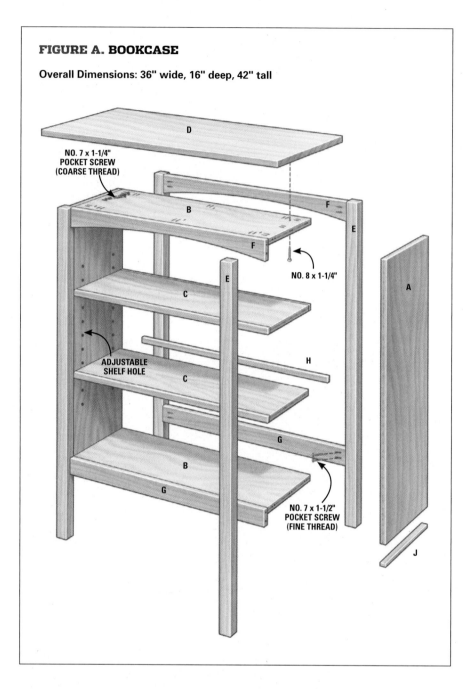

FIGURE A. BOOKCASE

Overall Dimensions: 36" wide, 16" deep, 42" tall

NO. 7 x 1-1/4"
POCKET SCREW
(COARSE THREAD)

D

F

B

F

E

A

NO. 8 x 1-1/4"

E

C

ADJUSTABLE
SHELF HOLE

C

H

G

B

G

NO. 7 x 1-1/2"
POCKET SCREW
(FINE THREAD)

J

Materials List

ITEM	QTY.
3/4" oak plywood	4' x 8'
1x4 solid oak	24'
1x10 solid oak	6'

Wood glue, pocket screws, stain, polyurethane,
adjustable shelf supports

Cutting List

KEY	PART	QTY.
3/4" Oak Plywood		
A	10-1/2" x 32" (sides)	2
B	10-1/2" x 29-3/4" (top and bottom)	2
C	9-1/2" x 29-5/8" (adjustable shelves)	2
3/4" Oak		
D	16" x 36" (top)	1
E	1-1/2" x 1-1/2" x 41-1/4" (legs; double up 3/4" stock)	4
F	2-1/2" x 29" (arched rails)	2
G	2" x 29" (bottom rails)	2
H	1/2" x 29-5/8" (edging for adjust. shelves)	4
J	3/8" x 10-1/2" (bottom edge sides)	2

the saw marks. If you are a beginning woodworker, congrats on taking on this project—but you might find curves are a little complicated and wind up slightly intimidated by the bookcase's arched upper rails (F). Never fear! Here's a neat trick for marking out a shallow arch **(Photo 5)**. Your first curved cut **(Photo 6)** might not be perfect, but a little sanding will smooth it out just fine **(Photo 7)**.

With the rails and legs complete, you are ready to drill pocket holes in the rails and assemble the face frames **(Photo 8)**. It's easy to make mistakes during face frame assembly, so—before driving any screws—clamp the frames together and then set them on the box to make sure everything is aligned correctly. Use similar caution when attaching the face frames to the box: Dry-fit the face frames **(Photo 9)** before you glue, and clamp them into place **(Photo 10)**.

TOP IT OFF AND FINISH UP

You might think that making the top (D) is a simple matter of edge-gluing two boards together **(Photo 11)**. That

boards—will look better. For that same reason, you should go ahead and choose boards with straight grain along the edges to form the bookcase top **(see Photo 11)**.

BUILD A BOX AND ADD FACE FRAMES

After cutting the plywood box parts to size **(see Cutting List)**, add the 3/8-in.-thick edging (J) to protect the bottoms of the cabinet sides (A; **Photo 1)**. Apply the same edging (H) to the plywood shelves (C). Then drill

the pocket holes in the box top and bottom (B; **Photo 2)**. After that, drill holes for adjustable shelf supports in the plywood sides and—finally— assemble the box **(Photo 3)**.

With the box assembled, turn your attention to building two identical face frames. (Since the bookcase has no back, it needs two face frames.) Unlike a standard face frame that has vertical stiles, our face frame has legs (E) made from two layers of 3/4-in.-thick boards. Glue up the leg blanks **(Photo 4)**, rip both blanks into two legs and sand out

4 GLUE UP THE LEG BANKS. Sandwich two 1x4s together and later cut the legs from this stock. Use scrap wood "cauls" to distribute clamping pressure evenly.

CAUL

LEG BLANK

5 MARK THE ARCHES. Make an "arch bow"—simply a 3/16-in.-thick strip of wood with slots cut into both ends. Hook a knotted string in one slot, tighten the string to bend the bow and tie off the other end.

ARCHED RAIL

6 CUT THE ARCHES. For a smooth cut, use a fine-tooth blade and move slowly, putting only light forward pressure on the saw. If your saw is variable speed, cut at full speed. If the saw has orbital action, switch it off.

7 SAND THE ARCHES. Smooth the arches with an orbital sander. Keep the sander moving so you don't sand too deep in one spot and create a wave in the curve.

8 ASSEMBLE THE FACE FRAME. Clamp the face frame together and drive in pocket screws. Pocket screws rarely strip out in hardwood, so you can skip the screwdriver and use only a drill.

9 DRY-FIT THE FACE FRAMES. Align the face frames, pocket-screw them to the box and check the fit. If your alignment is a bit off, you can drill new pocket holes and reattach the frames. If the fit is right, you're ready to remove the face frames and add glue.

FACE FRAME

is mostly true, but there are a few tricks to make it easier. First, always do a complete dry run by clamping up the boards without glue. That will alert you to any clamping or alignment problems before it's too late. Second, start with boards that are an inch or so longer than the final top. It's much easier to trim the boards later than to fuss with edge alignment during glue-up. Finally, to ensure that the tops of the boards meet flat and flush, use pocket screws on the underside of the top. A couple of pocket screws won't provide enough pressure to substitute for clamps, but they will hold the board flush while you crank on the clamps.

When the top is trimmed to size and sanded, drill elongated holes (**Photo 12**) and screw on the top (**Photo 13**). You might wonder why it pays to finish both sides of the top of the bookcase, rather than just the outside. There are two good answers. First, finishing is always easier when furniture is disassembled; second, and more important, both sides of the top need to be finished. Wood absorbs and releases moisture as humidity changes. Wood finishes slow that process, so wood with a finish on only one side will end up with differing moisture levels in the finished and unfinished sides. That will lead to warping and to a bookcase with a shortened life span down the road. And no one wants that!

Moral of the story, make sure you finish both sides of the top (and the rest of the bookcase) with a coat of Minwax PolyShades Oil-Based Mission Oak Satin interior stain or another comparable brand, followed by polyurethane.

That's it. Not bad for a weekend of woodworking. You now have a keepsake piece to pass down within your family—or just for you to use. With quality construction, you won't have to worry about this bookshelf's longevity. And it's fun to consider what your hard work might be worth to antiquers in about a hundred years!

10 GLUE ON THE FACE FRAMES. Apply a light bead of glue over the box edges and screw on the face frames as before. There are no screws fastening the legs to the box sides, so you'll need to clamp them.

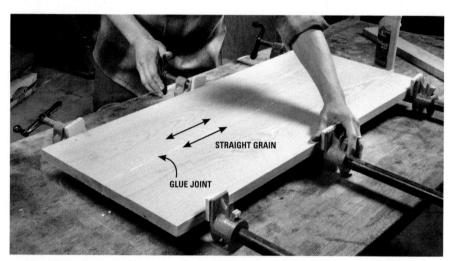

11 GLUE UP THE TOP. Edge-glue the boards together to form the top. Choose boards that have straight grain lines along one edge and place those edges together. A glue joint with straight grain on both sides is almost invisible.

STRAIGHT GRAIN

GLUE JOINT

12 DRILL SLOTTED SCREW HOLES. Drill screw holes in the shelf box to fasten the top. Rock the bit back and forth to bore enlongated slots that will allow the top to swell with changes in humidity.

13 SCREW ON THE TOP FROM BELOW. Drive the screws snug but not so tight that they won't allow for seasonal wood movement. Remove the top of the bookcase for sanding and finishing.

Adjustable spice shelf

Get spicy with this inexpensive shelf that's sure to become an indispensable part of your kitchen.

This in-cabinet spice shelf puts small containers at eye level and still leaves room in the cabinet for tall items. The materials are inexpensive, and building and installing it will take only an hour or so. You'll need a 4-ft. 1x3 for the top shelf and a 4-ft. 1x2 for the bottom ledger. You can find shelf pegs at home centers in two sizes, 1/4 in. and 3/16 in., so measure the holes in your cabinet before you shop. The secret is to assemble the shelf outside the cabinet and then set it on the shelf pegs.

Measure the sides and back of your cabinet, and then cut your shelf and ledger pieces. Subtract 1/8 in. from all sides so you can fit the unit into the cabinet. Attach the sides to the back of the bottom ledger and put two nails into each butt joint. Then nail the top shelf sides into place and pin the shelf back at the corners to hold it flush **(Photo 1)**. To install the shelf unit, carefully fit one end of the "U" into the cabinet, holding it higher at one end, and shimmy it down until it sits firmly on top of the shelf pegs **(Photo 2)**. Shift the pegs up or down to adjust the shelf height. Spray a quick coat of lacquer on the shelf before installing it to make it more scrubbable.

WHAT IT TAKES		
TIME 1 hour	**COST** Under $50	**SKILL LEVEL** Beginner
TOOLS Miter saw, drill/driver		

1 Nail the back and side ledgers together, then nail on the side shelves. Measure between the side shelves and cut the back shelf to fit.

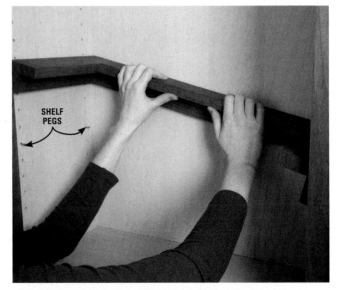

2 Set the spice shelf on adjustable shelf pegs. You may have to remove an existing shelf so you can tilt the spice shelf into place.

**FIGURE A.
CLOSET
SHELVES**

1-5/8"
SCREWS

MIDDLE SUPPORT

NEW TOP
SHELF

END SUPPORT

EXISTING
SHELF

No wasted closet space here—just storage on top of storage.

Two-story closet shelves

**Double the shelf space in your closet in a jiffy by adding a second shelf
above the existing one.**

There's a lot of space above the top shelf in most closets, and it is a fantastic place to store items or off-season clothing. Make use of this wasted space by adding a second shelf above the existing one. Buy enough closet shelving material to match the length of the existing shelf plus enough for two end supports and two middle supports over each bracket. Twelve-inch-wide shelving is available in various lengths and finishes at home centers and lumberyards. Cut the supports 16 in. long, or place the second shelf at whatever height you'd like. Screw end supports to the walls at each end. Use drywall anchors if you can't hit a stud. Then mark the position of the

middle supports onto the top and bottom shelves with a square, and drill 5/32-in. clearance holes through the shelves. Drive 1-5/8-in. screws through the shelf into the supports.

WHAT IT TAKES		
TIME 2-4 hrs.	**COST** Under $50	**SKILL LEVEL** Beginner

TOOLS
Tablesaw, drill/driver, basic hand tools

Stacked recycling tower

Does your recycling bin overflow, like a waterfall, with stuff? Then you need a better way to store it. Try this tower.

Five plastic containers, six 2x2s, screws and one hour's work are all it takes to put together this awesome space-saving recycling storage rack. Our frame fits containers that have a top measuring 14-1/2 in. x 10 in. and are 15 in. tall. The containers shown were made by Rubbermaid.

If you use different-size containers, adjust the distance between the uprights so the 2x2s will catch the lips of the containers. Then adjust the spacing of the horizontal rungs for a snug fit when the containers are angled as shown.

Start by cutting 2x2s to length according to the illustration. Then mark the position of the rungs on the uprights. Drill two 5/32-in. holes through the uprights at each crosspiece position. Drill from the outside to the inside and angle the

holes inward slightly to prevent the screws from breaking out the side of the rungs.

Drive 2-1/2-in. screws through the uprights into the rungs. Assemble the front and back frames. Then connect them with the side crosspieces.

WHAT IT TAKES		
TIME	**COST**	**SKILL LEVEL**
1-2 hrs.	Under $50	Beginner
TOOLS		
Miter saw, drill/driver		

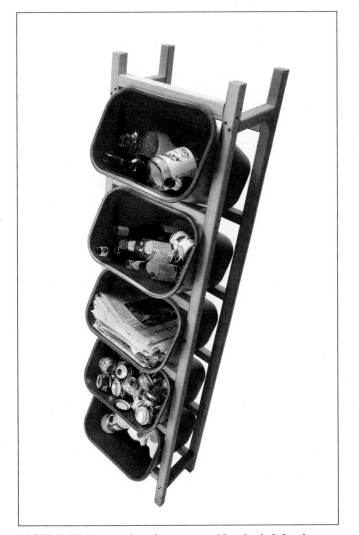

FIGURE A. STACKED RECYCLING TOWER

17"

7-1/2"

2-1/2"

ALL SUPPORTS 10-1/2" APART

70"

4"

CROSSPIECE 2-1/2" SCREWS

7-1/2"

ABOVE: Build this tower in an hour or two with a simple 2x2 and screw construction. **BOTTOM RIGHT:** Assemble the tower as shown, pre-drilling all through screw holes and pilot holes in the receiving parts, so they don't split.

DIY upholstery

Anyone can make a nasty seat nice—in just a couple of hours.

Reupholstering is a good way to bring tired-looking chairs—and even tired-looking rooms—back to life. The materials are relatively inexpensive, the tools are simple and it is a project almost anyone can tackle with success. Here's how.

CHAIRS ARE NOT ALL CREATED —OR UPHOLSTERED—EQUAL

Here we'll show you how to reupholster a chair with a "drop-in" or "screw-on" seat—a style shared by a wide variety of benches and stools. Seat bases can be constructed from a variety of materials: solid wood, plywood, pegboard and others. The seats are normally screwed on but can also be glued on or dropped in. The cushions can be foam, cotton or another natural material.

Our seats, for example, were made from a pegboard-like material secured to a 1x3 framework, covered with horsehair padding. Someone had already reupholstered the chairs, going directly over the old fabric. Expect the unexpected and adjust your game plan accordingly.

ROUND UP YOUR MATERIALS

When you shop, buy "upholstery grade" fabric because of its strength and stain resistance. Fabric prices vary wildly; you might find something for $5 in the bargain bin or you might spend 10 times as much. We bought our fabric, foam and batting at a fabric store. For the dust cover, we used landscape fabric from a home center.

REMOVE THE OLD AND GET READY FOR THE NEW

If you're re-covering more than one chair, number each chair and seat; that way, the screw holes will line up properly when you reinstall the seats. There are special tools just for yanking upholstery staples or tacks, but you can get by with basic hand tools **(Photo 1)**. Tip: Old, dull side cutters are perfect. They grip staples well but don't cut them off. Remove the padding and inspect the seat. If the wood base seems solid, reuse it. If it's cracked, use it as a template to make a new one **(Photo 2)**. We used a sander to taper the edges to match the profile of

A little DIY upholstering work took this sleepy chair from drab to eye-catching and stylish.

1 REMOVE THE OLD UPHOLSTERY. Pry and yank the staples with a screwdriver and pliers or side cutters. Remove the upholstery and cushion material.

Materials List

ITEM	QTY.
1/2" to 3/4" plywood (if needed)	1
30" x 30" quilt batting	1
1" x 24" x 24" high-density foam	1
30" x 30" upholstery fabric	1
24" x 24" landscape fabric (optional)	1

WHAT IT TAKES		
TIME 2 hours	**COST** Under $50	**SKILL LEVEL** Beginner
TOOLS Basic hand tools		

NEW PLYWOOD SEAT WITH BEVELED EDGES

OLD SEAT

3/4" PLYWOOD

2 MAKE A NEW SEAT. If the old seat is in bad shape, cut a new one from plywood. Trace around the old seat, then cut with a jigsaw or circular saw. Bevel or soften edges with a sander or router to match the old contour.

BREAD KNIFE

1" HIGH- DENSITY FOAM

3 CUT THE FOAM. Trace the outline of the seat onto 1-in.-thick foam. Cut the foam with a bread knife. To avoid tearing the foam, pull the knife toward you, using light pressure and short strokes.

ELECTRIC STAPLER

SINGLE STAPLE

PLYWOOD SEAT BASE

BATTING

FOAM

4 ADD THE BATTING. Cut the batting so it overhangs all sides of the seat by about 4 in. Then drive a single staple on each side to hold the foam in place.

5 CENTER THE PATTERN. Determine the best layout for your chosen material; make sure any patterns or stripes align correctly. Hang the edge of the seat over your work surface. Then drive a staple, from below, in the center of the front and back.

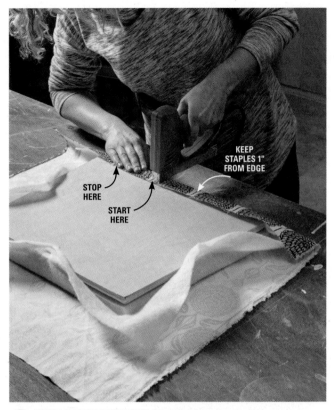

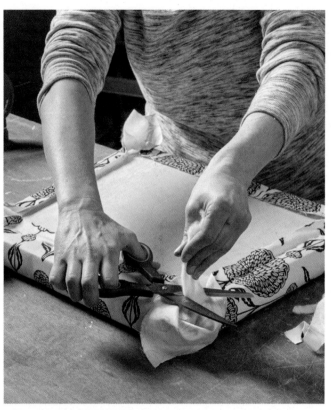

6 **STAPLE THE FRONT EDGE.** Working from the center outward, install staples along the front as you lightly tension the material with your hand. Stop 2 in. from the corner. Flip the seat over several times to check the pattern as you go. Repeat the process along the back edge and sides.

7 **TRIM THE CORNERS.** Cut off all of the excess batting and upholstery so you don't end up with ugly, unsightly lumps at the corners of your cushion.

Which stapler works best?

All the staplers shown will do the trick. The question is: How hard do you want to work—and squeeze—to "do the trick?" Your stapler-buying decision may also hinge on a few other factors, including how often you'll use it, what else you might use it for and whether you need a good excuse to buy an air compressor.

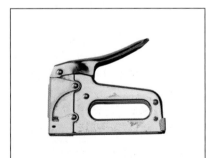

HAND STAPLER
It will give your hand a workout, and you may have to occasionally use a hammer to drive the staples all the way in, but you can still get good results. Make sure you hold the nose of the stapler firmly against the seat base when you pull the trigger.

ELECTRIC STAPLER
We used one for our project and it worked flawlessly. You still need to firmly press the nose against the fabric and plywood to get a well-seated staple—but it's way easier on the hand. As a bonus, some models also shoot 3/4-in. and shorter brad nails.

PNEUMATIC STAPLER
(plus air compressor)
If you're going to be stapling for hours on end, invest in a pneumatic stapler. These drive staples flush with the pull of a finger and allow you to be extremely accurate in the placement of your staples. Some tools also drive brad nails up to 1-1/4 in.

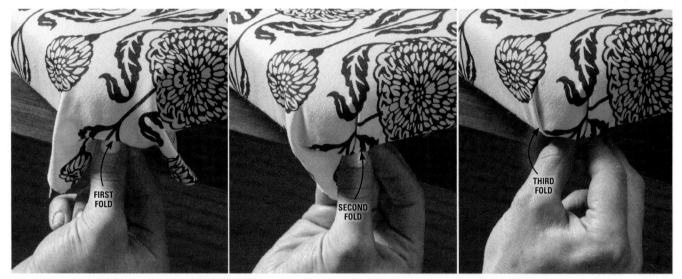

8 **WRAP THE CORNERS.** Create a "butterfly corner" by first tucking the center under, then folding and tucking the material from each side. Flip the seat over and drive staples to hold the corner tight.

the old one. Plop the seat on top of the foam and outline it with a marker. Use a serrated bread knife **(Photo 3)** to cut the foam just inside the line.

INSTALL THE NEW FABRIC

Place a section of batting—4 in. wider in all directions than the size of your chair seat—on a flat work surface, then set your foam and seat on top. Lightly stretch the batting and drive one staple **(Photo 4)** along each edge.

Flip the seat over, then center your material on top **(Photo 5)**. Cut the material so you'll be able to wrap it up onto the chair bottom at least 4 in. in each direction.

With the seat facing up and the front edge overhanging the work surface, drive one staple through the bottom to hold the material in place. Rotate the seat 180 degrees, then tack the back the same way.

PRO TIP

Don't worry about mistakes

Upholstery work is forgiving. If you make a mistake, just yank out the staples and try again.

Check your pattern alignment one more time, then flip the seat upside down. Starting at the front middle staple and working toward the corners, use the palm of your hand to lightly stretch the material, then drive a staple every 2 in. **(Photo 6)**. Keep the staples within an inch of the edge, and secure the batting and fabric at the same time. Use your entire hand, not just fingertips, to tighten the material. This way you'll avoid little dips and puckers in the pattern.

Repeatedly flip the seat over to check the pattern for straightness; it's easier to keep flipping and checking than to go back and pull staples.

Our expert flipped the seat over and checked the pattern a dozen times while stapling each edge. Stop stapling 2 in. from each corner.

Secure the back edge in the same way, stretching the material lightly as you work. Then complete the sides, again repeatedly checking the pattern.

CORNERS ARE THE KEY

You can make simple single-fold "hospital corners" if the edges of your seat are concealed by a frame. But in most cases the front corners will be exposed and will look better with "butterfly corners." Remove excess batting and material from the corners

9 Install the dust cover. After you trim the excess fabric and batting, staple on a dust cover—we used landscape cloth. A dust cover neatly hides the exposed fabric edges.

(Photo 7) then flip the seat right side up and experiment with a few corner tucks. Fold the center inward, then overlap each side onto that fold **(Photo 8)**. When the corner looks symmetrical and tight, flip the seat over and staple the folds in place.

When the corners are done, flip the seat over. Cut off the excess material. Staple on a dust cover **(Photo 9)**. Then put the cushion back on the seat and enjoy your "new" chair.

Entry bench

Despite its appearance, this is an easy piece of furniture to build—and handy, too. Besides giving storage space, it's the perfect perch for slipping on your shoes.

This bench starts with an unfinished upper kitchen cabinet—the kind sold in any home center. Cover the sides with primed beadboard paneling to make them flush with the front trim and to eliminate the kitchen cabinet look. The next step is to build a base (parts E, G and H) and wrap it with trim.

Your local home center may not carry the same chair rail molding we used, but it will have a similar profile. Glue fillers into the recess at the top and bottom of the cabinet. (Actually, most stock cabinets don't really have a "top" or "bottom"—just pick one.) Then screw the base to the spacers and add the bun feet (**Photo 3**).

We used 3/4-in. particleboard for the seat, though MDF or plywood would work just as well. For a better-looking upholstery job, round all the corners and edges of the seat. A router and 1/4-in. round-over bit will work best, but a sander will work, too.

Cut the foam to size so it overhangs all four sides of the seat by about 1 in. and glue it to the seat. Spray adhesive is the standard glue for this job, but you can just dribble a few lines of wood glue onto the seat and then set the seat onto the foam.

Cut the batting so it overhangs the seat by about 3 in. and the fabric so it overhangs by 4 in. Then stretch and staple the fabric (**Photo 1**). There are a few ways to deal with seat corners. **Photo 2** shows the easiest method. Don't worry about mistakes—the nice thing about upholstery work is that you can always pry out staples and fix mistakes. To fasten the seat to the cabinet, drive screws through the cabinet and fillers and into the seat.

1 UPHOLSTER THE SEAT. Lay out the fabric, batting and foam. Stretch and staple the fabric to the seat, starting at the middle of each side and working toward the corners.

Cheap trick: DIY bun feet

There are lots of online sources for bun feet, but you can make your own for free. Gather up some 3/4-in.-thick wood scraps, glue two layers together and cut out circles with a hole saw. After sanding the rough edges, screw each foot to a scrap of wood to hold it securely and round both sides with a round-over bit. A 3/4-in. round-over bit will cost you just as much as factory-made bun feet would. But spending on tools is always the right thing to do.

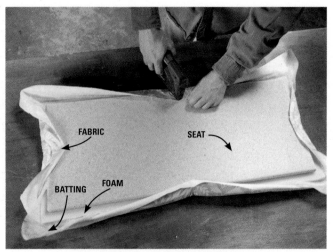

WHAT IT TAKES		
TIME	**COST**	**SKILL LEVEL**
2 days	$100 - $250	Intermediate

TOOLS
Miter saw, drill/driver, router, basic hand tools

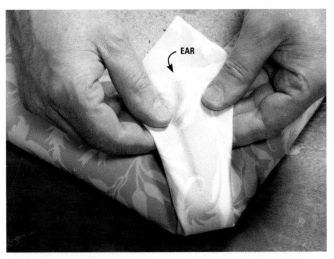

2 STAPLE THE CORNERS LAST. Fold the fabric inward to create an "ear." Then pull the ear back, staple it and cut off any and all of the excess fabric.

3 ADD THE BUN FEET. Drive dowel screws halfway into the bun feet. Drill pilot holes in the bench base 2-1/4 in. from the edges and then screw in the bun feet.

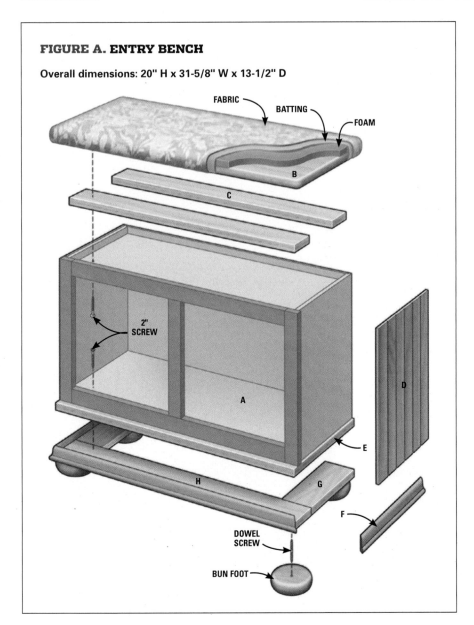

FIGURE A. ENTRY BENCH

Overall dimensions: 20" H x 31-5/8" W x 13-1/2" D

FABRIC
BATTING
FOAM
B
C
2" SCREW
A
D
E
H
G
F
DOWEL SCREW
BUN FOOT

Materials List

ITEM	QTY.
12" x 15" x 30" cabinet	1
3/4" x 4' x 4' plywood	1
Chair rail molding	6
3/16" beaded paneling	1 sheet
2' x 3' Fabric, batting, 1" foam	1
Scrap wood for bun feet, wood glue, cabinet knobs, 2" screws, dowel screws	

Cutting List

KEY	PART	QTY.
A	12" x 30" x 15" (cabinet)	1
B	3/4" x 13-1/2" x 31" (seat)	1
C	3/4" x 3" x 28-1/4" (fillers)	4
D	3/16" x 11-1/4" x 15" (side panel)	2
E	3/4" x 12-3/4" x 30" (base)	1
F	1-5/8" (chair rail molding; cut to fit)	3
G	3/4" x 3-1/2" x 9-1/4" (base side)	2
H	3/4" x 3-1/2" x 30" (base front)	1

WHAT IT TAKES		
TIME 4 hrs.	**COST** Under $50	**SKILL LEVEL** Beginner
TOOLS Tablesaw or circular saw, drill/driver, basic hand tools		

Rolling storage box

Use simple circular saw skills to build a storage box that's great on the go.

Make a box from one 8-ft. length of 1x12 pine, a circular saw, a drill and a few hand tools.

The handles are made by drilling two 3/8-in. holes through the sides and feeding 5/16-in. cotton sash rope through the holes. Tie each end of the rope, and add a drop of glue to prevent slipping. Add casters for mobility.

SPEED SQUARE

1 CUT THE PINE. Trim the ends of each board to make them square before marking and cutting them to the required length (see the Cutting List). TIP: Use a Speed Square to guide the saw.

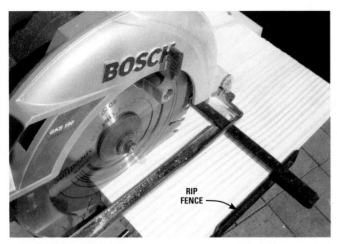

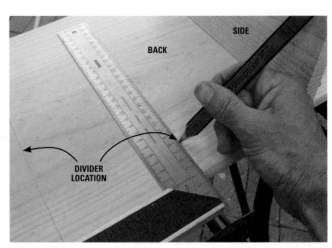

2 **TRIM THE DIVIDERS.** Set the rip fence on the saw to remove 3-1/4 in. from the sides of the dividers. Clamp the boards to cut them to the correct width. Check the sizes and label each piece. TIP: A 40- to 60-tooth blade cuts the pine cleanly.

3 **JOIN THE BACK AND SIDES.** Join sides to the back, securing with glue and 6d finish nails (see Figure A). Mark the divider locations across the back.

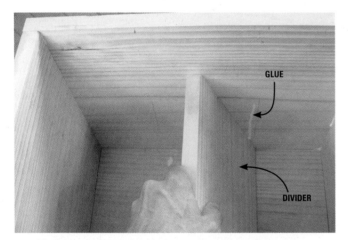

4 **ATTACH THE DIVIDERS.** Join the front and base to the frame with glue and nails. Apply glue on the divider layout lines, insert dividers, and secure with glue and nails.

5 **SMOOTH THE SURFACES.** Drive the nail heads below the surface with a nail punch and fill with wood filler. When dry, sand all surfaces, joints and sharp edges using 180-grit sandpaper. Finish with a clear coat of varnish or two coats of interior paint.

PRO TIP

Avoid splits

To prevent wood splitting at the edges, drill 3/32-in.-diameter holes for the nails before joining the panels.

Cutting List

KEY	PART	QTY.
A	15-3/4" x 11-1/4" x 3/4" (front and back)	2
B	11-1/4" x 11-1/4" x 3/4" (sides)	2
C	11-1/4" x 11-1/4" x 3/4" (base)	1
D	11-1/4" x 8" x 3/4" (dividers)	2

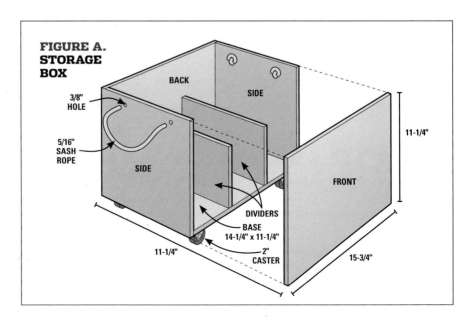

FIGURE A. STORAGE BOX

WHAT IT TAKES

TIME	COST	SKILL LEVEL
4-5 hours	$100-$250	Intermediate

TOOLS
Miter saw, circular saw, brad nailer, clothes iron, roller, veneer trimmer or razor blade

Shelf tower

This stylish-but-sturdy shelf unit will neatly hold your stuff.

This shelf unit may look lightweight and easy to topple, but don't be fooled. It's a real workhorse. The 33-1/2-in. x 82-3/4-in. tower features five unique tray-like shelves of different depths to hold a wide variety of items up to 13-1/4 in. tall. The unit is surprisingly sturdy despite its 10-degree lean, and its open design won't overpower a room.

Whether you choose to make this piece more functional, as in this office setting, or to place it in a family room to showcase treasures, the basic construction is the same. Select the type of wood, then stain or paint to dress it up or down to fit a room's look.

All the materials can be purchased at home centers or lumberyards. The only special tools you'll need are a power miter saw for crisp angle cuts and a brad nailer for quick assembly and almost invisible joints. Also, you'll have to rustle up an old clothes iron for applying oak edge-banding. Once you've gathered up all the materials, you can easily build the shelf unit in just one afternoon.

BUYING THE WOOD

This unit was built with red oak and oak veneer plywood and then finished with two coats of red oak stain. The beauty of this project is that any wood species will work. If you plan to paint it, select alder or aspen for the solid parts and birch for the plywood.

One note when buying boards: Use a tape measure to check the "standard" dimensions of 1x3s and 1x4s. They sometimes vary in width and thickness. Also, check the two full-length 1x4s you plan to use as the uprights to be sure they're straight, without warps or twists. And always examine the ends, edges and surfaces for blemishes or rough areas that won't easily sand out.

CUT PLYWOOD SHELVES FIRST

Lay a couple of 2x4s across sawhorses (**Photo 1**) to cut the half sheet of 3/4-in. plywood cleanly and without pinching the saw blade. Since all five shelves are 30-1/2 in. wide, cut this width first, making sure the grain will run the long way across the shelves. Remember to wear safety glasses, earplugs and a dust mask. Make a homemade jig to fit your circular saw and clamp it to the plywood.

Next, cut all five shelf depths, starting with the smallest (3-3/8 in.) first. Cut smallest to largest so you'll have enough wood to clamp the jig.

Important: Make sure you account for the width of your saw blade when you cut each shelf.

Now mark and cut the tops of all four 1x4 uprights (the ends that rest against wall) according to **Photo 3** and the two dimensions provided in the inset of **Figure A**. Use a sharp blade in your circular saw to prevent the wood from splintering.

Select the best front of each plywood shelf, clamp it to the bench on edge and sand it smooth with 150-grit paper on a sanding block. Then preheat a clothes iron to the "cotton" setting and run it over the top of the edge-banding veneer, making sure the veneer extends beyond all edges (**Photo 4**). Roll it smooth immediately after heating. Let each shelf edge cool for a couple of minutes before trimming and sanding the edges.

CUT THE UPRIGHTS AND SHELF FRAME NEXT

Now enter the miter saw, which you use to make all the 90-degree straight cuts first (five shelf backs and 10 shelf sides; see Cutting List). Important: Remember that one end of each shelf side has a 10-degree cut, so first cut them square at their exact length, then cut the angle carefully so the long edge of each piece remains the same.

Next, rotate the miter saw table to the 10-degree mark and cut all the angle pieces. First cut bottoms of both uprights so each one rests flat against the floor and wall (**see Figure A**). Then trim the top of the upright to

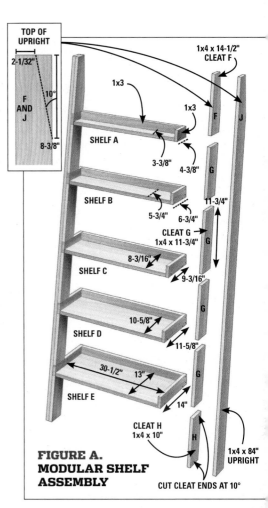

FIGURE A. MODULAR SHELF ASSEMBLY

Materials List

ITEM	QTY.
A half sheet (4' x 4') of 3/4" oak plywood	1
8' oak 1x3s	3
8' oak 1x4s	4
7/8" oak iron-on veneer (Band-It brand, The Cloverdale Co., band-itproducts.com, 800-782-9731, available at home centers)	1 package (25')
Wood glue	
1-1/4" brad nails	
Foam pads (3/4" round, self-adhesive non-skid pads)	

Cutting List

KEY	PART	QTY.
Shelf bases		
A	3/4" x 3-3/8" x 30-1/2" oak plywood (base)	1
B	3/4" x 5-3/4" x 30-1/2" oak plywood (base)	1
C	3/4" x 8-3/16" x 30-1/2" oak plywood (base)	1
D	3/4" x 10-5/8" x 30-1/2" oak plywood (base)	1
E	3/4" x 13" x 30-1/2" oak plywood (base)	1
Shelf sides		
A	3/4" x 2-1/2" x 4-3/8" oak (sides)	2
B	3/4" x 2-1/2" x 6-3/4" oak (sides)	2
C	3/4" x 2-1/2" x 9-3/16" oak (sides)	2
D	3/4" x 2-1/2" x 11-5/8" oak (sides)	2
E	3/4" x 2-1/2" x 14" oak (sides)	2
Shelf backs		
A-E	3/4" x 2-1/2" x 30-1/2" oak (backs)	5
Shelf cleats		
F	3/4" x 3-1/2" x 14-1/2" oak cleats (cut with 10-degree angles)	2
G	3/4" x 3-1/2" x 11-3/4" oak cleats (cut with 10-degree angles)	8
H	3/4" x 3-1/2" x 10" oak cleats (cut with 10-degree angles)	2
Shelf uprights		
J	3/4" x 3-1/2" x 84" oak uprights (cut with 10-degree angles)	2
*Front part of side cut at 10 degrees		

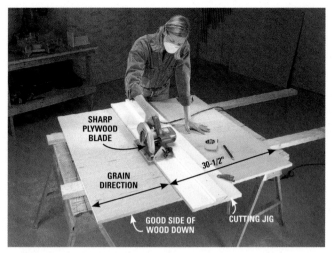

1 Cut 3/4-in. shelf plywood to width first, using a circular saw and a homemade jig for exact cuts. Use a sharp plywood blade and cut with the best side of the wood facing down to minimize splintering.

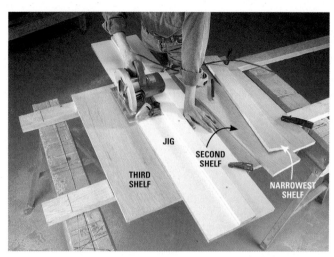

2 Cut the individual shelves, beginning with the narrowest, using the jig for perfectly straight cuts.

3 Cut both shelf uprights to length with a miter saw. Clamp to sawhorses. Mark the 10-degree angle at the top (dimensions in Figure A inset), then cut with a circular saw.

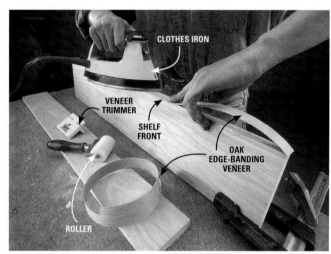

4 Iron edge-banding veneer to the front edge of all five shelves. Roll the entire surface to ensure a solid bond, and trim the edges.

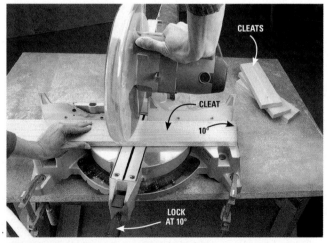

5 To maintain accuracy, lock the miter box at 10 degrees, then cut all angled pieces—uprights, cleats and one end of shelf sides—without changing the table.

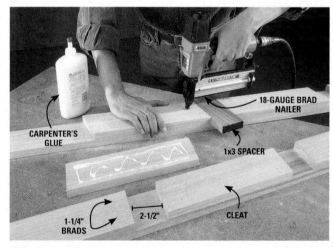

6 Glue and nail the shelf cleats to the uprights using a 1x3 spacer. Hold each cleat tight to the spacer.

match the bottom, being careful to maintain the 84-in. total length. Next, cut the cleats based on the Cutting List dimensions, which are measured edge to edge (**Photo 5 and Figure A**). Leave the top cleats long and cut them to exact fit during assembly. Then, to speed finishing, use an orbital sander with 150-grit sandpaper to smooth all pieces before assembly.

ASSEMBLE UPRIGHTS FIRST, THEN THE SHELVES

To begin assembly, lay out uprights and all cleats to ensure that the angles are correct so the shelves will be level when the unit is against the wall. Then glue and nail the first cleat flush with the base of each upright (using five or six 1-1/4-in. brads on each cleat). Work your way upward using 1x3 spacers (**Photo 6**). Make sure the spacer is the exact same width as the shelf sides! Set these aside to dry.

For shelf assembly, first glue and nail on the shelf backs. Next, apply sides with glue and nails (**Photo 7**). For final assembly, lay one upright on 2x4s, then clamp on shelves as shown in **Photo 8**. Apply the glue, position the second upright on top flush with the front edge of shelves, then sink four 1-1/4-in. brads into each shelf from the upright side. Carefully turn the unit over and repeat the process to attach the second upright. Work quickly so the glue doesn't set. Lift the ladder shelf. Place it upright against a straight wall. Check it with a framing square and flex it if necessary to square it up and make sure that it rests flat against the floor and wall (assuming your floor is level). Attach three bar clamps as shown in **Photo 9** while the glue dries.

The shelf is highly stable, but once you've stained or painted it, you can add self-adhesive foam gripping pads to the bottom of the uprights. And if you don't feel secure with the shelf on a slippery floor, the width is perfect for screwing the top of it into wall studs.

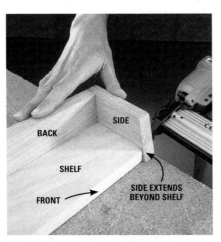

7 Glue and nail the shelf backs, then attach the sides to the plywood shelves. Position the sides to overlap the shelf base as shown.

8 Clamp the shelves into one upright. Spread glue in the shelf notches of the other upright, position it flush with the front of the shelves and nail. Flip the unit over and attach the other upright.

9 Set the shelf unit against a straight wall, check for squareness and apply three bar clamps until the glue dries.

Easy-to-build shoe storage

Banish bothersome shoe piles for good with this storage unit that is both simple to construct and simple to use.

Without constant vigilance, shoes tend to pile up, creating a mess next to entry doors. Untangle the mess with a simple, attractive shoe ladder that keeps everything, from boots to slippers, organized and off the floor.

Cut and drill the dowel supports **(Photo 1)**, then screw them to a 1x4 **(Photo 2)**. Cut each 1x4 to fit your shoes and the available space—an average pair of adult shoes needs 10 in. of space. Nail or glue the dowels into the dowel supports, leaving 2 in. (or more) extending beyond the supports to hang sandals or slippers.

Apply a finish before you mount the shoe ladder to the wall. Screw shoe ladder to studs or use heavy-duty toggle-bolt style anchors to hold it in place.

WHAT IT TAKES		
TIME	**COST**	**SKILL LEVEL**
2-4 hrs.	Under $50	Beginner
TOOLS		
Miter saw, drill/driver		

6-3/4"
1-3/8"
3-1/2"
5/8"
3/4" HOLE
5-1/8"

1 As you drill the holes, clamp the 1x3 support to a piece of scrap wood to prevent the wood from splintering.

45° CUT
2"
1-5/8" SCREWS
5/8" DOWEL

2 Predrill through the back of the 1x4 into the 1x3 supports, then glue and screw the pieces together.

Sturdy, stable stool

This stool is as practical as it is beautiful.

The crossed, flared legs on this stool make it stable, strong and quick to build. Start by gluing together 4-1/2-in.-wide boards **(Photo 1)** for the seat and 5-1/2-in.-wide boards for the legs. Rip 1/2-in.-wide contrasting accent strips on a table saw and glue them into place.

Next, mark the leg blanks, beginning with a center line **(Photo 2)**. To mark the angled end cuts, measure 10 in. from the center line at the bottom and draw a 15-degree angle. Make a trammel to mark the arcs: Drill a pencil hole in a strip of wood, then drive a screw 8 in. from the center of the pencil hole. Cut the arc with a jigsaw and sand it smooth. If the table saw is large enough, use it to cut the angled ends of the legs. If it is not large enough to cut the angled ends, use a circular saw and sand the cut smooth.

Cut notches in the legs with a small pull saw **(Photo 3)**. With both sides of the notch cut, break out the middle and smooth the bottom of the notch with a chisel. Slip the two legs together. If light hammer taps will not drive the legs together, hone down the tight spots with a file.

With the seat lying upside down, set the leg assembly on it and trace the outline of the legs. Drill marker holes through the seat from the underside at each of the four screw locations using a 1/16-in. bit. Then flip the top over and drill a 3/8-in. hole 3/8 in. deep at each marker hole. Use a brad-point bit for these holes to avoid splintering. Set the seat on the legs, drill 1/8-in. pilot holes and screw the seat to the legs. Then you're done, and you've got a good stool for your home.

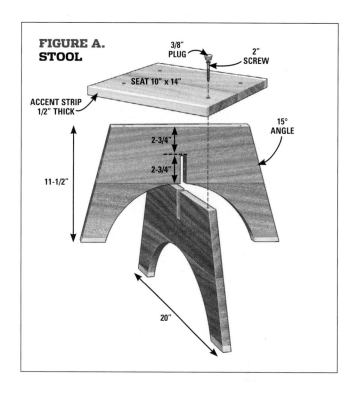

FIGURE A. STOOL

Materials List

ITEM	QTY.
10 ft. of walnut 1x6	1
2 ft. of maple 1x2	1
Wood glue	1
2-in. screws	
3/8-in. maple plugs	
Spray lacquer	

WHAT IT TAKES		
TIME 4-6 hrs.	**COST** Under $50	**SKILL LEVEL** Beginner/intermediate

TOOLS
Drill/driver, jigsaw, circular saw (optional), sander (optional), pull saw, basic hand tools

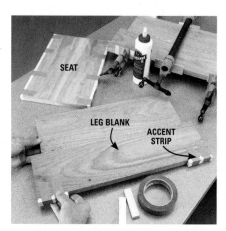

1 Glue and clamp the boards together to form the top and legs. Add accent strips, using masking tape to hold the strips until the glue dries.

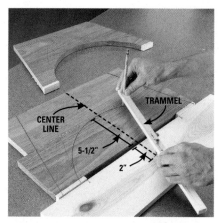

2 Mark arcs with a homemade trammel. Draw the center lines on the legs to accurately position the arcs, the end cuts and the notches that you'll cut next.

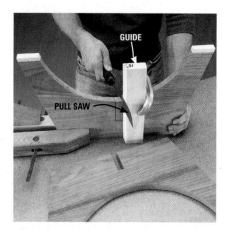

3 Cut perfect notches using a guide block to steer your saw. To make the guide, cut a scrap of wood on a table saw with the blade set to 15 degrees.

Fast furniture fixes

Easy repairs for everyday furniture pieces.

The creaking sound you hear each time you sit on that old kitchen chair is not a good sign. It has loose joints, and every time you sit on it, you're wearing them down and further loosening them. Someday the chair is going to fall apart. One of these tips is going to save that chair—and many other pieces of your favorite furniture will be rescued, too! But keep in mind that these are fast, easy, practical fixes. They are not meant for treasured heirlooms or valuable antiques.

A. FIX A WOBBLY TABLE

If you've got a table that rocks on an uneven floor, you've probably tried wedging something under the short leg. Doesn't last, does it? Here's a better way: Use washers and nail-on glides. First, drill holes for the nails with a 1/16-in. bit and install the glides. Then set the table in place and slip washers under the low leg until the table is steady. When you've determined how many washers are needed, pull off the glide and reinstall it along with the washers.

B. INJECT EPOXY INTO LOOSE JOINTS

When one or two joints loosen on a chair but you can't get the rest of them apart, here's an advanced repair technique to try: Inject epoxy into the loose joints using a syringe.

Once mixed, most epoxy is too thick to push through a syringe. However, an epoxy used for fiberglass boat repair (like the one shown here) has just the right consistency. To inject the glue, drill 1/8-in. holes in an inconspicuous place in line with the dowels. Aim for the cavity behind each dowel. Insert the syringe into the hole, then inject the epoxy until it runs out of the joint. Push the joint together, then wipe off the excess epoxy.

West System 101-TS packets are convenient for storing and dispensing epoxy. They are like ketchup packages—you just tear off the top and squeeze—and are available online.

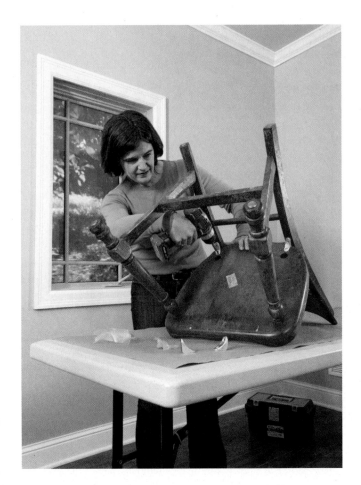

No workshop? No problem.

You don't need a workshop to make these repairs— a few simple tools and a sturdy table will do. And you don't need any special skills. If you know the most basic stuff—how to cut plywood and drive screws—you can do these fixes!

But at $31 for six packets, this epoxy is more expensive than the hardware store variety.

Plastic syringes are available at many pharmacies and online for less than $2 apiece, so they're easy to find and inexpensive.

A.

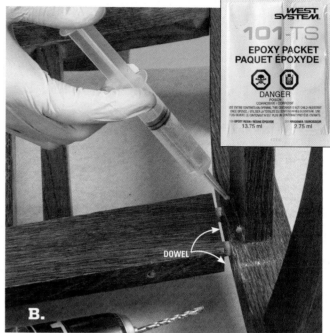

B.

C.

D.

C. RESCUE A DRAWER

Drawer fronts that are just nailed or stapled to the drawer box often come loose or even fall off completely. You could simply pound the parts back together, but that kind of fix won't last long. For a repair that's stronger than the original construction, add a backer to the drawer front.

Make the backer from 3/4-in. plywood and cut it to fit tight inside the drawer. Using a spade bit, drill 3/4-in.-diameter holes in the plywood so you can access the screws that hold the drawer's handle. Fasten the backer to the inside front of the drawer, then screw the drawer sides to the ends of the backer.

D. SUPPORT SAGGING SHELVES

If your shelves sag, sometimes you can simply flip them over—but eventually they'll droop again. Here's a permanent solution: Add supports that fit tight between the shelves.

Pine stair tread, which has a rounded front edge, is really perfect for this. It's available at home centers ($10 for 3 ft.). Many stores will cut it to length for you. You can paint or stain the supports to match the shelves, of course. But if the shelves hold books, consider staining the supports a color similar to your books. You'll wind up being surprised at how well they blend in.

E. ADD BRACES

Chair braces are an easy fix for a wobbly chair. They're better looking and much stiffer than L-brackets. Most hardware stores carry chair braces in finishes like chrome, brass or bronze. To avoid splitting the chair's wood, be sure to drill 1/8-in. pilot holes before you drive in the screws.

F. SAVE IT WITH SCREWS

When ready-to-assemble (RTA) particleboard furniture breaks—by being pushed across the floor, for example—the original knockdown fasteners often pull out of the wood and can't be replaced. The solution is to bypass them completely and screw the piece together from the outside.

Unfortunately, regular screws will not hold in particleboard. You need 2-1/2-in. to 3-in. screws with coarse threads and large, washer-style heads. Many home centers carry "cabinet installation screws" that are perfect for the job.

Be sure to drill pilot holes first, even if the screws have self-tapping points.

E.

F.

You can also buy colored self-stick caps to cover the screw heads.

G. FILL STRIPPED-OUT SCREW HOLES

Wooden drawer knobs tend to strip out and then come loose or even pull off. Using a fatter screw or shoving matchsticks into the hole might work, but here's a sure fix: Fill the hole with epoxy putty, and then drill a new hole. Epoxy putty is available at home centers and hardware stores. Epoxy putty is easy to use. You just cut off the amount you want, knead the piece until the inner and outer layers blend together, then roll it between your fingers to form a thin string. Push the string of putty into the hole with a screwdriver. Then scrape off the excess before it hardens.

H. HIDE SCRATCHES WITH WAX

To revive a finish, rub colored paste wax over the surface and buff. This isn't a perfect fix—heavy scratches or dents will still be visible—but light scratches and wear will almost disappear. For the best camouflage, pick a color that's slightly darker than the finish. You can find Minwax or Briwax colored paste wax at some paint stores or order it online ($10 to $20 for 16 oz.).

I. STRENGTHEN READY-TO-ASSEMBLE FURNITURE

New furniture that's put together with bolts and nuts often loosens up with

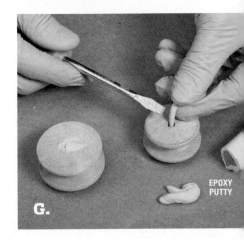
G. EPOXY PUTTY

---

3 classic tricks

People who repair furniture for a living have all kinds of simple tricks up their sleeves. Here are a few that anybody can do right at home:

- Lubricate a sticking drawer with canning wax, which is made from paraffin. Paraffin works much better than candle wax.
- When you are gluing a splinter or chip, use masking tape to hold it in place. A clamp isn't necessary.
- Use steam to raise a dent. Place a wet towel on the dent, then press the pointed end of a hot iron onto the towel, right above the dent, for 10 seconds or so. Two or three applications may be necessary.

PRO TIP

Add metal braces

If appearance doesn't matter, screwing a brace or T-plate onto a piece of furniture is often the quickest way to fix it. Adding metal may not make the piece totally sound, but at least it won't come apart any time soon.

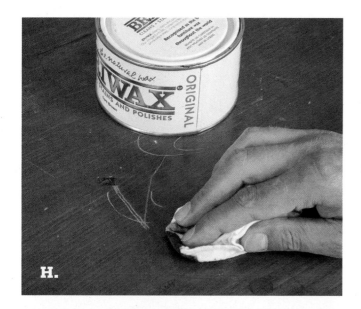

H.

I.

DOWEL

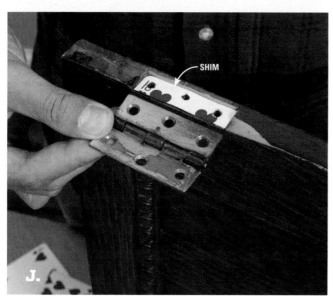

J.

SHIM

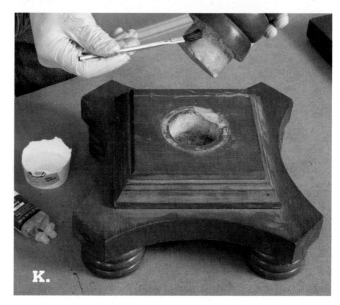

K.

use. If retightening the bolts every now and then seems like too much bother, you can take the piece apart and strengthen it with epoxy. Most RTA furniture uses loose-fitting dowels to align each part. Spread epoxy inside the dowel holes and on dowels themselves when you reassemble the piece. (If the dowels fit tight, use yellow glue.) Don't bother spreading glue on the ends of each part. They usually butt against a finished surface, and no glue will stick to a finish for very long.

J. SHIM A HINGE

When a door won't close or won't align with a catch, placing a shim behind one

of its hinges might solve the problem. The shim will kick out the upper or lower half of the door, depending on which hinge you choose.

Make the shim from one or more playing cards. Remove the hinge, then cut cards to fit into the hinge's recess. Place each piece in the recess and punch screw holes in it using an awl or a small Phillips screwdriver. Remount the hinge with the original screws.

K. EPOXY A SLOPPY JOINT

When parts don't fit tightly, epoxy is the best possible answer. Other woodworking glues, like yellow, white

or polyurethane, require a snug fit. The gap between parts can't exceed the thickness of a piece of paper, which complicates things when your piece of furniture has a wider gap. Epoxy, on the other hand, bonds across a gap of any size—making it perfect for your furniture repair.

Epoxy won't stick well to old glue, so remove as much of the old glue as you can with a file or coarse sandpaper. Most epoxies must be used within five minutes of mixing, but you can buy a slower-setting epoxy if you need more time. Devcon 2-Ton Epoxy gives you a leisurely 30 minutes to assemble parts and is available at many hardware stores.

Great Goofs®

Laughs and lessons from our readers

CUTTING THE DECK

I was demolishing a 1950s built-in buffet in my basement as part of a remodel, and I decided to cut it into pieces for easy removal. I didn't have any extra cash at the time to buy a reciprocating saw, but I felt my trusty chain saw would do the trick. First, I ripped off the plastic laminate top and took a quick look inside to avoid hitting any nails. With my next cut, I noticed paper flying out with the wood chips. I found that I had cut through five vintage baseball cards! They included 1954 editions of Willie Mays and Roy Campanella— valued at more than $400!

That money could have bought a nice reciprocating saw or helped pay for the remodel. I guess I'm just really unlucky at cards.

WILLIAM F. PRICE IV

WISHY-WASHY SURPRISE

My husband built a beautiful bookcase for our living room and put on the first coat of varnish. The next day, I thought I'd surprise him by applying the second coat while he was at work.

I carefully brushed on the varnish and was pleased that it dried quicker than I expected. The extra time allowed me to apply another meticulous coat. I had completely finished the project!

When my husband came home, he was certainly surprised. My "varnish" was really just the water he had been soaking the brush in.

KATHY CHARLES

RAINDROPS KEEP FALLING...

After I left for college, my father decided to empty my water bed. Unable to get a good siphon going, he gave up and dropped the hose on the floor and left the room to take care of other chores. Hours later he noticed water dripping through the ceiling below. The siphoning had started after all. When I went home that weekend, I saw several garbage cans in the living room. He had drilled holes all over the ceiling to let the water out. Poor Dad. I'd never seen him more frustrated or forlorn. I don't think we'll be shopping for another water bed any time soon!

KARIN CARR

TRANSPARENT CAULK JOB

As a professional handyman, I install dozens of doors every year. On one particular job, I installed five interior prehung doors, which the homeowner had painted white. After they were hung, I caulked all the gaps between the trim and the uneven wall surfaces with white caulk. I made sure the job looked flawless.

When I came back the next morning, none of the gaps looked like they had been caulked. After a Twilight Zone moment, I examined the caulk more closely. Sure enough, I had used clear caulk. It goes on white but dries clear. Moral of the story: Read the label twice and caulk once.

HARRY "THE HANDYMAN"

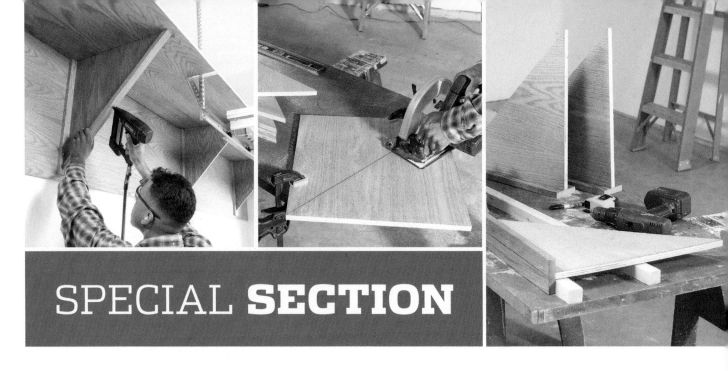

THREE-DAY PROJECTS

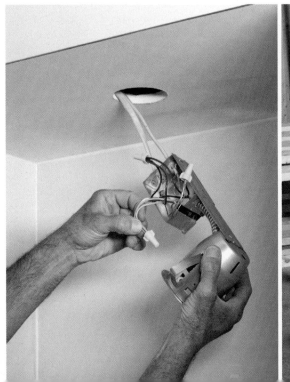

Showcase wall

Turn a bland wall into a showstopper!

There aren't many DIY projects that will give you quite as much bang for the buck as this dramatic drywall showcase. Granted, you'll have a chunk of time invested before you're done, but the materials are readily available and inexpensive. As you'll see, it's just 2x6 framing covered with drywall. And the beauty of this type of construction is that the design is limited only by your imagination. You can build shelves just like ours, or you can design any other size and shape you'd like. Here we'll show you how to build the frame, hang the drywall, and finish the project with corner bead and drywall tape. We'll also show you how to add an outlet for the TV and wire the switch and lights. For more information on how to hang and tape drywall and how to install outlets, switches and rough-in wiring, go to familyhandyman.com.

Dramatic results with cheap materials

Stunning projects usually carry a stunning price tag. Not this one. It requires only common 2x6 framing lumber, drywall, corner beads and joint compound, making it more affordable than other comparable projects. Best of all, you can get everything off the shelf at your local home center or hardware store.

This elegant shelving unit is limited only by your imagination (well, and your wall space). You can choose to make yours just like ours or you can choose your own DIYing adventure. Build the unit to fit whatever space you have—or to match how much storage you want.

WHAT IT TAKES

TIME	COST	SKILL LEVEL
40 hrs.	Over $500	Intermediate

TOOLS
Circular saw, drywall square, drill/driver, tin snips, 6- and 8-in. taping knives and mud pan, voltage sniffer, wire cutter and stripper, painting tools

1 MARK IT OUT ON THE WALL. Mark the location of the framing and snap chalk lines on the wall. Make sure that there's at least 1/2 in. between the outside lines and the walls, floor and ceiling, and that the lines are level and plumb.

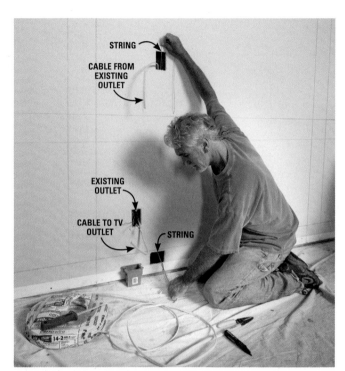

STRING

CABLE FROM EXISTING OUTLET

EXISTING OUTLET

CABLE TO TV OUTLET

STRING

2 ADD A SWITCH AND OUTLET. If your project includes a TV and lights, you'll need another outlet and a switch. Start by turning off the power to the existing outlet. Cut a hole for the new TV outlet and another hole directly below, near the floor. Extend NM electrical cable from the existing outlet to the new TV outlet. Run another cable from the new outlet through the hole near the floor. Leave enough cable to reach your switch location, plus at least 12 in. of extra cable (Figure B).

COLUMNS

SHELF

3 BUILD THE FRAMES. Pick the straightest lumber for the long lengths and cut the parts. Mark the front and back of each base and top for the column locations. Mark column sides for the shelves. Build the U-shape and box-shape backers, and nail the parts together.

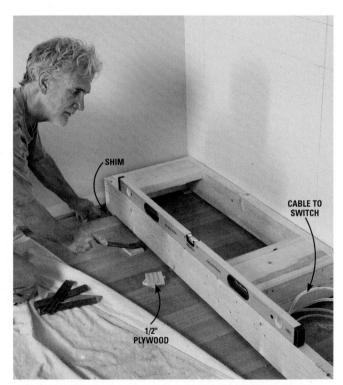

SHIM

CABLE TO SWITCH

1/2" PLYWOOD

4 LEVEL THE BASE. Shim the base with 1/2-in. scraps of plywood on all four corners. Then use a level and add shims as needed to level the frame across the front and from front to back. Add shims under each column. Screw the frame to the wall studs.

Our wall is 12 ft. wide with a 9-ft. ceiling. We designed these 18-in.-deep shelves to accommodate home theater gear and the center rectangle to fit around a 60-in. TV screen. This arrangement also looks great even if your ceilings are only 8 ft. high. And keep in mind that you don't have to build your shelves wall to wall. You can leave one or both ends exposed and simply finish them with drywall.

We used a computer drawing program called SketchUp to design these shelves, but you can use graph paper or just map it out on the wall. We first added about 5 in. to the width and height of the TV, and then we centered this rectangle on the wall. When we were satisfied with the design, we marked the wall at the vertical and horizontal framing locations and chalked lines to get a better sense of how it would look **(Photo 1)**. We left a 1/2-in. space between the 2x6 framing and the floor, walls and ceiling. The 1/2-in. space serves two purposes. First, it allows you to prebuild the framing and slip it in without trying to fit it exactly to the room. Second, the 1/2-in. space creates a perimeter that's the same width (6-1/2 in.) as the rest of the vertical and horizontal dividers after they're covered with drywall.

GETTING STARTED

If your room is carpeted, you can either build right over the carpet or peel it back and hire a carpet layer to reattach it after you're done. You can cut the baseboard molding in place or remove it like we did and reinstall it when the shelves are done. Make sure the framing isn't going to cover an electrical outlet. If it is, you'll have to relocate the outlet or change your design. We've included a Materials List on p. 270, but you can adjust the quantities for your design.

Measure the distance from the floor to the ceiling at both ends of your proposed shelves. Then measure the

5 **SET THE COLUMNS.** Screw the outside columns to the base. Plumb them and attach them to the wall with your screws or drywall anchors. Position the center columns, plumb them and attach them the same way.

6 **MOUNT THE TOP FRAME.** Slide the top into place over the columns. Line up the columns so the shelves fit and screw them to the top frame. Then screw the top frame to the wall.

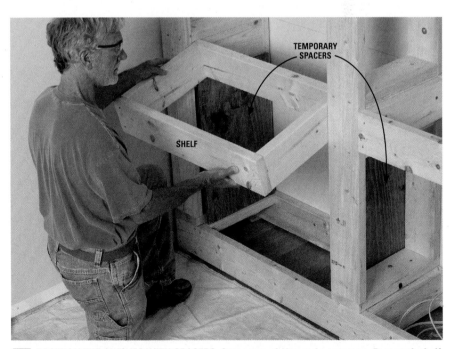

7 **POSITION THE SHELVES WITH SPACERS.** Cut scraps of plywood as spacers. Rest each shelf on the spacers and screw them to the columns. This will ensure that the shelves are lined up precisely. You'll need another set of spacers for the top shelves.

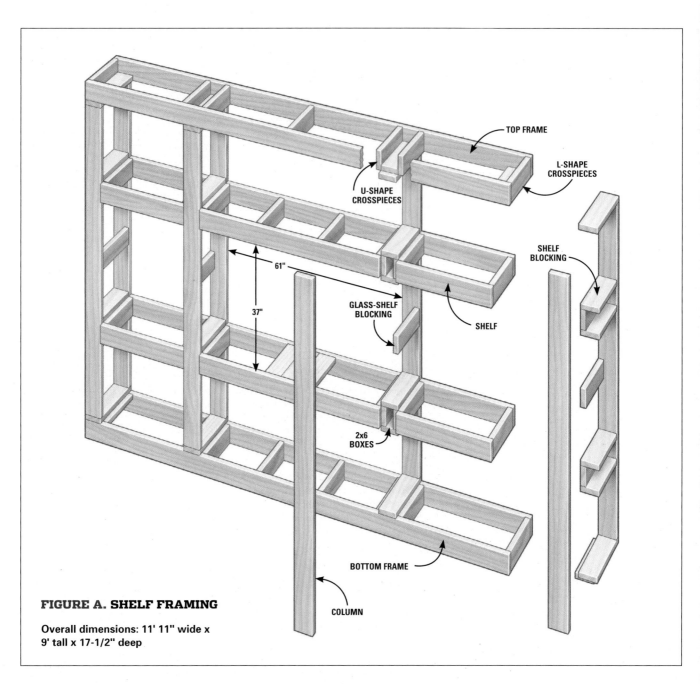

FIGURE A. SHELF FRAMING

Overall dimensions: 11' 11" wide x
9' tall x 17-1/2" deep

Labels in figure:
TOP FRAME
L-SHAPE CROSSPIECES
U-SHAPE CROSSPIECES
SHELF BLOCKING
GLASS-SHELF BLOCKING
SHELF
2x6 BOXES
BOTTOM FRAME
COLUMN
61"
37"

Materials List

ITEM	QTY.
2x6 x 8' SPF (spruce, pine, fir)	22
2x6 x 12' SPF (spruce, pine, fir)	4
4' x 8' x 1/2" drywall	8
8' drywall corner beads	14
Scraps of 1/2" plywood	
Shims	2 pkgs.
16d nails	2 lbs.
3" construction screws	2 lbs.
1-1/4" drywall screws	2 lbs.
1-1/4" ring-shank drywall nails	2 lbs.
1" long, 1/4" crown staples (optional)	1 box
45-minute setting-type joint compound	2 bags
Premixed joint compound	1 bucket
Paper tape	1 roll
Mesh tape	1 roll
Optional (not included in materials cost)	
1/4" glass shelves	2
Glass-shelf supports	8

Electrical List

ITEM	QTY.
3" recessed lights*	6
Dimmable LED flood bulbs	6
14-2 or 12-2 NM cable with ground	80
Single-gang remodel box	1
Single-gang new-work box	1
Cable connectors (optional)	
Wire connectors	30
1/2" staples	30

distance between the walls at both the top and the bottom. Subtract 1 in. from the smallest measurement of both the width and the height. Use these dimensions to build the frames.

BUILD THE FRAMES

The 2x6 framing consists of a full-length base and top, four vertical columns and shelves. You can build all of the parts in your garage or backyard **(Photo 3)** and move them into your room to assemble. Cut the 2x6s for the top and bottom to length and mark the

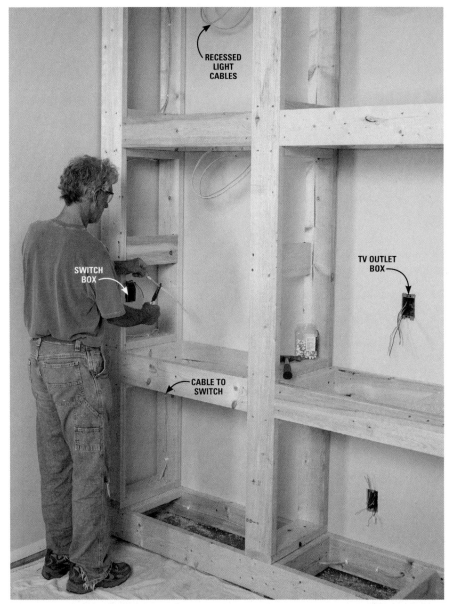

RECESSED LIGHT CABLES

SWITCH BOX

TV OUTLET BOX

CABLE TO SWITCH

8 **ROUGH-IN THE ELECTRICAL WIRING.** Drill holes and run the cable to the switch box and then to the recessed light fixture locations. Leave at least 2 ft. of extra cable at each light. Secure the cables with 1/2-in. plastic staples.

1-1/4" DRYWALL SCREW

1/2" DRYWALL

9 **INSTALL THE DRYWALL.** Attach the drywall with screws. If you plan to caulk the back edges, get a tight fit between the drywall and wall. Shave off overhanging edges at the front so they don't interfere with corner bead installation.

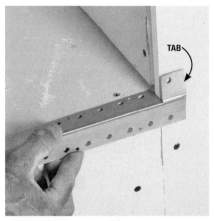

TAB

10 **NAIL ON THE TOP AND BOTTOM CORNER BEADS.** Notch one of the corner beads as shown here. Push it into the corner and mark the opposite end. Notch the other end the same way. Fit the corner bead into the opening and staple or nail it. Repeat on the opposite side of the opening.

column locations. If you have a miter saw, set up a stop and cut all the short crosspieces you'll need.

You can see from **Figure A** that you'll need three crosspieces, assembled into a U-shape, at each column location. Use L-shape crosspieces at the ends. Nail the top and bottom frames together. Then build the columns. The center columns have 2x6 boxes at each shelf location to provide backing for the drywall on both sides. We added flatwise 2x6s to provide the backing for our glass-shelf supports. Finally, build the shelves.

PREPARE FOR WIRING

If you're going to add lights and another outlet, add the new outlet box and the cable that runs to the switch before you install the framing **(Photo 2)**. The first step is to turn off the power to the outlet, and double-check that the power is off by testing the wires with a noncontact voltage detector. Then remove the outlet and twist wire connectors onto the black wires as an extra precaution. Determine whether the wires are 12 or 14 gauge. Then count the wires in the box and calculate

the box size required, including the extra hot, neutral and ground wire you'll be adding. Go to familyhandyman.com and search for "dimmer switch" for information on calculating box sizes. If the box is too small, cut it out and add a larger one.

Remove a knockout from the top of the box for the new cable. If the box is metal and doesn't include built-in cable connectors, add a cable connector to the new cable.

Next, cut the hole for the TV outlet. To make running new cable much easier,

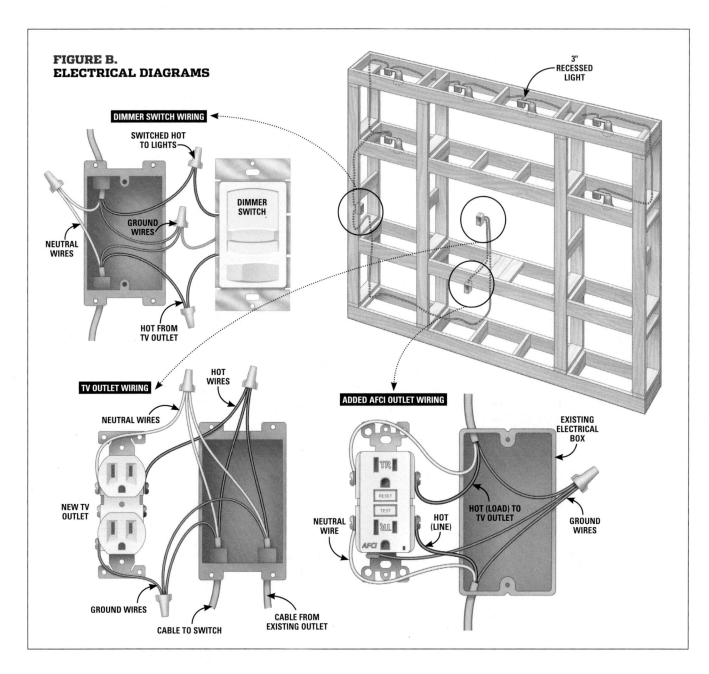

FIGURE B. ELECTRICAL DIAGRAMS

3" RECESSED LIGHT

DIMMER SWITCH WIRING

SWITCHED HOT TO LIGHTS

DIMMER SWITCH

GROUND WIRES

NEUTRAL WIRES

HOT FROM TV OUTLET

TV OUTLET WIRING

HOT WIRES

NEUTRAL WIRES

NEW TV OUTLET

GROUND WIRES

CABLE TO SWITCH

CABLE FROM EXISTING OUTLET

ADDED AFCI OUTLET WIRING

TR

RESET

TEST

TR

AFCI

NEUTRAL WIRE

HOT (LINE)

HOT (LOAD) TO TV OUTLET

EXISTING ELECTRICAL BOX

GROUND WIRES

try to choose a location that's in the same stud space as the existing outlet. If this isn't possible, you'll have to cut out some drywall to drill through studs. Mark around the remodel box and cut the hole. Also cut a hole near the floor, directly under the TV outlet hole.

Match the gauge of the new cable, 12 or 14 gauge, to the gauge of the wire in the existing box. Run the NM (nonmetallic) cable with ground from the existing outlet to the new outlet and from the new outlet to the hole near the floor. Leave 12 in. of extra cable at the new outlet. Then run enough cable

from the new outlet through the hole near the floor to reach your new switch location. Be generous with the cable to the switch to be certain you'll have at least an extra foot at the switch location.

INSTALL THE FRAMING

Tack small squares of 1/2-in. plywood to the four corners of the bottom frame. Drill a 3/4-in. hole in the back 2x6 to feed the cable through. Set the frame in place and level it by adding shims if necessary **(Photo 4)**. When the frame is level, add scraps of 1/2-in. plywood and shims under the two column locations.

Make sure the frame is centered, with a 1/2-in. space on each end, and screw it to the wall. Next, install the columns **(Photo 5)**.

Use a level to make sure the end column is plumb, and screw it to the bottom frame and to the wall. If there is no stud to drive screws into, use toggle-type drywall anchors to hold the column against the wall. Then use the shelves as spacers to make sure the columns are in the correct locations before you screw them to the base. There should be a 1/2-in. space between the wall and the end columns.

Next, set the top frame in place on the columns. Screw the top frame to the wall, and screw the top of the columns to the top frame (**Photo 6**). Finish the framing by installing the shelves (**Photo 7**).

ROUGH-IN THE WIRING

Before you start your project, contact your local inspections department to find out if an electrical permit is required. In most cases the wiring will need to be inspected before you cover it with drywall. The new electrical code requires an AFCI (arc-fault circuit interrupter) in many areas when new wiring is added. Ask your inspector if an AFCI is required in your situation. If so, simply replace the existing outlet with an AFCI receptacle, and run power from the "load" side of the AFCI outlet to the new TV outlet and then on to the switch and lights. Any new receptacle outlets must also be tamper resistant.

Start wiring by nailing a switch box to the frame in a convenient location and then drilling 3/4-in. holes through the framing to make a path for the new cables (**Photo 8 and Figure B**). Run lengths of cable from the TV outlet to the switch, from the switch to the first light fixture, and between light fixtures.

Leave a 2-ft. loop of extra cable at each light fixture location. For details and tips on rough-in wiring and more, go to familyhandyman.com and search for "wiring."

We ordered our 3-in. recessed light fixtures online because the fixtures we found at a home center were too tall to fit in the drywall space and still meet the electrical code requirement of 1/2-in. space between the fixture and the combustible surfaces. We chose remodel-type fixtures, which are installed after the drywall is finished. You can choose any non-IC (insulation contact) fixture you like as long as there's at least 1/2 in. between the fixture and any combustible material and insulation is kept more than 3 in. away. You can use any IC-rated fixture that will fit in the space.

When the wiring is in place, call for a rough-in wiring inspection. After the wiring is approved, then go ahead and move on to the next steps: drywall and corner bead.

11 **ADD CORNER BEADS TO THE SIDES.** Cut the side pieces to fit between the top and bottom notched corner beads so they overlap the metal tabs. Line up the corners and attach the beads with nails or staples.

SIDES OVERLAP TABS

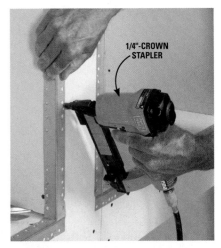

1/4"-CROWN STAPLER

12 **ATTACH CORNER BEAD WITH A STAPLER.** Using a 1/4-in.-crown, pneumatic stapler and 1-in.-long staples, drive staples every 6 in. and wherever the corner bead is buckled out. Then cover the edge of the bead with mesh tape.

MESH TAPE

JOINT COMPOUND

PAPER TAPE

13 **TAPE THE INSIDE CORNERS.** Spread a layer of joint compound on both sides of the corner. Cut a piece of paper tape and fold it to fit in the corner. Press the tape in with your fingers. Then embed it with your taping knife. Spread a thin layer of compound over the top of the tape.

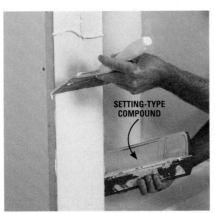

SETTING-TYPE COMPOUND

14 **FILL THE BEAD.** Mix about a half bag of setting compound with water. Spread a thick layer of compound between the corner beads, and smooth it with an 8-in. taping knife. Fill both sides of all the beads. Recoat after the compound firms up.

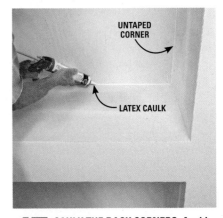

UNTAPED CORNER

LATEX CAULK

15 **CAULK THE BACK CORNERS.** Avoid a plethora of tricky corner taping by caulking the back inside corners. Cut the tip of the latex caulk tube carefully to create a very small hole. Then apply a neat bead of caulk and smooth it out with your finger.

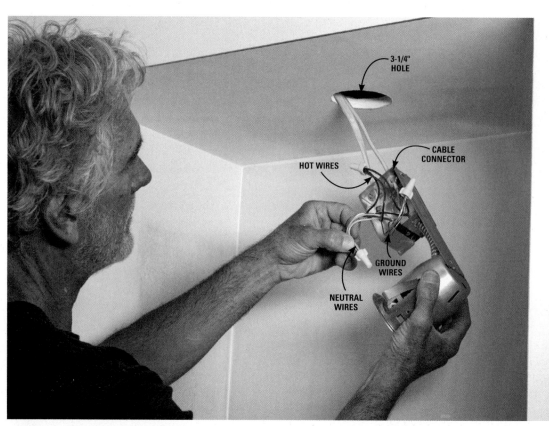

3-1/4"
HOLE

CABLE
CONNECTOR

HOT WIRES

GROUND
WIRES

NEUTRAL
WIRES

16 INSTALL THE RECESSED LIGHTS. Cut holes for the lights using the template provided or a large hole saw mounted in a drill (we used a 3-1/4-in. hole saw). Remove the cover and knockouts, and add cable connectors if they're not built into the fixture. Push the cable(s) through the connectors and connect hot, neutral and ground wires with the appropriate wire connectors.

COVER THE FRAME WITH DRYWALL

You can cut the drywall in the usual way by scoring one side with a utility knife, bending it to break at the scored line and then cutting the paper backing. But for fast, super-clean cuts, we used a table saw to cut the drywall. We have a table saw with a good dust collection system, so it wasn't too dusty. But you could also cut the drywall outdoors with a circular saw and a straightedge. Stack four pieces of drywall and cut all of them in one pass. We started by cutting a 2-1/2-in.-wide strip from the edge of each sheet to remove the tapered section. We did this to avoid having a tapered edge under the corner bead or at the back where we wanted to caulk the back edges rather than tape them **(Photo 15)**. If you're using the score-and-break method, clean up cut edges with a rasp.

Once the pieces are cut to width, it's easy to cut them to length and screw them to the framing. Mark the length

and use a drywall square to score them. All drywall cuts should be 1/8 in. to 1/4 in. less than actual measurements. You can easily fill gaps, but drywall will break along the edge if you try to force it in. Attach the drywall with 1-1/4-in. drywall screws. Use a special drywall screw gun, or buy a special bit for your cordless drill that sets the screws just under the surface without driving them too deep.

NAIL ON THE CORNER BEAD

There are several types of corner bead. You can buy perforated plastic corner bead that attaches with spray adhesive or paper-faced corner bead that you embed in a layer of joint compound. We decided to use conventional metal corner bead. To speed up the process, we used a 1/4-in.-crown, air-powered stapler to fasten the beads **(Photo 12)**. You can buy a stapler for as little as $30. Or you can simply fasten the

corner bead with some 1-1/4-in. ring-shank drywall nails.

You'll need a tin snips to cut the corner bead. **Photos 10 and 11** show an easy method for cutting the metal beads to length and creating a strong corner. The key to installing corner beads is to press them in until the outside corner is just slightly proud of the drywall before driving the fasteners. Also, adjust the position of the bead so the corners of adjoining beads line up. For extra insurance against cracking, cover all the corner bead edges with adhesive-backed mesh tape.

TAPE THE CORNERS AND FILL THE BEAD

To save time, we decided to confine our taping to the intersection of the sides and tops of the drywall recesses **(Photo 13)**. We caulked the back edges later **(Photo 15)**. Start by taping the inside corners. Then fill the corner beads with joint compound. Use 45-minute

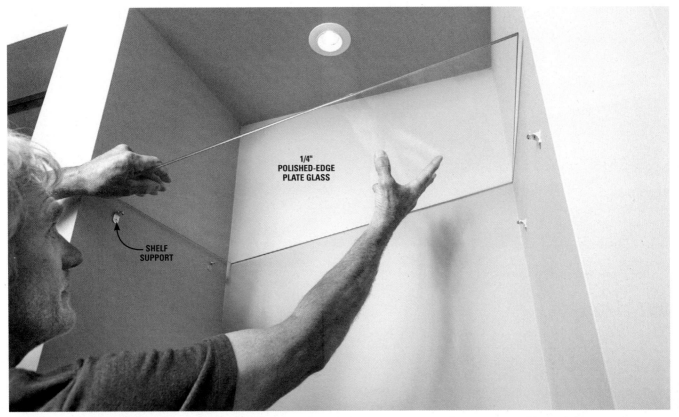

**1/4"
POLISHED-EDGE
PLATE GLASS**

**SHELF
SUPPORT**

17 **ADD GLASS SHELVES.** Screw shelf supports into the 2x6 backer, making sure they're level with each other. Set the 1/4-in.
polished-edge glass shelves on the supports.

setting-type compound for this. Mix the powder with water according to the instructions on the bag. Then use an 8-in. taping knife to fill the corner beads **(Photo 14)**. We used almost two full bags of setting compound for this project. When the joint compound has firmed up to the consistency of soap, carve off any lumps and high spots with your taping knife. You can add another coat as soon as the compound hardens. You don't have to wait for it to dry.

Don't rush this part of the job. Plan on spending a few hours a day for several days. Use premixed joint compound for the final coats, letting it dry between each coat. Trowel on thin coats until you've got a smooth, flat surface. Let the final coat dry. Then sand carefully with 120-grit drywall sandpaper mounted on a drywall sander. Use a fine sanding sponge with an angled edge to sand the inside corners. Vacuum all the dust from the surfaces and check your work with a strong

raking light. Fill any imperfections, resand, and then it's time to prime and paint.

FINISH THE WIRING

When you're done sanding the drywall, you can install the recessed lights. Then when the painting is complete, finish the wiring by adding the outlets and connecting the switch or dimmer switch. For more help with installing switches and outlets, go to familyhandyman.com and search for "switch" or "outlet." **Figure B** shows how to wire the outlets and dimmer switch. **Photo 16** shows how to install the recessed lights.

We used 6-watt dimmable LED flood bulbs in our fixtures. If you're using LED bulbs and want to install a dimmer, check the manufacturer's instructions to make sure the switch is compatible with the brand of LED bulb you're using. When the wiring is complete, turn on the circuit breaker

to check your work. Then call the electrical inspector for a final inspection.

FINISHING TOUCHES

Since we wanted to use the shelves as an entertainment center, we cut holes for low-voltage old-work brackets in the back wall of the TV compartment and the compartment below it. That way we could run HDMI and any other necessary audio/video cables through the wall from the components to the TV. Make sure the cables are rated for in-wall use—look for CL2- or CL3-rated cables.

We also installed 1/4-in. polished-edge plate-glass shelves in two of the compartments **(Photo 17)**. To protect the drywall from wear and moisture, consider having more glass pieces cut that you can use to cover the bottoms of the other compartments. Reinstall the baseboard molding and you're ready to move in and enjoy your dramatic new display wall.

Build the best-ever garage storage shelves

These shelves help you get organized by using space you didn't know you had.

The average two-car garage has an upper region on three 24-ft.-long walls ready and available for big-time storage. Add a continuous 2-ft.-deep shelf on all three walls and you're talking about a huge, accessible storage platform that takes up no floor space whatsoever. This project will work in just about any garage, although you may have to customize it a bit for your space. (More on adapting it later.) Shown here is a garage with finished walls, but the assembly techniques will also work on garages with open studs.

While these shelves aren't sturdy enough to store hundreds of pounds of stuff, they're definitely strong enough for off-

season clothes, sporting goods and camping gear—in short, just about anything you'd want to hoist onto an 8-ft.-high shelf and out of the way. In general, keep the weight under

WHAT IT TAKES		
TIME 1 weekend	**COST** $250-$500	**SKILL LEVEL** Beginner
TOOLS Circular saw, miter saw, stud finder, drill/driver, nailer, compressor, basic carpentry hand tools		

about 30 lbs. per linear foot (you wouldn't want your stuff to come crashing down).

The 23-in.-high apron under the shelf is a perfect place to drive nails and hooks for hanging garden tools, cords and hoses. Add a closet rod between a couple of braces and you have a convenient place to hang jackets, raincoats or other clothes. Cutting and installing the parts for an entire garage will take you only a weekend. As for skills, it's a project almost anyone can tackle. If you can handle a circular saw,

TOP LEFT: If you're not using the wall space in your garage for storage, you're missing out.
ABOVE: Look how much you can store on these shelves!

Planning your shelves

No magic heights or widths can be given for your shelves; you'll want to customize them for your garage and needs. The best strategy is to build a 3-ft.-long mock-up of the shelf shown and hold it against the walls in various positions to test the fit. This just takes a little effort and may help prevent headaches later. Then you can decide what height and size the shelves need to be to clear obstacles.

Some rules of thumb for sizing and positioning:

- Choose shelf heights that will allow for enough space between the ceiling and the shelf for the tall items you plan to store.
- Make sure that shelves and braces will clear obstructions like garage doors, garage door tracks and, of course, service doors.
- In foot traffic areas (near car doors, for example), keep braces above head level and back from doorways so you don't bump into them.
- If you have an SUV or a pickup truck, make sure the braces won't end up obstructing the doors.
- If you need to build narrower shelves, just shrink the plywood braces and shelves by the same amount.

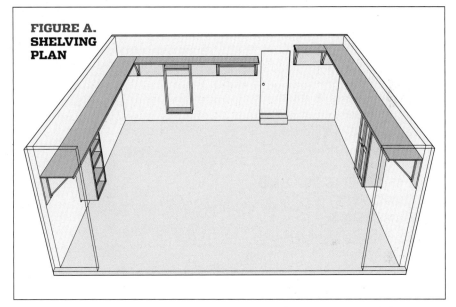

FIGURE A. SHELVING PLAN

Position shelves in all unobstructed zones along the ceiling. Customize by varying heights and adding shelves, racks and cabinets for special items.

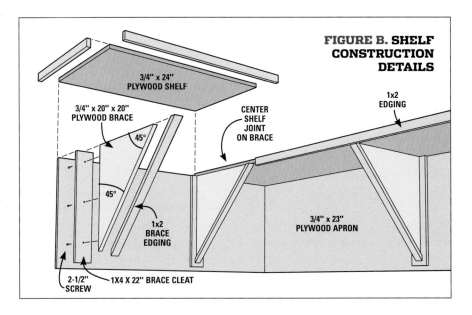

FIGURE B. SHELF CONSTRUCTION DETAILS

3/4" x 24" PLYWOOD SHELF
3/4" x 20" x 20" PLYWOOD BRACE
CENTER SHELF JOINT ON BRACE
1x2 EDGING
45°
45°
1x2 BRACE EDGING
3/4" x 23" PLYWOOD APRON
2-1/2" SCREW
1X4 X 22" BRACE CLEAT

a screw gun and basic hand tools, you will have no problems. For the cleanest look, use a miter saw to cut the trim. And to speed up the job, use a brad nailer for most of the nailing.

CHOOSING THE MATERIALS

This shelving system, made from oak plywood and solid oak trim, costs about $60 per 8 ft. of length. If you choose 3/4-in. CDX (construction grade) plywood and pine trim, you'll whittle down the cost to about $40 per 8-ft. section. Everything here is shown with two coats of polyurethane. If you choose to finish your shelves, roll the finish on the full sheets of plywood and brush the finish on all of the trim boards before cutting.

Measure the overall length of shelving you intend to build and then use the dimensions in **Figure B** to help calculate the materials you need.

LAY OUT THE WALLS AND MOUNT THE APRONS

Rip each sheet of plywood into one 23-in.-wide apron and one 24-in.-wide shelf. Then use the factory edge of a cut shelf as a saw guide for straight cuts on the other shelves and aprons **(Photo 1)**, or use a table saw.

Snap a level line on the wall to mark the top of the apron and then mark all of the studs with masking tape. Take your time with this step; it's important that the apron nails anchor into solid framing since they support the entire weight of the shelf. To be sure, poke nails through the drywall to find the centers of studs. Start the first apron somewhere in the middle of the wall, making sure that both ends fall on the centers of the studs. Then work toward the corners where the freehand crosscut ends will be hidden. If you're working alone, partially drive a couple of "stop" nails at the chalk line to help align the apron **(Photo 2)**. That will eliminate any guesswork. Prestart a

1 Rip 24-in.-wide shelves and 23-in.-wide aprons from each 3/4-in. sheet of plywood. Use a factory edge as a straightedge guide.

2 Snap a chalk line to mark the top of the apron and then mark the stud locations. Hold the plywood apron even with the line and nail the apron with 16d finish nails, four to each stud.

couple of nails at stud locations before hoisting the apron into place so you can tack it to the wall while supporting it with one hand.

CUT AND MOUNT THE BRACES

Cut the triangular braces from 20-in. squares **(Photo 3)**. You can cut the diagonal freehand because the trim will hide minor cutting flaws. Use two 1-3/8-in.-wide spacers to center and support the brace while you're screwing the 1x4 brace cleat to the back side **(Photo 4)**. Drill 1/8-in. pilot holes into both pieces and countersink

holes in the cleats to prevent splitting. Use three 2-1/2-in. screws, one about 2 in. in from each end and one more centered. Run the wood grain the same direction on each brace.

Drill four pilot holes in the cleats, two 1-1/2 in. from the top and two 3 in. from the bottom. Then screw each brace assembly to the apron **(Photo 5)**. Use finish washers under the screws for a polished look. Position a brace directly over each apron seam, and place one more in the center so no shelf span is more than 4 ft. Make sure they're flush and square with the top of the apron. When shelving turns

3 Rip 20-in.-wide lengths of plywood and cut them into 20-in. squares. Draw a diagonal line and cut the triangular braces. Use a sharp blade to minimize splintering.

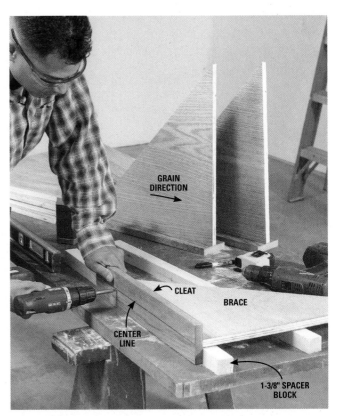

4 Rest the braces on 1-3/8-in.-thick spacer blocks, then mark the center of each 1x4 cleat. Predrill 1/8-in. holes and screw the cleat onto the brace with three 2-1/2-in. screws.

5 Fasten each brace to the apron, flush with the top, with four 1-5/8-in. screws. Space the braces at the ends and middle of each full sheet.

6 Nail the shelves to the apron and to the braces with 2-in. nails spaced every 8 in. Make sure joints meet at the center of the 3/4-in. braces.

CLEATS

Customized shelving

You can easily customize this shelving to fit special items like golf clubs, hanging clothes or anything else that's best stored in a cabinet or on open shelving. Just assemble a cabinet box like the one shown here so that the sides fall over the wall studs. Go as narrow as 16 in. or as wide as 4 ft., but make sure you can attach the cleats directly to wall studs. Attach those cleats to the back of the cabinet with 2-in. screws placed every foot, just as you did with the braces, and then screw the assembly to the wall. The cabinet sides replace the 45-degree braces and support the shelf. A simple unit like this one takes no more skill than was required for the shelves. If you're interested in drawers or fancier cabinetry work, you're limited only by your cabinetmaking skills.

45° BEVEL

NOTCH

1x2 TRIM

7 Cut the 1x2 brace trim pieces to fit with opposite 45-degree bevels at each end. Glue and nail the trim to the braces with 2-in. brads.

1x2 EDGE TRIM

8 Cut the 1x2 edge trim to length, then glue and nail it to the front edge of the shelf with 2-in. brads.

a corner, center a brace exactly 24 in. from one wall **(Figure B)**. This brace will support the front edge of the shelf on the adjoining wall and a shelf end.

NAIL ON THE SHELVES AND ADD THE TRIM

Lay the shelves in place so joints fall over the braces, and nail them to the braces and the apron with 2-in. brads

spaced every 8 in. As with the apron, start in the center of each wall so you'll have factory edges abutting each other at joints and the saw cuts will be hidden at the ends. Angle nails slightly at the joints so they hit right at the center of the braces.

Add trim to the plywood edges for a finished look. Trim also strengthens the assembly and stiffens the shelves.

Cut the brace trim to fit with opposing 45-degree bevels at each end. Then glue and nail the trim to each brace with 2-in. brads **(Photo 7)**.

Starting at one end of each wall and working toward the other, cut edging to fit **(Photo 8)**. Overlap plywood joints by at least 2 ft. for better support. The plywood will be a little wavy, but it'll straighten as you nail on the trim.

WHAT IT TAKES

TIME	COST	SKILL LEVEL
40 hours	Over $500	Intermediate

TOOLS
Gas-powered masonry saw, masonry hand tools, wheelbarrow, landscaping tools, plate compactor, level, heavy landscaping equipment

A good retaining wall will stand the test of time, so we went to work with the pros to learn how to build one that'll be timeless.

Build a long-lasting retaining wall

This wall will stand for decades and laugh in the face of Mother Nature.

Anyone with a strong back can stack a bunch of blocks and build a pretty retaining wall. But it takes skill and planning to construct an attractive wall that can also handle immense pressure and shrug off the forces of gravity. That's the kind of stuff that keeps a retaining wall around—and doing its job in your yard.

Unsurprisingly, that's the kind of wall we wanted to learn how to build. We went to work with Joe and Jake Blakeborough of Blakeborough Hardscapes in Prior Lake, MN. They showed us that it's all about a solid base, proper drainage and the right materials for the job. They also shared a few handy tips they've picked up over the years.

STORY POLE
FOR LASER
LEVEL

PLATE
COMPACTOR

1 MAKE THE TRENCH WIDE, DEEP AND LEVEL. Size the trench so there's enough room for the block and at least 8 in. of space behind it. Excavate deep enough to completely bury at least one full course, including space for 6 to 8 in. of base material. Establish a level trench to ensure an even layer of base material. That will help prevent the wall from tipping after freeze/thaw cycles. Our experts use a laser level and a story pole to determine the depth of the trench.

2 COMPACT THE TRENCH. Compact the soil in the trench bottom with a hand tamper or vibrating plate compactor. This step is often neglected. The excavator, and even hand shovels, can disturb and loosen the top inch or two of soil, and that's enough to make your wall settle—settling is bad!

3 LAY A CRUSHED STONE BASE. Our experts prefer crushed stone for the base rather than naturally occurring gravel dug from a pit. Crushed stone is a little more expensive. However, it provides better drainage, and because of the sharper angles on the stone, it requires less compacting. And once it's compacted, it stays that way. Joe and Jake have found that crushed stone sized between 1/2 in. and 3/4 in. is best suited to handle the heaving forces created by the harsh freeze/thaw cycles in Minnesota. Avoid rounded stones like pea gravel or river rock; they don't form strong interlocking bonds like angular stone. Leave the stone no more than 1/2 in. higher than you want the final height to be, and then make a couple of passes with a hand tamper or plate compactor. You'll notice the stone is almost 100 percent compacted as soon as it's laid in the trench. The same type of stone will be used for backfilling, which also eliminates the need for hauling in multiple materials.

GRATE

TEE

SILT SOCK

4 **GET THE FIRST COURSE RIGHT.** Use a torpedo level to level each block front to back and a 4- or 6-ft. level to keep each course level and even. Set the blocks with a heavy rubber or plastic mallet. Getting the first course flat and level is extremely important, so take your time. Try to lay the course as close to the center of the trench as possible.

TORPEDO LEVEL

5 **PROVIDE DRAINAGE.** Once a few rows have been stacked, backfill the wall with rock so it matches the grade height in front of the wall, and then lay down perforated drain tile on top of the rock. Install drain tee fittings and a drain grate every 25 ft. to 50 ft., depending on how much rainwater is expected to run down to the wall. Cut one block down to accommodate the drain grate. Screw the drain tile parts together so they won't come apart when they get covered with more rock. Drain the tile to daylight at the ends of the walls whenever possible.

FIRST BLOCK IN SECOND BASE COURSE

LESS- EXPENSIVE STONE

6 **SWEEP BEFORE STACKING.** Even a pebble on the surface of a block will throw the one above it out of alignment. And that crooked block will affect the one above it, and so on. That little stone will eventually create an unattractive hump in the top course.

7 **STEP UP AFTER TWO FULL COURSES ARE BELOW GRADE.** If the wall runs up a hill, continue each base course into the hill until the top of the second course is level with the grade, and then start your second base course at that point. If you have the option, it can be easier to excavate and lay the lowest course before excavating the trench for the next step, especially if you have to step up several times. Save yourself some money and install the cheapest style/color that matches the wall style (usually the gray ones) on the bottom course since it won't be seen.

8 MARK CUTS WITH A SOAPSTONE PENCIL. These pros like soapstone because the lines created by grease pencils and markers can stay visible for a very long time, whereas soapstone washes off. The downside? Soapstone doesn't work as well on wet blocks. You can find these pencils at online retailers for as little as 25¢ each.

Which blocks are best?

Solid blocks are heavy. Lighter, hollow blocks are available but can't be split because cutting will expose the voids. Many pros prefer blocks that are held together with pins rather than a lip on the bottom because pinned blocks work better on tighter curves and the flat bottom makes them easier to stack. Also, the small lip on some lipped blocks can be prone to cracking, which weakens the wall.

PRO TIP

Keep space between tiers

If you're building tiered retaining walls, set each tier back far enough to prevent the weight and pressure of the wall above from destroying the one below. The rule of thumb is to separate wall tiers by a distance that's no less than twice the height of the wall below. So if the bottom wall is 4 ft. tall, the wall above it should be built at least 8 ft. behind it.

9 SPLIT BLOCKS FOR A ROUGH FINISH. If the end of a block will be visible and you'd like it to match the other rough surfaces, use a block splitter. You can rent one like this for about $85 per day — or cheaper.

10 MAKE SMOOTH CUTS WITH A SAW. Use a gas-powered cutoff saw like this one for a smooth cut. This saw can cut with or without water. Water eliminates the dust but creates a messy slurry that can permanently stain surfaces like driveways and sidewalks. You can rent a saw like this for about $80 per day.

LOCKING PIN

11 **KEEP THE JOINTS TIGHT.** Stagger the overlaps (at least 4 in. for this Versa-Lok product) and try to keep the butt joint between the blocks as tight as possible. Large gaps can create a pathway for water and sediment. Whichever type of block you use, make sure you follow the manufacturer's instructions.

ADHESIVE

2x4 GUIDE

12 **KEEP THE CAPSTONES EVEN.** Secure the capstones with a specialty landscape block adhesive, which stays flexible over time. Make sure the blocks are dry before applying the adhesive. Overhang the capstones about 1 to 1-1/2 in. Joe and Jake use a scrap 2x4 as a guide.

Tall walls need engineering

Walls more than 4 ft. tall will likely require a building permit and a plan made by a licensed engineer. The engineer will specify the base's width and depth, how far down the base course should be buried, and whether or not a geogrid (soil reinforcement system) should be used.

13 **BACKFILL WITH STONE.** Versa-Lok recommends compacting the angular stone as you backfill, but check the installation instructions for the type of block you're using. Backfill about 8 to 10 in. below the top of the capstones. This will allow enough room for the topsoil and turf.

PROJECT INDEX

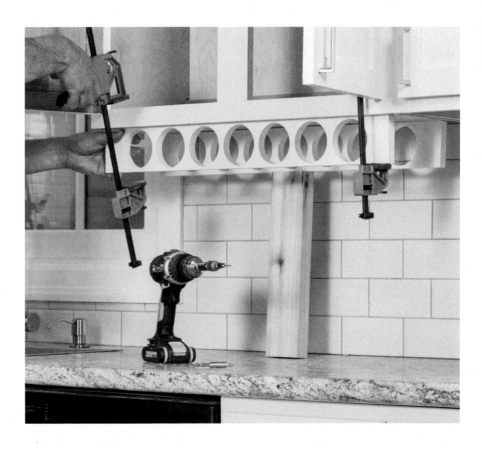